HAGAKURE

THE SECRET WISDOM OF THE SAMURAI

YAMAMOTO TSUNETOMO
Translated by ALEXANDER BENNETT

HAGAKURE

THE SECRET WISDOM OF THE SAMURAI

TUTTLE Publishing

Tokyo | Rutland, Vermont | Singapore

Published by Tuttle Publishing, an imprint of Periplus Editions (HK) Ltd.

www.tuttlepublishing.com

Copyright © 2014 Alexander Bennett

Library of Congress Cataloging Number 2013040332

ISBN: 978-4-8053-1198-1

Distributed by

North America, Latin America & Europe
Tuttle Publishing
364 Innovation Drive,
North Clarendon, VT 05759-9436, USA
Tel: 1 (802) 773 8930; Fax: 1 (802) 773 6993
info@tuttlepublishing.com
www.tuttlepublishing.com

Japan
Tuttle Publishing
Yaekari Building 3rd Floor
5-4-12 Osaki Shinagawa-ku, Tokyo 141 0032, Japan
Tel: (81) 3 5437 0171; Fax: (81) 3 5437 0755
sales@tuttle.co.jp
www.tuttle.co.jp

Asia Pacific
Berkeley Books Pte Ltd
3 Kallang Sector #04-01, Singapore 349278
Tel: (65) 6741 2178; Fax: (65) 6741 2179
inquiries@periplus.com.sg
www.tuttlepublishing.com

First edition
27 26 25 24   16 15 14 13 12   2403VP

Printed in Malaysia

CONTENTS

FOREWORD

When I heard that Dr. Alexander Bennett was going to translate *Hagakure* by Yamamoto Jōchō (Tsunetomo), my initial thought was that the final result would surely be very interesting. This is because Dr. Bennett possesses a profound knowledge of, and deep insight into, the world of Japanese bushido. This expertise has been enhanced by his extensive practical experience of the traditional martial arts of Japan, and his proficiency in this domain is highly acclaimed.

First of all, I would like to briefly introduce Dr. Bennett's extraordinary background and unique experiences in Japan, as doing so will illuminate the reasons why he is such a worthy translator of this classic text. He was born in New Zealand in 1970. In 1987, he came to Japan for the first time as an exchange student. Through participating in club activities at his host high school in Chiba Prefecture, Dr. Bennett stumbled across the traditional budo art of kendo. This experience led to an insatiable fascination with Japan's martial culture. When his year-long sojourn in Chiba finished, he returned to New Zealand, but it wasn't long before he was back in Japan for another couple of years, from 1989 to 1991, to further his study of kendo and other martial arts.

Dr. Bennett graduated from the University of Canterbury in his hometown of Christchurch in 1994. He received his Ph.D. in Humanities and Sciences from Kyoto University in 2001. His doctoral dissertation, written in Japanese, was an impressive investigation of bushido that was eventually published in 2009 by Shibunkaku in Kyoto as *The Bushi Ethos and its Evolution: An Investigation of Bushidō from the Perspective of the History of Social Thought*.

In 2002, Dr. Bennett became a research associate at the International Research Center for Japanese Studies, where I met him for the first time. Following his tenure of research at the IRCJS, he taught Japanese culture at the Faculty of Liberal Arts in Teikyo University, and then moved to his current position as an associate professor at the Division of International Affairs, Kansai University. For many years he has been the driving force behind *Kendo World*, an endeavor he was instrumental in establishing as the world's first English language kendo magazine in 2001. Dr. Bennett currently holds the ranks of 7th-dan in kendo, 5th-dan in iaido, and 5th-dan in naginata, and is a living embodiment of the ideal of *bunbu-ryōdō*—being accomplished in both the literary and military arts.

For quite some time now, he has advocated the practical teaching of *zanshin* as a key concept in the culture of bushido. What is *zanshin*? Literally "lingering heart," simply put it is an important principle in the martial arts which means to maintain psychological and physiological alertness at all times, even after achieving victory in combat or a match. It entails remaining vigilant, calm, and collected after the engagement, and mustering complete control over the surge of adrenaline in your blood. Expressing emotions of joy in victory or anguish in defeat are unacceptable. Throwing one's arms up in exhilaration shows a lack of vigilance and respect.

Thus, *zanshin* can be described as a state of mind in which one shows constant awareness and self-control. Dr. Bennett contends that, in the world of the samurai, such a mind-set was developed through the accumulated experience of mortal combat. Showing respect towards one's adversary in a life-and-death situation, and reminding oneself of the grave danger of dropping one's guard, even for an instant, is the kind of encounter that nurtures a sense of *zanshin*. I feel his observations of the importance of *zanshin* is a critical reminder of an all but forgotten element of samurai culture, that once lost, will also lead to a fading in comprehension of the true essence and lessons of bushido.

When I first came across Dr. Bennett's theory of *zanshin*, I was reminded of another Japanese word, *mushin* ("no-mind"), or *mushi* ("selflessness"). The term *zanshin* sounded foreign to my ears, as it does to most Japanese people. In actual fact, *zanshin* sounds like quite an inconsistent or unstable state of mind to Japanese people, who have long believed that an "empty mind" and "selflessness" is a profound way of living, representing the highest plane of spiritual attainment. How does the lingering mind of *zanshin* compare with the state of no-mind in *mushin*? Is it really so important, as Dr. Bennett maintains, that it should be considered the ultimate state of mind in the Japanese martial ways known around the world as budo? These are questions that smolder in the back of my mind. I feel compelled to confess that I have been obsessed with these questions ever since Dr. Bennett brought to my attention the concept of *zanshin*.

As I ponder such matters, I am intrigued as to what kind of attitude the author of *Hagakure* had towards ideals reminiscent of *zanshin* and *mushin*. Given his acute understanding of such tensions inherent in the lifestyle of the samurai, it is a point of great interest to me to see how Dr. Bennett interprets Yamamoto Jōchō's theory of bushido. I look forward to scouring his translation of *Hagakure* to see how he encountered Yamamoto Jōchō, and communicated with him between the lines of the text.

Yamaori Tetsuo
(Former Director of the International
Research Center for Japanese Studies)
June 2, 2013
Kyoto

HAGAKURE
IN CONTEXT

INTRODUCTION

B ushido[1] tends to stir people's imaginations. The term is synony-
mous on the one hand with strength, masculinity, fearlessness,
honor, and transcendence, and on the other, callousness and cold-
hearted brutality. The most visible vestige of samurai culture in the
modern age is budo, that is, the Japanese traditional martial arts, and
these are indisputably Japan's most successful cultural exports, with
literally tens of millions of enthusiasts around the world. People practice these arts not only as a means of self-defense or as competitive
sports, but also in the pursuit of spiritual development.

Another factor that sparked interest in bushido—although by no
means a driving force now—was Japan's remarkable postwar economic success. In the days of the bubble economy in the late 1980s,
the belief that Japan's economic and business accomplishments could
be attributed to management practices deriving from "samurai strategy" was widely held. The Japanese culture boom of the 1980s and
1990s encouraged many people to take up martial arts, and to study
translations of famous warrior books, such as Miyamoto Musashi's
The Book of Five Rings, Daidōji Yūzan's *Budō Shoshinshū,* and of

---

1 *Bushidō* (武士道)—literally "the Way of the warrior." "*Bushi*" is the common Japanese
word denoting warriors in academic circles, although "samurai" is probably better
known in the West. Nowadays, both terms are used interchangeably; however, the
word samurai is used most frequently in this book.

course, Yamamoto Jōchō's (Tsunetomo)[1] *Hagakure*. Nowadays, Japanese culture has been embraced by a new generation of "*anime otaku*," or diehard devotees of Japanese animation and pop culture.

There have been many popular movies over the years promoting samurai ideals, including *The Last Samurai*, starring Tom Cruise and Watanabe Ken. This film sparked a resurgence of interest in samurai ethics. Also of note was the critically acclaimed 1999 film, *Ghost Dog*, starring Forest Whitaker, which used *Hagakure* aphorisms as reference points throughout the story about an African-American hit man. He worked for a Mafia mobster, seeing himself as a devoted "retainer," unflinching in his loyalty to the man who saved his life years ago.

Despite the noble depictions in modern pop culture and literature, some scholars have described samurai as nothing more than "valorous butchers." Indeed, there is no denying that throughout *Hagakure* death sentences are violently dished out for the most trivial of offenses. From the standpoint of contemporary morality, the apparent cheapness of life in samurai society seems truly obscene. Texts such as *Hagakure*, which advance death so matter-of-factly, shock our sensibilities, especially in an age when people have a propensity to avoid contemplating their own mortality.

For example, our society denounces suicide, and capital punishment for murder is a highly contentious issue. To the samurai, however, death was celebrated as being integral to their honor and way of life. Attachment to life hindered a warrior during a catastrophe, and so it was deemed virtuous to train one's mind and spirit to be able to choose death with firm resolve if the situation called for 'decisive action.' As such, while the extremist attitudes and scenes portrayed so vividly in *Hagakure* may repulse the modern reader, the aphorisms provide a window on an age and a society that, although foreign to our own lifestyle, will serve to stimulate readers

---

1 Tsunetomo is written with the *kanji* characters 常朝. When Tsunetomo took the tonsure following the death of his lord in 1700, he began using his Buddhist name, Jōchō, which uses the same *kanji* characters in their *on* reading. Discussions of *Hagakure* are divided as to which reading is used. As *Hagakure* was written after Jōchō became a monk, throughout my translation he is mostly referred to as Jōchō rather than Tsunetomo.

into contemplating challenging questions regarding the human experience. In order to appreciate the content, it is important to first put things into context.

THE *HAGAKURE* PHENOMENON

Properly titled *Hagakure-kikigaki* (literally "Dictations given hidden by leaves"), *Hagakure* is now one of the most famous treatises on bushido. Completed in 1716, the content consists of approximately 1,300 vignettes and contemplations of varying lengths, divided into 11 books. It covers the people, history, and traditions of the Saga domain[1] in the southern Japanese island of Kyushu, and also records anecdotes about warriors from other provinces. Although some of the content is abstract in nature, the pages are filled with engaging stories about the feats of individual samurai and the maelstrom of retainership, premised by a balance of insanity and equanimity, rather than a convoluted philosophical discourse.

The first two books of *Hagakure* are believed to have been dictated by Yamamoto Jōchō (1659–1719), a middle-ranking retainer of Nabeshima Mitsushige (1632–1700), daimyo of the Hizen (Saga) province, to fellow clansman Tashiro Tsuramoto (1678–1748). Books 3 to 6 are about the Nabeshima lords and episodes that occurred in the Saga domain; Books 7 to 9 delve into the "meritorious feats" of Saga warriors; Book 10 is a critique of samurai from other provinces; and Book 11 provides supplementary information about miscellaneous events and various aspects of warrior culture.

Although Jōchō undoubtedly provided a fair proportion of the information contained in Book 3 onwards, given that some of the entries relate to people and happenings after his death, Tashiro

---

1 The Saga domain is also known as the Hizen domain and Nabeshima domain. It is located in the Hizen province in the modern-day prefecture of Saga on the southern island of Kyushu. The region was originally controlled by the Ryūzōji clan, of whom the Nabeshima were originally vassals. Nabeshima Naoshige became the guardian of Ryūzōji Takanobu's son, Takafusa, when he was killed in battle in 1584. In 1590 Toyotomi Hideyoshi allowed the Nabeshima clan to usurp the region, and the Ryūzōji hegemony was superseded with Naoshige becoming the first Nabeshima daimyo of the fiefdom.

Tsuramoto clearly pieced together much of the content from other sources. Thus, although the book is commonly attributed to Jōchō, it was ultimately Tsuramoto's abiding efforts that brought it to fruition.

The content is censorious of the Tokugawa shogunate (the warrior government based in Edo) in some sections as a reaction to restrictive decrees that reduced samurai to a "mechanical cog in the bureaucratic wheel of state."[1] It was also critical of the actions of certain eminent warriors of the Saga domain. Because of its somewhat guileless critiques of local dignitaries, and the effete ways of metropolitan "Kamigata" warriors of Edo and Kyoto, *Hagakure* was treated cautiously as a "forbidden text," and secretly circulated only among members of the Saga domain until it was thrust into the limelight and popularized in the militaristic atmosphere of the 1930s and 1940s. The content was considered too inflammatory for *Hagakure* to be openly endorsed within the Saga domain, and it was not even used as a text in the domain school, Kōdōkan, where young Saga warriors were educated. Given the book's far-reaching recognition today, however, it has become a source of great pride for the people of modern-day Saga Prefecture.

Modern interest in *Hagakure* transpired through a resurgent fascination in the traditions of bushido, ironically after the samurai class had been dismantled as Japan embarked on its quest to modernize. Although the samurai class was brought to an end during the Meiji period (1868–1912), it did not mean the end of bushido as a gripping, emotive force. Many samurai traditions, including the martial arts, were briefly suspended in the early Meiji surge of modernization, only to be revived from the mid-1880s. At this time, the cultural pendulum began to swing in a more blatantly nationalist direction, where Western technology was complemented by "Japanese spirit" (*wakon-yōsai*).

By the later 1880s, as Garon observes, "intellectuals, local elites, and officials broadly agreed on the need to foster 'a sense of nation' in the masses if Japan were to modernize and compete with Western

---

1 Eiko Ikegami, *The Taming of the Samurai*, p. 297

rivals."[1] It is precisely in this period that questions of "Japaneseness," that is, the essence of what it meant to be Japanese, became a prominent matter of debate. In many ways, the Japanese were feeling their way as they attempted to form a national identity, and according to Doak, this epoch signified the "first important moment in Japanese nationalism when culture, as a code for conceptualizing the collective identity of the Japanese as a single people, was mobilized in agendas that spanned the political spectrum."[2]

Prominent scholars such as Inoue Tetsujirō sought to bind bushido to the service of the state by associating it with patriotism and devotion to the emperor. His contemporary, the passionate Christian Uchimura Kanzō, reinterpreted the meaning of bushido, equating it with loyalty to Jesus Christ. The most influential bushido commentator of modern times is undoubtedly Nitobe Inazō. He published *Bushido: The Soul of Japan* in English, in which he portrayed a Christianized account of bushido for Western readers as the backbone of Japanese morality, and suggested it was a perfect base upon which Christianity could be grafted and evangelized in Japan. He stressed such virtues as honesty, justice, courtesy, courage, compassion, sincerity, honor, duty, loyalty, and self-control. He argued that bushido had evolved among the feudal warriors, but its values had been inherited by all echelons of Japanese society.

With momentous popular and symbolic appeal, bushido and other vestiges of warrior culture, such as the traditional martial arts, seemed an increasingly irresistible, albeit highly romanticized, feature of the cultural makeup of the Japanese nation. Harumi Befu referred to this phenomenon as the "samuraization" of the Japanese people, in which "characteristics such as loyalty, perseverance, and diligence that were said to be held by a small (but elite) segment of the population—the samurai—were gradually extended through propaganda, education, and regulation to cover the whole of the population."[3]

---

1 S. Garon, *Molding Japanese Minds*, p. 8
2 Kevin Doak, *A History of Nationalism in Modern Japan: Placing the People*, p. 195
3 H. Befu, *Japan: An Anthropological Introduction*, pp. 50–52

In particular, *Hagakure's* underlying theme of absolute loyalty to one's lord to the extent that a warrior must be prepared to die in the course of duty, a notion symbolized by the legendary phrase, "The Way of the warrior is to be found in dying" (*Bushidō to iu wa shinu koto to mitsuketari*) fitted well with Japan's burgeoning militarism because, as Ikegami points out, of the "combination of the cult of death with the ideal of faithful and efficacious devotion to the public good."[1]

The first time *Hagakure* was published in print and became known outside the province of Saga was in March 1906. Elementary school teacher Nakamura Ikuichi compiled a selection of aphorisms and published them in book form. It was not until 1935 that the entire text was published in Kurihara Arano's *Hagakure Shinzui* ("Essence of *Hagakure*"), followed by the carefully annotated *Hagakure Kōchū* ("*Hagakure* collation") in 1940. It was from this juncture that *Hagakure* finally emerged from the mists of obscurity. Its popularity was further facilitated by prominent Japanese philosopher Watsuji Tetsurō and ethics historian Furukawa Tetsushi's combined work, *Hagakure*, which was also published in 1940 by the major publishing house Iwanami Bunko. This pocket-sized, three volume set made *Hagakure* available to the masses. Although there was no major *Hagakure* boom *per se*, it was still a popular read among soldiers mobilized by the Japanese war machine.[2]

Following the phenomenon of the suicidal *kamikaze* pilots, and the actions of Japanese soldiers in World War II who were feared for their fanaticism in the face of death, books such as *Hagakure* were later subject to intense criticism as being tools for militaristic propaganda that sought to instil Japanese youth with an indomitable sense of patriotism, and prepare them to sacrifice their own lives for the emperor and the mother country. *Hagakure* provided a powerful and emotive creed for wartime ultranationalists, in no small part due to its one-dimensional affirmation of loyalty to the point of sacrificing one's life by entering a 'death frenzy' (*shini-gurui*) of deadly fury. Was this, however, an accurate interpretation of *Hagakure's* true intent?

---

1 Ikegami, Op. Cit., p. 288
2 Koike Yoshiaki, *Hagakure–Bushi to Hōkō*, p. 44

Foreign and Japanese critics in the postwar period blamed bushido as representing all that was most detestable in Japanese wartime behavior. Many Japanese renounced bushido as part of the misguided militaristic ideology that resulted in Japan's ensuing defeat and shame, and also as unsuited to a new post-war democratic society.

In this context, *Hagakure* became by association a book at the root of intense controversy. Depending on one's point of view, *Hagakure* represents a mystical beauty intrinsic to the Japanese aesthetic experience, and a stoic but profound appreciation of the meaning of life and death. Conversely, it may be regarded as a text that epitomizes all that is abhorrent in terms of mindless sacrifice, as well as a loathsome depreciation of the value of life and blind obedience to authority.

It is fair to say that *Hagakure* is a vastly misunderstood book both inside and outside of Japan. Perhaps this is why Yamamoto Jōchō implored Tashiro Tsuramoto to burn the text upon completion to prevent it from getting into the hands of those who could never appreciate it for the spirit in which it was written. This directive seems almost prophetic in light of the conflicting appraisals it has been subjected to in the modern era.

In Japan, a wide range of pundits, ranging from distinguished scholars to jingoistic right-wing ultranationalists, lazily quote from *Hagakure* to both highlight Japan's supposed "uniqueness," as well as attempting to draw a tenuous connection between the noble culture of the samurai and the spirit of modern Japanese people. Likewise, judging from the various steadily-selling foreign language translations available outside Japan, there are many non-Japanese who are captivated with the romanticism of Japan's feudal past and notions of bushido, maybe as a curio, or perhaps hoping to find some useful tenet of wisdom. There are also people who totally disregard *Hagakure* as nefarious nonsense used as a medium for malevolent brainwashing by the Japanese military.

Foreign scholars of Japanese history and culture tend to take a sceptical view of the modern cultural nationalistic constructs of bushido as "invented tradition." The historical value of *Hagakure*— as a window into the complex, sometimes incredibly violent, but generally peaceful world of Tokugawa period warriors—is often dismissed as being the radical, seditious ramblings of a disgruntled old curmudgeon, grumpy at the degeneration of the age. All of these attitudes, positive or negative, are understandable. But if read with a sympathetic understanding of the man and his times, the content of *Hagakure* makes much more sense.

CONTEXTUALIZING THE HISTORICAL SETTING AND SOCIAL MILIEU

As professional warriors, samurai were distinctive from peasant or civilian conscript soldiers of the ancient (*kodai*) and modern (*kindai*) periods. Their existence differed greatly to the officials who were merely assigned military duty in ancient times, and also to the modern career soldier.[1] The gradual rise of the samurai to political prominence on a national scale was activated by the on-going dismantling of military obligations forced upon the general populace under the *ritsuryō* system. The system encouraged a rigid hierarchy in court, where certain offices became hereditary among a select but small group of nobles.

These families, determined to maintain their privileges and monopoly on government posts, increasingly sought affiliation with burgeoning warrior groups, or created private armies of their own. This, in turn, provided useful opportunities for career advancement among the middle- to lower-ranked nobles. They were quick to realize that martial ability was their ticket to a successful career in a mutually beneficial arrangement with the powerful aristocratic families that controlled the seat of government in Kyoto. "The greater such opportunities became, the more enthusiastically and the more seriously such young men committed themselves to the profession of arms."[2]

Men from powerful local families in the eastern frontier lands entrusted with governmental titles formed bands and took up arms to defend their own estates, and helped quell other local disputes with the impending threat of violence. Provincial bands of samurai

---

1 Motoki Yasuo, *Bushi no Seiritsu*, p. 1
2 Karl Friday, *Samurai, Warfare and the State in Early Medieval Japan*, p. 6

eventually formed feudal ties bound by a strong sense of identity as warriors. They maintained intense bonds of loyalty born of their shared experience in combat, as well as the promise of financial reward for services rendered. By the time Minamoto-no-Yoritomo set up the first bakufu, or warrior government, in Kamakura in 1192, warriors had already developed their own unique culture based on a ferocious appetite for fame, glory, and honor. Although it was not codified at this early stage, warrior culture was referred to by an array of terms, such as *bandō musha no narai* ("customs of the Eastern warriors"), *yumiya no michi* ("the way of the bow and arrow"), *kyūba no michi* ("the way of the bow and horse"), and so on. The term bushido was not coined until much later, in the 1600s.

To the samurai, martial ability was an expression of individual strength and valor, and symbolic of their distinctive subculture as specialist combatants. From the ninth century (or arguably, perhaps, even earlier), Japanese warriors developed and cultivated an idiosyncratic culture based largely on the ability to utilize violence. Warrior ideals evolved over many centuries. They abided by idioms of honor and upheld bonds of fealty forged between the retainer and lord, for whom—the classic war tales (*gunki monogatari*) frequently inform us—the warrior would gladly forfeit his life.

Generally speaking, by the Kamakura period (1185–1333) samurai had developed a distinct ethical code to the extent that they would, ideally, risk or sacrifice their lives to maintain honor. Other members of society were not nearly as enthusiastic about the idea of demonstrating valor to the point of death. They created unique rules of interaction utilizing honorific expressions that directed the relationships between samurai individuals of all rank. It was the adhesive for the political and social life of the samurai. Warriors also developed an unquenchable desire to enhance the name of their families, or *ie*, and were fiercely competitive in ensuring that their name, or *na*, would last into posterity. In this sense, the quest to seek honor and avoid shame became inextricably linked to prowess and unremitting courage, and an eventual monopoly of the right to wield violence.

Naturally, as expressions of honor were demonstrated through martial skill and violence, the question of death has always been central to the samurai's way of life. As is the case with Western medieval knights, the job of killing was certainly not condoned as a moral act in itself, although it was both justified and vindicated in a number of ways. A yearning for posthumous recognition, and an obsession for personal and familial glory, was all the motivation and justification the samurai needed to kill and die for. This provided the emotional impetus to fight bravely for one's lord (along with the promise of financial reward), and the stigma of cowardice would be too much shame to bear, for both a samurai personally and his descendants.

Despite the honorable depictions of samurai in the popular medieval genre of literature known as "war tales," greed for land, power, and self-advancement was always prevalent in the larger picture. This peaked at one of the most turbulent times in Japanese history, the Warring States period (1467–1568) where rival warlords, or daimyo, vied to conquer and eventually rule over a united Japan. This was a period where loyalty to one's overlord was often conveniently flouted in favor of personal advancement, and alliances and promises of fealty were broken as often as they were made.

It was a volatile era in which the rise or demise of a great daimyo, his *ie* ("house") and its members was only a treacherous back-stab away. The precariousness of the times led to a proliferation of "house rules" (*kakun*), laws (*hatto*), and prescripts defining consummate samurai deportment—obviously an indication that model behavior was far from the norm. Nevertheless, the perilous lifestyle of Sengoku warriors and their exploits were looked upon nostalgically by future generations as "the good old days" where samurai were real men, and those who dared won, or died in the process.

When Japan was finally ushered into an era of peace under the Tokugawa shogunate (1603–1867), samurai were faced with a dilemma. How could the warrior class, constituting just five or six per cent of the total population, justify their existence at the top of the newly-established social order, or *shi-nō-kō-shō*,[1] when there were

---

1 Although the lines were often blurred and inter-class mobility certainly existed, *shi-nō-kō-shō* represented the social strata enforced by the shogunate which placed samurai at the top of the pyramid, followed by farmers, artisans, and merchants respectively.

no more wars to speak of?

A number of military and Confucian scholars started formulating and refining protocols to guide warriors in their peacetime role, which became referred to as "*shidō*" or "*bushidō*." The groundwork for a new system of political thought and awareness emerged over time, and arguments were circulated among the upper echelons of government advocating the centrality of warriors in affairs of state, offering validation for the existence of the privileged warrior class even though peace prevailed.

For example, in his famous military treatise *Heihō Kadensho* (1632), Yagyū Munenori (1571–1646) clarified how a virtuous ruler maintains the capacity to use military force to protect the masses. Thus, he argued, maintenance of a benevolent military government was vital for the wellbeing of the realm. "At times because of one man's evil, ten thousand people suffer. So you kill that one man to let the tens of thousands live. Here, truly, the blade that deals death becomes the sword that saves lives." In other words, the way of war was also seen as the way of peace.

This justification works on a governmental level, but by the time *Hagakure* was written in the middle of the Tokugawa period, it was the lower and middle tiers of samurai, now fully transformed into non-combatant salaried bureaucrats, who sought meaning to their existence. Prominent scholars such as Yamaga Sokō (1622–1685) and Daidōji Yūzan (1639–1730) provided samurai with standards for achievement in lieu of battlefield feats. Yamaga Sokō asked rhetorically: "The samurai eats food without growing it, uses utensils without manufacturing them, and profits without selling. What is the justification for this?" His solution was that the function of peacetime samurai was to serve his lord loyally, and be a moral exemplar to the commoners by demonstrating dedication to duty—by living in strict observance of protocols of etiquette, maintaining military preparedness through ascetic training in the military arts, while also nurturing aesthetic sensibilities in scholarly and cultural pursuits.

The quest for perfection in daily life and dedication to duty provided samurai with an alternative paradigm for accruing honor other than fighting bravely in battle. It was a far safer and less exciting substitute for war, but the shogunate was content for samurai to be tamed in this way, fearing that the intrinsic volatility of warrior culture could threaten its hegemony if not kept in check.

Interestingly, although the prospect of being killed honorably in battle was no longer a reality, the concept of death was idealized, and manifested in the attitude of self-sacrificing commitment to service and unequivocal loyalty to one's lord. This could take the form of a self-willed death for some transgression, or suicide through fidelity.

Celebrated episodes during the Tokugawa period demonstrate just how 'faithful' a samurai could be to this extent. The most obvious example is the revenge of the 47 *Rōnin* (master-less samurai). In 1701, Asano Naganori, daimyo of the Akō domain, drew his sword and assaulted Kira Yoshinaka in the Edo Castle while in attendance because of a slight on his honor. Asano was immediately ordered to commit *seppuku* (ritual suicide by disembowelment) for this serious breach of etiquette. His retainers plotted for two years and enacted a vendetta culminating in the successful assassination of Kira at his mansion. This in turn led to their own termination by ritual suicide. They remain celebrated heroes in Japan to this day as paragons of loyalty.

The propriety of their actions attracted both praise and criticism from all quarters. The reaction shows the complex nature of the Tokugawa warrior's "community of honor." Should Asano have showed more restraint when goaded by Kira? To what extent can the sacred line of one's personal honor be crossed before retaliation is acceptable? Given the inviolability of personal honor for a samurai, should the shogun Tsunayoshi have been more judicious before immediately meting out punishment to Asano for breaking castle protocol which prohibited the drawing of weapons? Should he not have punished Kira as well for being the other party in the altercation? Should the 47 Asano retainers have abided by the strict law preventing retribution, or were they justified in their actions? Was their vendetta motivated out of loyalty to their wronged lord, or for maintaining the reputation of their clan, or were they driven by egocentric desires to uphold their personal pride and names in their community of honor? Should they have been executed as criminals instead of given the chance to die honorably by their own hands?

All of these questions were important considerations of the day.

Jōchō's opinion on the incident is representative of his no-nonsense stance with regards to appropriate warrior conduct.

> The rōnin of the Asano clan were culpable for not immediately committing seppuku at the Sengakuji Temple [after the night raid on Lord Kira's mansion]. Moreover, it took too long to exact revenge after their master was killed by the enemy. What if [their intended victim] Lord Kira had died of illness in the interim? It would have been a disgrace. Warriors of the Kamigata region are clever and shrewd in finding ways of being showered in praise. (1-55)

Indeed, *Hagakure* provides a frank commentary on the multifarious issues that samurai had to contend with as they navigated their way through Pax Tokugawa. The life philosophy of Yamamoto Jōchō highlights the tension and contradictions endured by a warrior subculture that had primed itself for war over many centuries, but was stuck in the limbo of peace.

CONTEXTUALIZING THE CONTENT

The subject matter of *Hagakure* was dictated by Yamamoto Jōchō. He was born on the eleventh day of the sixth month in 1659 to Yamamoto Jin'uemon Shigezumi, a retainer of the Saga domain. Jōchō talks of his childhood days in Book 2. He mentions that his father was 70 years old when he was born, and given the encumbrance of rearing a child at his age, Jin'uemon quipped that he should like to off-load his new child to a salt merchant. His unit captain, Taku Zusho, advised against such rash disposal of the lad, as his illustrious lineage guaranteed usefulness as a retainer in the future.

Jōchō was first named Matsukame, and when he was nine years of age, he was renamed Fukei when called into service as an errand boy by Nabeshima Mitsushige (1632–1700), second lord of the Saga domain. His father was strict and gave him all manner of laborious chores to build his strength and stamina. Evidently the boy was of weak constitution, and it was said that he would probably not live past the age of 12. Showing the dogged qualities that pepper the text of *Hagakure*, he spent his youth in personal training to prove his doubters wrong.

Jōchō's father died when he was 11. Following his father's passing, he was cared for and austerely educated by his nephew, Yamamoto Tsuneharu, who was actually 20 years his senior. He was made a pageboy of Nabeshima Mitsushige and given the name Ichijūrō at the age of 14. In 1678, he underwent the coming-of-age ceremony (*genpuku*), taking the name Gon'nojō, and was promoted to the position of close attendant and scribe's assistant.

Unfortunately, his lord Mitsushige showed displeasure at Gon'nojō's complicity in his son Tsunashige's fixation with poetry, and he was temporarily discharged from duty. During this time, he visited his father's old friend Tannen Oshō, a Zen monk at the Kezōan, and there he was taught the teachings of Buddhist Law. When he was 21, he was administered the *kechimyaku*, a document that signifies the "bloodline" or succession of various masters in a particular Zen school. He was given the Buddhist name Kyokuzan Jōchō (which can also be read as Tsunetomo). Around this time, he also frequented the abode of Saga's renowned scholar of Confucianism and thought, Ishida Ittei. The teachings of both these men had a profound effect on Jōchō, and this is evident by the numerous times their wisdom is quoted in *Hagakure*.

Jōchō married at the age of 24 and was reappointed as an officer of document writing. He was dispatched to Edo in this capacity when he was 28, and then deployed to Kyoto later on. He took his father's name, Jin'uemon, upon returning to Saga at the age of 33. Five years later, he was sent to Kyoto again by Mitsushige on a special mission to acquire a copy of *Kokin-denju*, a rare corpus of teachings which illuminated the inner meaning of the poems contained in the tenth century anthology of poetry known as the *Kokin Waka-shū* (commonly called *Kokin-shū*). For this purpose, he visited an authority on *waka* poetry, the nobleman Sanjō-nishi Sanenori, and finally managed to acquire copies of valuable documents for his lord in 1700. Through some premonition, he realized he had to return to

Saga quickly, and did so just in time to present the bed-ridden Mitsushige with the prized teachings.

With Mitsushige dying that year, this turned out to be the culmination of Jōchō's service to his lord, and his greatest exploit. One gets the impression that he strongly regretted that his career was bound by a forced association with the arts. This ultimately prevented him from achieving his goal of reaching the lofty heights of chief retainer, where he dreamt of occupying an influential position to counsel his lord for the good of the domain.

It was Jōchō's stated desire to martyr himself and commit the act of *junshi*, or self-immolation, to follow his lord in death. Such a self-willed death was considered to be the highest expression of loyalty to one's deceased lord, and thought to be an honorable end to the life of a dedicated retainer. To the disappointment of Jōchō however, *junshi* (or *oibara* as it was also known) had been prohibited in the Nabeshima domain by decree in 1661, and indeed by the Tokugawa government in 1663. His only recourse to demonstrate his integrity and devotion as a loyal warrior of the Nabeshima clan was to commit a form of "social *junshi*." He took the tonsure, shaved his head, and retired to a hermitage in the hills in Kurotsuchibaru.

It was here, ten years later, that Tashiro Tsuramoto visited him to seek his counsel. Jōchō's wife had already died, and he had no children. Jōchō's adopted son Tsunetoshi (also named Gon'nojō) died while on duty in Edo aged 38, so it is understandable that Jōchō took a liking to his Nabeshima domain junior, and the relationship they forged was one of deep, almost paternal, respect.

Tsuramoto was born in 1678, and his scholastic talents were recognized from a young age. He was appointed as a copyist for Nabeshima Tsunashige when he was 19, and continued in this role with the fourth lord of the Nabeshima clan, Yoshishige. He was relieved of duty for some unknown transgression in 1709. Despairing, Tsuramoto visited Jōchō at his hermitage in Kurotsuchibaru in the third month of the following year. Deciding to live close to Jōchō, Tsuramoto visited often, and wrote down the stories relayed to him over a period of seven years. The first copy of *Hagakure* was completed on the tenth day of the ninth month, 1716.

The original manuscript of *Hagakure* has long since been lost, but important handwritten copies made during the Tokugawa period include the "Kōhaku-bon," transcribed by Kamohara Kōhaku, who was five years Tsuramoto's junior, as well as the "Kashima-bon," and "Koyama-bon" ("Yamamoto-bon" and "Gojō-bon")—in addition to subsequent copies of these copies, which total around 40. Each copy contains slight differences, and exist in varying degrees of completeness. This translation is based on the Kōhaku version, as this is generally considered to be the closest to the original.

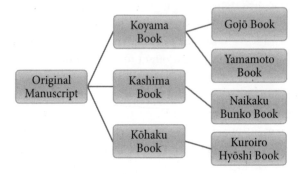

UNRAVELING THE ESSENCE OF *HAGAKURE*

The content of *Hagakure* is complicated, and unashamedly contradictory and ambiguous in places. Even the origin of the book's name is open for conjecture. One theory cites a poem by the famous Buddhist bard Saigyō Hōshi (1118–1190) in the *Sanka-shū*. "*Hagakure ni chiri-todomareru hana nomi zo, shinobishi hito ni au kokochi suru*" ("**Hidden away under leaves**, a blossom still left over makes me yearn to chance upon my secret love this way.")[1] Another hypothesis suggests that "hidden by leaves" was a reference to the secluded environment in which Tsuramoto interviewed Jōchō. Other scholars allude to the fact that Jōchō often makes reference to stalwart service from behind the scenes, or "service from the shadows," with no desire for recognition. It has even been postulated that the fifth Nabeshima lord, Muneshige, visited Tsuramoto and conferred the title himself.

---

1 William R. Lafleur, *Awesome Nightfall: The Life, Times, and Poetry of Saigyo*, p. 653

It would seem that the most plausible of all these theories is the Saigyō one. Nevertheless, it has been discounted by distinguished *Hagakure* expert, Furukawa Tetsushi, due to a passage that indicates Jōchō's contempt of Saigyō. "Kenkō and Saigyō were no more than lily-livered cowards. They masqueraded as writers because they were afraid to serve as samurai." Still, Jōchō concludes this vignette with the observation: "A man who has renounced the world to become a monk, or old men retired from duty, may become absorbed in such books. But to be a useful vassal to his lord, a warrior must be completely devoted to him amidst his pursuit of glory, or even after falling into the chasms of hell" (2-140) Thus, it seems logical that Saigyō's poem is the most conceivable derivation of the book's title, especially with the added allusion to "secret love," an important theme in *Hagakure* analogous with devotion and loyalty. "At a recent gathering I declared that the highest form of devotion is 'secret love' (*shinobu-koi*)." (2-2)

The premise for writing *Hagakure* stems from a vexation at the disintegration of warrior norms over previous decades, anti-shogunate sentiment, and nostalgic longing for the previous regimes of Lord Nabeshima Naoshige, first daimyo of the Nabeshima fiefdom, and his son and heir Katsushige (1580–1657).[1] Jōchō laments how young samurai "talk of money, about profit and loss, their household financial problems, taste in fashion, and idle chatter of sex." (1-63) Preoccupation with frivolities and consumerism was symptomatic of new generations of warriors who had never experienced battle, and therefore lacked discipline and the purity of intent reminiscent of earlier generations.

Jōchō's discourse is multifaceted and ostensibly chaotic, but the spirit of *Hagakure* can best be summed up by the four simple oaths he alludes to throughout the text:

> *I will never fall behind others in pursuing the Way of the warrior.*
> *I will always be ready to serve my lord.*
> *I will honor my parents.*

---

1 See the timeline for a chronological list of events outlining the history of the Saga domain from the time of the Ryūzōji clan and the transition to the Nabeshima clan.

I will serve compassionately for the benefit of others.
(See "Idle Talk in the Dead of Night")

At face value, the morals Jōchō is purporting here seem universal in nature, and not particularly burdensome. Underlying these outwardly serene pledges are powerful, emotive sentiments that penetrate to the very core of the samurai culture, in which life can be forfeited in an explosive instant of insanity for the sake of honor and loyalty. From the outset, Jōchō's sermon is pragmatic and affirms what could be described as a cult of death.

Indisputably the most famous phrase in *Hagakure* is "The Way of the warrior (bushido) is to be found in dying." Despite its seeming straightforwardness, this sentence is completely open to interpretation. Did Jōchō really mean that warriors should gleefully seize any opportunity to make the ultimate sacrifice? "If one is faced with two options of life or death, simply settle for death. It is not an especially difficult choice; just go forth and meet it confidently." (1-2) This would suggest that this was, indeed, the case. Conversely, the very next sentence in the text provides a literal and figurative juxtaposition: "Only when you constantly live as though already a corpse (*jōjū shinimi*) will you be able to find freedom in the martial Way, and fulfill your duties without fault throughout your life." (1-2) In other words, adherents of bushido should seek to nurture an indomitable fighting spirit free from concerns of life and death.

Within the context of yeomanly service (*hōkō*) and daily duties, bushido also implies commitment, perseverance, and devotedness. In this sense, the ideal of death can also be interpreted as a selfless application to service in the leader-follower relationship of vassalage, and the correct mind-set required. Consequently, as well as being a declaration of "death over life" in the literal sense, it also implies the nuance of "live as if dead," where each and every second of one's life is a precious, unrepeatable moment, and should never be used in vain.

The following passage confirms this. "With regards to the way of death, if you are prepared to die at any time, you will be able to meet your release from life with equanimity. As calamities are usually not as bad as anticipated beforehand, it is foolhardy to feel anxiety about tribulations not yet endured. Just accept that the worst possible fate for a man in service is to become a *rōnin*, or death by *seppuku*. Then nothing will faze you." (1-92) That is to say, as long as one knows that the most appalling thing that can happen is disassociation from one's *raison d'être* or death, then one should be able to live an uninhibited and productive life before meeting death in a dignified manner. *Hagakure* professes that life is a set that is completed by death; they are inextricably linked, and the nobler the death, the better the life it was. Furthermore, a noble death is the result of living life as if one were already dead.

This is an almost existential attitude, and Jōchō advocates not becoming confused in the face of a meaningless or absurd world. "Are men not like masterfully controlled puppets? It is magnificent craftsmanship that allows us to walk, jump, prance, and speak even though there are no strings attached. We may be guests at next year's Bon festival. We forget it is an ephemeral world in which we live." (2-45) For this reason, living with single-minded resolve (*ichinen*) and becoming a heroic warrior, the all-reliable supreme samurai referred to as *kusemono*, is the only way to liberate one's self and add meaning in this fleeting existence.

But still, *Hagakure* is fraught with contradictory messages about death and service which cause confusion. Although the Tokugawa period was an epoch of relative stability, and warriors would rarely if ever smell the stench of death in their nostrils on the battlefield, there was always an undercurrent of honor-fuelled tension ready to erupt into fatal clashes of violence in the course of daily life. *Hagakure* abounds with stories of fights which generally extol the actions of warriors who unflinchingly despatch their foe in spite of the impending dire consequences of *seppuku*, or even the disgrace of execution as punishment for breaking the law.

For example, a story in Book 10 relays an incident in Kyoto in which a samurai hears from a passer-by that one of his peers is involved in a brawl. He rushes to the scene to find he is about to be finished off, so he charges in with suicidal intent, and kills the two attackers. He is arrested and tried by the Kyoto magistrate. In his defense he says, "I was told 'your colleague is in a fight,' and thought it would dishonor the military way if I ignored the situation. That is why I dashed to the scene. What's more, it would have been unforgivable had I done nothing after witnessing the murder of a fellow clansman. I would extend the duration of my own life, but the spirit of bushido would perish in me. Thus, I dispensed with my cherished life to preserve the Way of the samurai. By forfeiting my life, I have observed the law of the samurai and upheld the warrior spirit. I have already laid down my life, and therefore humbly request that my punishment be meted out swiftly." (10-63) Following this statement, the magistrate released him, and sent notice to his lord: "Your retainer is a praiseworthy fellow and should be treasured."

On the other hand though, in another story contained in *Hagakure*, seeking a peaceful resolution is the recommended course of action for a samurai to take. It tells of two warriors meeting on a one-lane bridge, both refusing to give way to the other and threatening to resolve the situation with sword diplomacy. Then, a lowly radish seller comes between the two warriors and, "catching each one on either end of his shoulder carrying pole, picks them up and spins them around to the opposite ends of the bridge." It is concluded that "There are many ways of solving problems, and this counts as constructive service to one's lord. It is most unfortunate to see precious retainers die needlessly, or create needless discord." (2-124)

Some passages advise that the warrior should be reserved and discreet when offering counsel to his lord. "If admonishment and opinions are not communicated carefully with a spirit of accord, it will amount to nothing. Insensitive protests will cause umbrage, and even simple problems will not be resolved." (1-152) At the same time, Jōchō encourages samurai to actively seek recognition in the quest for honor and glory. "A samurai who does not care much for his reputation tends to be contrary, is conceited, and good-for-nothing. He is inferior to a samurai who craves glory, and is thus completely unusable." (1-154) Or, "In matters of military prowess, train with all of your might to never be surpassed by others, and think to yourself, 'My valor is beyond compare.'" (1-161)

Similarly, warriors are encouraged to vicariously support others to benefit the clan as a whole. For example: "It is an act of loyalty to educate others to become better retainers. Therefore, those with the will to learn should be given instruction. Nothing is more joyous than passing on knowledge to be vicariously useful in service through others." (1-124) Nevertheless, another passage shows Jōchō's defiance of orders so that he could accompany his lord in battle. "I cannot comply with this order when it will keep me away from His Lordship in battle. Please bear witness as I swear an oath to the god of war (Yumiya Hachiman) that I cannot possibly attach my seal of acceptance to this order… If it is determined that I should commit *seppuku*, then I will willingly comply."

He then finishes with a comment urging warriors to surpass colleagues and prevail amid the rivalry that characterized warrior life. "A young warrior should be strong headed." (1-106) Furthermore, "A samurai should be excessively obstinate. Anything done in moderation will fall short of your goals. If you feel that you are doing more than is needed, it will be just right." (1-188)

Jōchō also advises prudence. "The best course of action is to first take a step back, understand the depths and shallows of various matters, and avoid provoking indignation in your master." (2-8) Then again, he advises against judiciousness. "A calculating man is a coward. This is because he considers everything from the perspective of loss and gain, and his mind never deviates from this track. To him, death is a loss, and life is a gain." (1-111) Often he sponsors rash acts, completely disregarding the outcome. "To retaliate entails just frenetically throwing yourself at your adversary with the intention of being cut down. Being killed this way brings no shame. Thinking about how to win may result in missing the best opportunity to act." (1-55) This action is represented by another couple of keywords in *Hagakure*—*kichigai* and *shini-gurui,* or the "mad death frenzy." "In any case, just give yourself over to insanity and sacrifice yourself to the task. That's all you need to do. If you attempt to solve problems through careful manoeuvring, doubts will creep in and paralyze your mind, and you will fail miserably." (1-193)

If all these incongruities were not confusing enough, the conflict that arises between "secret love" in loyalty and in the man-love relationships called *shudō* adds to the complexity of the dynamics of human relations depicted in the book. "The essential point in *shudō* is preparation to forfeit your life for the sake of your lover. Otherwise you risk humiliation. On the other hand, though, this means that you would be unable to surrender your life in the service of your lord. Through this contradiction, I came to realize that in *shudō*, you should love your partner, but not love him at the same time." (1-181) *Shudō* is depicted as the purest form of reverential bonding between two males, based on ineffaceable trust and appreciation of each other's inner qualities.

These are just a few examples of the multifarious nature of the content and contradictory tenets of advice that create a degree of abstruseness that leaves the message of *Hagakure* open for interpretation. This is precisely why reading *Hagakure* without a basic understanding of the complexities of the Tokugawa warrior community of honor, the samurai ethno-mentality, and, to a degree, local knowledge of Saga and its personalities, leaves one with the impression that the content is just the mad ramblings of a disgruntled old man. To be sure, the text undeniably contains a degree of this, too, and like any human being, Yamamoto Jōchō certainly had good and bad days when reminiscing to Tsuramoto. In fact, some sections of *Hagakure* were probably relayed with a grin, and even an element of humor can be detected, if one looks for it.

Many of the apparent inconsistencies in *Hagakure* can be assuaged by simply being aware of who—or what—level of samurai each vignette is directed toward. It is a common mistake to lump all samurai together, but there were many ranks within their world, and the responsibilities and expectations of each were markedly different. Therefore, the ideal deportment and style of loyalty differed as well. For instance, Olivier Ansart makes a distinction between two broad types of loyalty: middle-ranked samurai and below personified "symbolic service," whereas "loyalty of counsel" was required of high-ranked warriors.[1]

Middle- to lower-ranked samurai were encouraged to engage in

1　Olivier Ansart, "Embracing Death: Pure will in *Hagakure*," *Early Modern Japan: An Interdisciplinary Journal v. 18*, (2010): pp. 57–75

unconditional service and blind obedience, being prepared to fre-netically sacrifice their own lives by entering a "frenzy of death" with purity of intention. The low-ranked warrior had no influence on how the domain was governed, or what his lord thought. The only realistic homage they could pay to their lord was expressed using their martial skill and spirit in violent or self-sacrificial acts. This included frenzied fights to the death that reflected on the lord's reputation of having valorous, decisive warriors in his domain. The samurai were essentially expendable pawns who could only dream of upward social mobility premised on selfless service from a young age. If he was noticed by his lord for acts of gallantry, or for is outstanding attributes, he could live in hope of being promoted to a higher position up the ranks. This, however, was very much the exception rather than the norm.

On the other hand, the "loyalty of counsel" was reserved for upper-ranking samurai. To fulfill their important duty of counselling the lord, as well as remonstrating with him for his transgressions for his and the domain's benefit, required skills in diplomacy, selfless resolve, wisdom, and prudence. Honor was found in the act of offer-ing judicious, yet discreet, advice. This, too, was a precarious exis-tence, as it might mean sacrificing one's life to take the blame for a lord's foolishness, or to atone for angering him. In both virtual and counsel-based forms of loyalty, the important mind-set was to act in accordance with a single-minded, pure will and intention, referred to throughout the pages of *Hagakure* as *ichinen*.

> All that matters is having single-minded purpose (*ichinen*), in the here and now. Life is an ongoing succession of 'one will' at a time, each and every moment. A man who realizes this truth need not hurry to do, or seek, anything else any-more. Just live in the present with single-minded purpose. People forget this important truth, and keep seeking other things to accomplish. (2-17)

A warrior who can demonstrate such resolve and purity in thought and action is hailed as a *kusemono*. In modern Japanese parlance, *kusemono* has negative connotations, indicating an eccentric or abnormal person—a quintessential weirdo. The *kusemono* depicted in *Hagakure*, however, represents the supreme warrior. Such an ideal man could be relied upon to always be there in a calamity, but remained behind the scenes when not needed. "Exceptional warriors (*kusemono*) are dependable men. Dependable men are exceptional warriors. I know this through considerable experience. Dependable men can be relied upon to keep away when things are going well, but will come to your aid without fail when you are in need. A man of such temperament is most certainly a *kusemono*." (1-132)

The presence of the *kusemono* is pervasive throughout *Hagakure*. The *kusemono* is the archetypical warrior whom Jōchō aspired to be, and the unnamed hero of the book. It is the *kusemono* who embodies the essence of *Hagakure*'s bushido.

CONCLUSION

This introductory chapter was written with the intention of contextualizing the myriad of influences that resulted in the writing of, and subsequent fascination with, this collection of guileless but sometimes quixotic aphorisms known as *Hagakure*. Controversial from the beginning, modified interpretations of the text's mentality in the twentieth century made the book particularly useful for stirring ultra-nationalistic sentiment and inculcating militarism. Consequently, *Hagakure* temporarily became a "forbidden text" of sorts again in the aftermath of World War II. Gradually, though, Japan entered a period of renewed interest in *Hagakure* from the 1960s. Renowned historians such as Furukawa Tetsushi and authors such as Mishima Yukio acclaimed *Hagakure* as representing the most exquisitely "beautiful" aspects of Japanese culture that had been indiscriminately purged in the immediate post-war period.

Western interest in the book was also piqued with a growing fascination for samurai culture and philosophy, especially following Japan's rise as an economic superpower in the 1980s. In recent years, a handful of translations into modern Japanese have become available, as have several English language translations that seek to introduce the "wisdom" of *Hagakure* to a wide international readership.

Given the historical importance of the work for understanding the samurai psyche, it is hardly surprising that a number of English translations have already been published. This begs the question as to why it is necessary to produce yet another. Although the extant translations are reliable to varying degrees, they often tend to gloss over the finer nuances in the original Japanese. In addition, to date there have been no complete translations of *Hagakure* in book form. This book is by no means complete, but it is the first to contain translations of all the vignettes in the first two books. These two are particularly important as they were dictations of Yamamoto Jōchō. The remaining books were comprised of information possibly from Jōchō, but a considerable portion of the material was collated elsewhere by Tashiro Tsuramoto. In the third section of this translation, I have included a selection of these later aphorisms which I find interesting, or have used in previous research.

This translation is based on the *Hagakure* version contained in Saiki Kazuma (et al eds.), *Mikawa Monogatari, Hagakure* (*Nihon Shisō Taikei* 26), which I consider to be the most academically rigorous. It is based on the aforementioned Kōhaku Book and makes exhaustive comparisons with the other extant copies, providing many notes which aid in the understanding of the obscure references in the text. I have incorporated relevant notes in the hope that this translation of *Hagakure* will facilitate the reader's understanding of this complex yet profoundly interesting window on human experience in eighteenth-century Japan, when warriors struggled to find equilibrium between their honor and the dictates of social order.

Finally, I would like to thank Professor Lachlan Jackson, Professor Uozumi Takashi, Professor Yamaori Tetsuo, Trevor Jones, and my research assistant for this project, Remi Yamaguchi, for their opinions and invaluable assistance in completing this translation.

IDLE TALK
IN THE
DEAD OF NIGHT[1]

Our first meeting was on the fifth day of the third month,
in the seventh year of Hōei (1710).[2]

How far away from the wretched world,
Are the mountain cherry trees? (Komaru)[3]

We met at last under the white clouds,
With cherry blossoms blooming.[4] (Kisui)[5]

---

1 This title is written in the Yamamoto-bon variant of *Hagakure*. Although it is not titled as such in the *Hagakure* reproduced in *Nihon Shisō Taikei 26, Mikawa Monogatari, Hagakure* edition (Tokyo: Iwanami Shoten, 1974), I decided to add it anyway.

2 This was ten years after Yamamoto Jōchō (Tsunetomo) took up the tonsure. Jōchō was 52 years old and Tashiro Tsuramoto was aged 33. The meeting place was Jōchō's thatched hut, secluded in the mountains.

3 Jōchō's pseudonym.

4 These poems represent Jōchō wistfully sharing his thoughts with an open heart and purity represented by the beauty of the cherry tree (*yama-zakura*) far removed from the hustle and bustle of the mundane world, and Tsuramoto's reply expresses his gratefulness for his counsel.

5 Tashiro Tsuramoto's pseudonym.

All retainers of the Nabeshima clan must be familiar with the lore and customs (*kokugaku*) of the domain.[1] It is lamentable that such learning has been neglected of late. Why is it necessary? It helps one understand the origins of the Nabeshima clan, and appreciate the great sacrifices and generosity of the domain's forefathers to ensure its continued prosperity. Gratitude is owed to Lord Gōchū[2] for his compassion and valor, and to Lord Risō[3] for his benevolent deeds and faith. For it was thanks to them that the might of Lord Takanobu[4] and Lord Nippō[5] ensured the clan's longevity and an enduring, honorable reputation in the world still unmatched.

It is incomprehensible how warriors these days have forgotten the magnitude of these historical events, and even revere unrelated lords instead.[6] Sakyamuni, Confucius, Kusunoki Masanari, and Takeda Shingen were never a part of the Ryūzōji-Nabeshima brotherhood, and are not compatible with the customs of our domain. In times of both peace and war, it is important for men of high or low status to revere our own clan's ancestors and abide by their teachings. Disciples of a school or tradition[7] venerate the master of their style. But retainers of the Nabeshima clan need not study anything outside

---

1 The term *kokugaku*, literally "national learning," is more commonly associated with the textual and interpretive study of classical Japanese literature, a field of academic inquiry that flourished during the Tokugawa period. In the case of *Hagakure*, it refers to the formation of the Nabeshima domain, the genealogy of its lords, and its political systems and customs.

2 Originally Ryūzōji Iekane (1454–1546), he was a formidable warlord during the Warring States period, whose many victories culminated in the Ryūzōji family's hegemony over the Saga domain. He changed his name to Gōchū when he entered the priesthood.

3 Risō is the posthumous name of Nabeshima Kiyohisa (1468–1552), a retainer of Iekane. He was also the grandfather of Nabeshima Naoshige, who was to take over control of the Saga domain from the Ryūzōji family.

4 Ryūzōji Takanobu (1529–1584) was a powerful warlord who gained hegemony over the province of Hizen and surrounding districts. His mother remarried Nabeshima Naoshige's father, thus making the two brothers-in-law and close allies.

5 Nippō was the posthumous name for Nabeshima Naoshige (1538–1618). He formally became the lord of Saga in 1607, inheriting it from the Ryūzōji family, and was referred to as the *hanso*, or Nabeshima domain founder. His son, Katsushige, became the first lord (*shodai*) of the domain after his father's death.

6 Worshipping the ancestral spirits of people not related to the Nabeshima clan or the domain.

7 Buddhism, Confucianism, the martial arts, or aesthetic pursuits.

the domain. Only after becoming familiar with the lore of our own principality is it permissible to learn other things. A retainer does not require anything more than a comprehensive understanding of the ways of the Nabeshima clan.

What if a warrior from another clan was to ask about the origins of the houses of Ryūzōji and Nabeshima, and how the domain came to be governed by the latter? Or, "I hear that the Ryūzōji-Nabeshima clans are known as the boldest in Kyushu. What are some of the heroic deeds that have been achieved by your warriors?" If the Nabeshima clansman has no knowledge of the history, customs, and traditions of his domain, he will be unable to answer these inquiries.

What's more, all that a retainer needs to do is to energetically execute his assigned duties. Even so, many have an aversion to their responsibilities, and look on with envy at the duties of others, leading to considerable negligence. Lord Nippō and Lord Taisei-in (Nabeshima Katsushige) set a wonderful example of how duties should be discharged faithfully. Their vassals also did their part and executed their duties with great dedication. Those above sought expedient men for retainers, and those below strived to be of use. In this way, the wills of men high and low were in accord, and so the clan was strong.

Lord Nippō endured indescribable hardships, often bloodied and tested in battle, and there were many occasions in which he was prepared to take his own life by *seppuku*. Despite the odds, he was also blessed with good luck, and succeeded in keeping his house in tact. Similarly, after almost committing *seppuku*, Lord Taisei-in came to govern the province [as the first Nabeshima daimyo]. Apart from fighting hard in many a battle, he withstood ordeals in administering the clan, protecting the province, and managing domain policies. He was also devoted in his faith. He said, "I would surely be punished if I thought to neglect the house revived by Lord Nippō. I am duty-bound to ensure that the clan enjoys peace and prosperity down through the generations. With peace, the world will become exquisitely extravagant. People will forget about the harsh times of war and increase their expenditure as they seek a life of luxury. Thus, living beyond their means, warriors of high and low station will fall into abject poverty, incurring much shame in the eyes of the people in and outside the domain, and finally their household will collapse. The veterans in the warrior houses all pass away, and the younger generations of samurai learn only the current trends. For this reason, it is my hope that what I wrote will be talked about by future generations. If my writings are passed on when headship of the clan is transferred, by reading this, the new leader will be able to appreciate the things that have come to pass before his time." For this purpose, Lord Nippō spent his entire life surrounded by scrap paper as he recorded his thoughts.

There is no way that we can know the secrets of the clan. According to the domain elders, the secret military tactics of *kachikuchi*[1] for achieving absolute victory are conveyed orally from one generation of Nabeshima heirs to the next at the time of accession. Also, in the house safety box there are two texts—*Shichōkakuchishō* and *Senkōsan'i-ki*.[2] These two military texts are handed down personally to each successive lord.

Furthermore, Lord Nippō recorded in great detail on high-quality *torinoko* paper the arrangement of matters in the house, outlines for all the various organizations in the domain, protocols for relations with the shogunate, and all financial matters.[3]

The enduring prosperity of our clan is owed to the hard work of Lord Nippō. We must be eternally grateful. Thus, with all due respect to new lords, I sincerely hope that they take the time to contemplate the hardships of their ancestors, Lord Nippō and Lord Taisei-in, and at least peruse the writings passed down, taking the content to heart. As new lords are mollycoddled from birth by attendants, they rarely experience hardship, and do not know the customs or history of the domain. They simply do as they wish with little consideration of the immense weight of responsibility a lord must shoulder. In recent years,

---

1 Literally "the mouth of victory."
2 Nabeshima Katsushige ordered that these two books on military tactics be compiled by Ishida Ittei and others in 1651.
3 *Torinoko* is eggshell-colored traditional Japanese paper made primarily of high-quality, glossy *Diplomorpha sikokiana* fibers. This domain procedural guidebook was known as the *Torinoko-chō*.

many new initiatives have been enacted and the domain's administration is faltering.

In such times, crafty retainers who know little of the world put on pretences of their facile wisdom as they think of new schemes, hoping to receive their lord's favor. They become arrogant and do as they please, causing no end of trouble. To give some examples: the discord between the three branch families of the Nabeshima clan;[1] the establishment of the rank of *chakuza* [directly under chief retainers] to control the domain's administration; the employment of outsiders into service; promoting *teakiyari* (reserve warriors) to the higher position of *mono-kashira* (unit captain); frequent reshuffling of members in *kumi* (military units); the changing of mansions; appointing chief retainers to the same status as the lord's kinfolk (*shinrui-dōkaku*); dismantling of the Kōyōken mansion; amending the domain rules (*okitechō*); the creation of a system of rank for temples [for exclusive audiences with the lord]; using significant funds for building the west mansion (Nishi-yashiki) by Tsunashige; restructuring the units of *ashigaru*;[2] dividing the lord's items [after he dies] among retainers; dismantling of the west mansion [by Yoshishige]; and so on. The manner for dealing with such matters changes each time a new lord ascends, and problems arise when they succumb to the lure of pursuing something new.

Nevertheless, the enactments of our ancestors are stable, and the foundations of the clan have not been unsettled in the slightest. Even with a degree of maladministration, if all men abide by the instructions bequeathed by Lord Nippō and Lord Taisei-in, the clan will not suffer, and stability will enable effective governance of the domain.

In any case, not one of our ancestral lords has been a tyrant or of sinister disposition. Not one of our lords has ever been negatively compared to any of other provinces. Our excellence is unquestionable thanks to the inviolable faith of our revered ancestors. In accordance with our customs, Nabeshima clansmen were never exiled to other provinces even when dishonorably discharged (*rōnin*), and

---

1 See Book 1-101.
2 See Book 2-69.

few outsiders from other clans have been employed here. Even a warrior dismissed from his post, or the offspring of men ordered to commit *seppuku,* are permitted to reside within the principality.

With such strong bonds of fealty, being born into this clan and basking in the munificence and compassion passed down through generations, bears a debt of gratitude which can hardly be expressed with words, written or spoken, for retainers, and even the farmers and townsmen. When employed as a retainer, harden your resolve to repay this debt of largesse through selfless service. If you are made a *rōnin,* or ordered to commit *seppuku,* think of this as service also.

Even living deep in the mountains, or from under the ground, continue to wish for the continued prosperity of the clan. This must the first and foremost aspiration of a Nabeshima samurai.

Although presumptuous of me as a hermit, one who has taken the holy orders, not once have I desired to attain Buddhahood in death; instead, I only want to be reincarnated seven times as a Nabeshima clansman, with the determination resolutely etched in my gut to uphold the tranquillity of the Saga domain.

No particular talent is needed. In a word, all that is required is the fortitude to declare that you alone will shoulder the burden of responsibility. As a man, who can I be inferior to in matters of cherishing and serving the lord? As is usually the case with a man's training, one will not succeed without being haughtily believing in your true worth as a man of service. Each samurai must believe that he alone will carry the clan. Like the axiom, *yakan-dōshin* ("searching for the Way in a kettle"), one's feelings can run hot and cold, but there are attitudes that should never be forsaken. The following is my own professed oath:

> *I will never fall behind others in pursuing the*
> *Way of the warrior.*
> *I will always be ready to serve my lord.*
> *I will honor my parents.*
> *I will serve compassionately for the benefit*
> *of others.*

By chanting these four oaths (*shiseigan*) every morning and night to the deities and to Buddha, you will become imbued with double your strength, and will never lag behind. Like an inchworm, it is simply a matter of advancing forward, little by little. Even the gods and Buddha started by pledging an oath of allegiance.

Book 1

闘書一

1. Although it stands to reason that a warrior must abide by the tenets of the martial Way,[1] it seems that many are guilty of dereliction in this respect. If asked, what is the essence of *budō*? there are few who can answer this question without hesitation because it has not been taken to heart. This clearly shows negligence in understanding the warrior's Way. This is appallingly careless.

❀ ❀ ❀

2. The Way of the warrior (bushido) is to be found in dying.[2] If one is faced with two options of life or death, simply settle for death. It is not an especially difficult choice; just go forth and meet it confidently. To declare that dying without aiming for the right purpose is nothing more than a "dog's death"[3] is the timid and shallow way of Kamigata warriors.[4] Whenever faced with the choice of life and death, there is no need to try and achieve one's aims. Human beings have a preference for life. As such, it is a natural tendency to apply logic to justify one's proclivity to stay alive. If you miss the mark and

---

1 *Budō* (武道) is used here as an alternative word to *bushidō*. In fact, *budō* was more commonly used during the Tokugawa period to refer to warrior ideals. However, this tends to cause confusion nowadays, as *budō* is the designation used for the modern (post-Meiji) martial arts. Bushido became a popular generic term from the Meiji era (late nineteenth century) to describe the distinctive culture, ideals, and lifestyle of samurai from all time periods. The term itself did not even exist until the end of the Sengoku period (1467-1568); and even during the Tokugawa period (1603-1867) it was not widely used. *Hagakure* is actually one of the few examples of Tokugawa literature that uses the term extensively. More common appellations representing "the Way of the warrior" during the Tokugawa period include *budō* and *shidō*.

2 This is undoubtedly the most famous phrase in *Hagakure*. There are differences in modern Japanese and foreign language translations of exactly how it should be interpreted. Some prefer "**I have found** the Way of the warrior is in death." It seems that the verb *mitsuketari* ("found") is either attached to the author's discovery of the meaning of bushido, or that the meaning of bushido is found in embracing death. I prefer the latter interpretation, but either is possible linguistically.

3 The word used here is *inu-jini* (犬死), a term that was widely used during the Tokugawa period to express the pathos of a wasted or meaningless death.

4 The term "*kamigata*" usually refers to the Osaka and Kyoto region, but in this case also implies the city of Edo. The word is often mentioned in *Hagakure* to contrast the mannerisms of sophisticated, urban warriors with the rustic ways of samurai in the Saga domain.

you live to tell the tale, then you are a coward. This is a perilous way of thinking. If you make a mistake and die in the process, you may be thought of as mad (*kichigai*), but it will not bring shame. This is the mind-set of one who firmly lives by the martial Way. Rehearse your death every morning and night. Only when you constantly live as though already a corpse (*jōjū shinimi*) will you be able to find freedom in the martial Way, and fulfill your duties without fault throughout your life.

3. A man in service (*hōkōnin*) needs only to place his lord at the center of his heart. Nothing is more desirable than this. Having been born into the service of the honorable house of Nabeshima, a clan that extends back many generations, we should appreciate the magnitude of the largesse (*on*) successive lords have bestowed upon our ancestors, and be prepared to sacrifice body and soul in reverential servitude. On top of this, it is beneficial if one has wisdom and other talents that can augment competent service. Even a man who is useless and unable to accomplish anything effectively, however, will be a trusted servant so long as his allegiance is wholehearted. Relying only on cleverness and talents [devoid of single-minded devotion] is a lower form of service.

4. There are those who are born with a quick wit, and others who need to withdraw and contemplate matters carefully to find an answer. Although there is considerable disparity in natural talent between men, by discarding one's own predispositions and carefully contemplating the "Four Oaths" (*shiseigan*)[1] tremendous wisdom will emanate from within. People are apt to think that serious matters

---

1 "I will never fall behind others in pursuing the Way of the warrior."
  "I will always be ready to serve my lord."
  "I will honor my parents."
  "I will serve compassionately for the benefit of others."

can be solved through meticulous introspection, but the predominance of egocentric motivations leads to malevolent ideas that come to no good. It is too much to ask for foolish men to become selfless. Therefore, if one seeks to resolve a problem, let it sit for a while, take time to think about the "Four Oaths" and subdue any self-centered thoughts, and then you will be able to proceed without faltering.

❄ ❄ ❄

5. As actions are typically based on one's own limited intelligence, selfish desires transpire and men inadvertently turn their backs on the Heavenly Way (*tendō*), resulting in wickedness. Others will view this as repugnant, weak, constricted, or lax. When it is difficult to invoke true wisdom unimpeded by selfish motivations, consult a man with insight. He will be able to offer selfless and candid advice as the matter is of no concern to him personally, and he will thus be able make rational judgments. Such recourse will be viewed by others as being firmly-rooted and prudent. It is akin to an enormous tree with many roots; by contrast, the self-centered wisdom of one man is like a small tree precariously placed in the ground.

❄ ❄ ❄

6. We can tap into knowledge that serves to steer us away from egotism by studying the aphorisms and deeds of the ancients. If we discard our own prejudices and invoke the maxims of our forebears, or consult with others on such matters, we can proceed without impediment and not wane into iniquity. Lord Katsushige often consulted [his father] Lord Naoshige. This information is recorded in the *O-hanashi-kikigaki*—and demonstrates fine judgement.

Likewise, there was a man who employed several of his younger brothers as retainers, and they accompanied him when he visited Edo and the Kamigata region. Being able to consult with them in matters of both personal and official nature, it is said that his affairs were conducted efficiently without any oversights.

❈ ❈ ❈

7. Sagara Kyūma[1] was at one in body and soul with his lord, and he attended him with selfless dedication as if he was 'already dead.' He was one in a thousand. Once, in the seventh year of Enpō (1679), a conference was convened at Lord Sakyō's[2] Mizugae residence, where it was decided that Kyūma must commit *seppuku*.[3] At that time, there was a teahouse in Lord Taku Nui's[4] three-storied suburban villa in Ōsaki. Kyūma rented the building, and invited all the scoundrels in Saga to a party. They even staged a derisive puppet show in which he operated the lead puppet himself. They drank the days and nights away in a raucous cacophony overlooking Lord Sakyō's residence. Purposefully instigating this commotion with the gallant intention of vicariously committing suicide for his lord was truly commendable.[5]

❈ ❈ ❈

8. Ishida Ittei[6] relayed the following: "Sagara Kyūma probably appeared on the scene thanks to the prayers of Lord Katsushige. He was a man of impressive capacity. Lord Katsushige had him write his supplications to the deities and Buddha each year. The one he wrote the year before his death is possibly stored in the repository. Kyūma behaved in a somewhat unsatisfactory manner towards the end. He said, 'I am receiving a stipend that is overly generous, and I am unable to repay the debt of obligation. My son Sukejirō is an infant, and as I do not know how competent he will be, I feel obliged to return my stipend. Should His Lordship appoint my son as my successor, I would appreciate it if you would issue him a stipend in

---

1 Sagara Kyūma was a high-ranking vassal of Nabeshima Mitsushige.

2 Nabeshima Katsushige's tenth son, Shindai Naonaga.

3 At the meeting, Lord Mitsushige's transgressions were deliberated on, and it was decided that Kyūma should atone for his master's wrongdoings by sacrificing his own life.

4 Yasuhide.

5 The inference here is that by participating in such shameful revelry, observers would conclude that he was ordered to commit suicide for his own transgression, diverting attention away from his lord's blunders.

6 Jōchō's teacher of Confucian ethics.

accordance with his capabilities.' Normally, one would never expect a man of Kyūma's caliber to make such an excuse. Maybe it was because of some ailment. It is sad, but the house of Sagara will see its demise within three years. The favor he has received from his lord is a debt so heavy that it cannot be repaid."

Ittei also remarked to somebody else: "That man is very clever, and has an unblemished service record. Still, his house will also come to an end in four or five years." Everything he predicted came to pass. He had uncanny powers of observation. I also started to take notice of men in service of the lord, and gradually came to see how long an inadequate samurai would last in service.

Kyūma later became a *rōnin*. His expulsion happened after a notice was attached to the *o-metsuke* (inspector) Yamamoto Gorōzaemon's[1] gate, which stated how Kyūma's brutalizing of farmers was unacceptable. It was found that the allegations were true after an investigation. Several retainers were rebuked, and Kyūma was removed from service.

❀ ❀ ❀

9. A true retainer is his lord's greatest follower, entrusting all matters, good or bad, to him in selfless deference to his authority. Two or three men of this caliber will ensure the wellbeing of the clan. After observing the world for some years, I noticed that when things are going well many come forth and make pretences of their usefulness on the grounds of intelligence, judgment, and artful talents. However, when the lord decides to retire or passes away, they are quick to turn their backs on him and ingratiate themselves with his successor. It pains me to recall such reprehensible behavior. Men of high and low status, clever men, and artistic men all vie to exhibit their merit as loyal servants, but become limp and craven when it comes to actually sacrificing their lives when calamity strikes. This is inexcusable behavior indeed.

A seemingly useless retainer becomes superior to a thousand

---

1 Also known as Tsuneharu, he was Jōchō's nephew, but 20 years his senior.

men of this ilk if he has already resolved to cast away his life and become one with his lord. This was evident with the passing of Lord Mitsushige. I was the only one determined to follow him in death by relinquishing my privileged status and becoming a lay monk. Some others followed my lead later on.[1] Distinguished men of rank, who expounded their views pompously when Lord Mitsushige was alive, turned their backs on him the moment he died. The pledge of devotion between lord and follower bound by the weight of *gi*[2] is thought to be very difficult to abide by, but it is in fact very simple. A retainer who has made up his mind without hesitation [to die for his lord] will be without peer.

❀ ❀ ❀

10. Some people showed a tendency to procure the lord's items meant for disposal, and keep them for themselves. Such men cannot be trusted. It is sacrilege to take items permeated with the lord's soul and then to use them in one's own household—such as elaborate pouches that he cherished—and evaluating various belongings in boxes before pilfering them. Although it may not be a punishable offence, I question their sense of right and wrong. Such superficial service lacks the moral obligation binding a lord and his retainer.

❀ ❀ ❀

11. Throughout his life, Yamasaki Kurando[3] refused to accept any cast-off paraphernalia from his lord. Nor did he once visit the abodes of [well to do] townsmen. This is precisely the modest attitude

---

1 Yamamoto Jōchō wished to follow his lord in death by committing ritual suicide (*junshi*). However, the act of *junshi* had been outlawed in the Saga province in 1661 and later by the bakufu in 1663. Being denied his right to a "self-willed death," Jōchō decided to take holy orders instead, and gave up life in the mundane world. In this passage he shows his disdain for other attendants who appeared more calculating in their actions following Mitsushige's death.

2 *Gi* (義) has a number of meanings, including morality, righteousness, justice, and honor; it also alludes to non-consanguineous relationships.

3 A clan elder (*toshiyori*).

expected of a retainer. On no occasion did Ishii Kurōuemon[1] use any secondhand equipment, either. These days, people show a disturbingly selfish tendency to try and outdo others in acquiring used trappings. They make uninvited visits to townspeople, imposing on their hospitality, and then take pleasure in purchasing frivolities off merchants on the pretense of inspecting the marketplace. Such licentious behavior makes a mockery of the code of the samurai.

❀ ❀ ❀

12. During my sojourn in the Kamigata region before the passing of Lord Mitsushige, I was suddenly gripped by a strong desire to return to the domain.[2] I made arrangements with Kawamura[3] to convey my intentions to his master (Sanenori) and embarked on the long journey traveling day and night back to Saga.[4] I was blessed to complete the voyage in time for His Lordship's demise. It was quite a miracle, for news of his sudden turn for the worse had not yet reached Kyoto when I departed. I feel that I was alerted to his looming death by the gods because of my steadfast conviction that I was the only retainer who thought of him above all else. Although my service was not discernible by any particular deed of note or virtue, I alone upheld my lord's reputation when he died.[5] When the lord of a domain

---

1 A clan elder (*toshiyori*).

2 This is referring to Jōchō's time spent in Kyoto. He returned to Saga in 1700.

3 Kawamura Gonbei, who served the famous poet and aristocrat Sanjō-nishi Sanenori (1619–1701). This journey and the patronage of Sanenori was highly significant as it enabled him to fulfill the important self-appointed task of acquiring the rare teachings, *Kokin-denju,* and related documents back to Mitsushige. The teachings were an explanation of the *Kokin-shū,* a compilation of tenth century poems, and was greatly desired by Mitsushige, who was a keen enthusiast of poetry.

4 Through Kyoto, Osaka, and Edo.

5 Jōchō is alluding to his expressed desire to demonstrate his loyalty by committing ritual suicide (*junshi* or *oibara*). However, this act was prohibited by Nabeshima Mitsushige's decree of 1661. The bakufu (shogunate) also prohibited *junshi* nationally in 1663. The practice of self-immolation to follow one's lord in death, had become a relatively common occurrence in the early modern period, when there were no more wars in which samurai could demonstrate their valor and manliness. This was considered a valid way of expressing one's excellence as a faithful retainer. The Nabeshima domain had a history of such personal sacrifice. The founder of the domain, Naoshige, died

passes, it is tragic when none of his retainers are prepared to follow him. I know this because nobody was inclined to make such a personal sacrifice when Lord Mitsushige died. All that is required is to surrender one's life for the sake of the lord. This world is full of cowardly, spineless men who think only of self-gratification and satisfying their own greedy desires. This is why my heart was full of despair for many years after my lord breathed his last.

❀ ❀ ❀

13. There are certain procedures that should be observed when sorting what items [of a deceased lord] are to be preserved and those to be burned. I will only mention the main points here, and specifics will be imparted verbally: The world has changed and this is no longer the duty of official attendants. Some of the effects may be discarded and some retained. After boxing an item up, receive a seal of proof from an elder lest people become suspicious that you may have taken it. Verify if either measure has not already been deferred. Ask questions to ensure agreement. Check the inventory.[1]

❀ ❀ ❀

14. Presenting one's opinions to others to help them rectify their faults is an important act of great compassion, and is the duty of a retainer. Nevertheless, the way in which an opinion is offered is of the essence. It is easy to discern good and bad points in others, and anybody can offer criticism. In many cases, people think they are being considerate by pointing out wrongdoings that are usually unpleasant or difficult to broach. If their advice is not received with

---

in 1618, and 13 retainers committed suicide. When his son Katsushige died in 1687, 36 of his retainers chose to kill themselves. Jōchō strongly desired to martyr himself in the same way as his predecessors had done in the ultimate demonstration of loyalty, but was instead forced to take the tonsure, as an alternative to *junshi*. To Jōchō, at least by expressing this desire, he had saved his lord from the shame of not having anybody prepared to die with him in accordance with the old customs of military houses.

1 The list of instructions outlined is vague in the original Japanese and open to interpretation. Possibly instructions from Tsunashige regarding Mitsushige's belongings.

the grace it is given, then the remonstrator is resigned to think that little else can be done. Such an attitude is of little use. It is analogous to shaming somebody, or disparagement simply to get something off your own chest.

In offering one's opinion, one must first ascertain whether or not the recipient is in the right frame of mind to receive counsel. Strive to become a trusted colleague, and ensure that he has faith in your words. Start by broaching matters that he is interested in, and devise various ways of making your thoughts known. Decide on an appropriate time, and whether you should express your ideas in writing, or talk to him on the way home. Mention your own failures, and try to evoke his understanding indirectly. Or, while complimenting his finer attributes, present your views in such a way that he will happily take your advice to correct his shortfalls, just as a man with a dry throat reaches for water to quench his thirst.

To achieve this is very challenging. If a bad habit has become ingrained over many years, it cannot be remedied easily. I have also had experience with this. Being convivial and cooperating with one's companions to rectify each other's inadequacies to be of better use to the lord is what constitutes genuinely compassionate service. Remember though, how can you expect a man to become a better person just through humiliating him?

❋ ❋ ❋

15. Making an opinion known to somebody verbally. Regarding a *rōnin* who loathed his master: Painfully aware of his transgressions, a certain *rōnin* returned to serve his lord after five or six years' absence. At first, he rejected the offer to return to service, but made a pledge after accepting the second invitation. Having refused the first time he should have resigned once and for all. Or, he could have shaved his head to become a monk.

Similarly, a *rōnin* who does not acknowledge his mistakes and begrudges his master should not be allowed to return. If he persists in bewailing the "unsympathetic" treatment he received, or continues to feel "animosity," the heavens will spurn him all the more. A man once said: "It is a heavenly reprimand. Simply acknowledge that you are solely at fault and repent, otherwise you will never be able to resume service again."

❀ ❀ ❀

16. After serving as Sawabe Heizaemon's second (*kaishaku*) on the event of his *seppuku*, I (Jōchō) received a letter of appreciation from clan elder Nakano Kazuma of Edo.[1] In it he stated in the most elaborate terms that the family's reputation had been restored. At the time, I thought that it was excessive to write such a letter for assisting in Sawabe's suicide. After further consideration, I realized that it was quite tactful. It is important to commend young warriors if they perform their duties well in order to motivate them, even if it was only a trifling achievement. That is why he wrote the letter. Not long after, I also received a note of praise from Nakano Shōgen.[2] I have kept both letters safe. Yamamoto Gorōzaemon presented me a gift of saddle and stirrups.

❀ ❀ ❀

17. Yawning in the presence of others is impolite. If the urge to yawn suddenly arises, rub your forehead in an upward stroke to suppress it. If this is not enough to restrain the yawn, use the tip of your tongue to lock your lips shut, and cover your gaping mouth with your hand or sleeve to conceal it from others. Sneezes should also be stifled. Sneezes and yawns make you look very silly. There are many other points of etiquette that you should be mindful of at all times.

❀ ❀ ❀

18. Master Jōchō pondered tasks for the coming day and wrote them

---

1 Sawanabe Heizaemon was Jōchō's nephew. He committed *seppuku* for an indiscretion in 1682. Yamamoto Gorōzaemon was also a nephew of Jōchō.

2 Nakano Shōgen was Jōchō's uncle (the grandchild of Jōchō's father's older brother). He was an elder councilor (*toshiyori-yaku*) of the domain, and committed *seppuku* in 1689.

down. Being organized keeps you a step ahead of others. When scheduled to meet somebody the following day, make a careful assessment the night before, contemplating appropriate greetings, topics of conversation, and points of etiquette. He relayed the following advice when we travelled somewhere together. It is good practice to think things through when going to visit somebody. This is to ensure that harmony prevails. It is also a matter of protocol. Furthermore, if one is invited by a man of high standing, it is not good to be too nervous beforehand as you will be unable to converse properly at the start. Instead, one should feel genuine gratitude for the opportunity to meet, and embark with feelings of joyous anticipation.

It is generally best to avoid visiting somebody unexpectedly when you have no business there. On the other hand, if you are invited you should act in such a way that your host regards you as an "agreeable visitor;" otherwise you have no place as a guest. In any case, it is important to organize yourself well beforehand. This is most important at a drinking party. The best time to excuse yourself is hard to discern. Your stay should not become wearisome, but care should be taken not to be in a hurry to leave early, either. Usually, it is inadvisable to be too restrained when offered morsels to partake of. Politely refrain from accepting once or twice, but then capitulate to your host's kind generosity. This also applies when you meet somebody by chance on the road and are invited to their home.

19. In essence, the "Four Oaths" have the following meaning:[1] "Never fall behind others in pursuing the Way of the warrior" means you must be prepared to demonstrate your gallantry to all and sundry and always be ready to die for your cause. This is recorded in more detail in *Gukenshū*.[2] The second pledge, "be ready to serve one's lord," means aspiring to becomes a *karō* (chief retainer), a position in which

---

1 See Book 1-4.
2 The *Gukenshū* was a book of precepts given by Jōchō to his adopted son Gon'nojō in 1708.

you remonstrate with your lord for the sake of the clan. "Filial duty" (*kō*) is connected with "loyalty" (*chū*). They are the same. "Serve compassionately for the benefit of others" means encouraging other men to be exemplary servants.

❀ ❀ ❀

20. When discussing paraphernalia needed for a wedding, one person made the observation: "A *koto* and *shamisen*[1] are not included in this list, but we will need them." Another person remarked curtly, "We don't need them at all." This individual made his comments fully aware of the company present, but contradicted himself the following day by stating that the two instruments were in fact essential for weddings after all, and that two of each, of the highest quality, should be acquired. Upon hearing this story, I thought: What a venerable fellow [for admitting he was wrong]. Master Jōchō said to me: "It is wrong to think like that. He acted that way simply to assert his authority. Such conduct is often encountered among outsiders of equivocal loyalty employed in our domain. First of all, it is rude to behave in such a way to a person of higher station; and it does not benefit his lord at all. To an adherent of the Way of the warrior, even if an item is reckoned to be completely unnecessary, correct deportment dictates that one first acknowledge the other person's assessment, and mention that it can be discussed later on so as to not cause embarrassment. Furthermore, the items in question were actually necessary, so he requested that they be added to the list the next day. This was devious, discourteous behavior that consequently humiliated his colleague publicly, and was very careless."

❀ ❀ ❀

21. There is disparity in the military tactics and strategy (*gungaku*) demonstrated by men who are prepared, and those who are not. The prepared warrior is not only able to solve problems in a quick and

---

1 Traditional stringed musical instruments.

commendable fashion by virtue of his life experience, but he can react appropriately through his comprehension of measures to meet any scenario. He is always ready. The unprepared warrior lacks foresight, and even if he succeeds in solving a problem, it is merely through good fortune rather than good planning. A warrior who doesn't think things through beforehand will be ill-equipped.

❀ ❀ ❀

22. Master Jōchō said, "It would be wonderful to have all the *rōnin* in attendance at the centenary of Lord Nippō's[1] death. I am certain that he would be pleased, although it is probably not feasible, as the clan needs to be prudent with expenses. In recent years, *rōnin* and the descendants of samurai from our clan who committed *seppuku* have been neglected. Reserve warriors of the lower rank of *teakiyari* and *rōnin* are hardly considered for promotion. I did hear, though, that through a lack of knowledge of the history of the Nabeshima clan, a *teakiyari* was promoted to the middle-rank of *monogashira*.

❀ ❀ ❀

23. One should always be careful to behave properly at social gatherings. Careful observation of revelries show that the majority of men are resigned to getting totally drunk. Partaking in alcohol is pleasurable so long as one ceases consumption at an appropriate time. It looks vulgar if one behaves recklessly, and it is an indication of one's character and [low] level of refinement. When drinking, the warrior should be aware that eyes are always upon him. Act appropriately in public.

❀ ❀ ❀

24. A certain person suggested itemizing expenditures in the domain, but this is not always wise. There is an old adage that goes 'Fish avoid

---

1 Nabeshima Naoshige.

streams with clear water."[1] Fish are able to survive and thrive by hiding under weeds and in the shadows of objects in the water. Overlooking the odd shortcoming enables the lower classes to live with peace of mind. This is also pertinent to matters of conduct."

❋ ❋ ❋

25. At the central domain office, a commoner wished to file a petition but was refused by a certain official, and thus a quarrel erupted. Another person intervened and said, "Accept the petition first, and if you decide later that it shouldn't be filed, then you can return it." Another official commented cynically, "How can you settle matters without accepting submissions?" Master Jōchō said he thought that Mr. So-and-so had mended his ways, but it seems he is still prickly. One can act with familiarity in everyday life, but must demonstrate strict adherence to courtesy in official dealings. That is the protocol of the samurai. Disgracing a visitor in such a way is unseemly, and runs counter to the warrior code.

❋ ❋ ❋

26. A certain official of high standing asked a samurai if he could acquire his residence. He agreed, but just as he was arranging to relocate, he was suddenly informed that his house was no longer needed. This change of mind upset the samurai, and he complained of the disruption. The senior official who reneged on the arrangement apologized, and offered a monetary settlement, to which the complainant agreed. This is a truly risible affair. Generally speaking, nobody likes to be tricked and come out on the losing end, but this is completely different. Nor did it have anything to do with being silenced because the other man was of high station. This instance was a matter of 'profit and loss.' Its basis is reprehensible to begin with. Even so, insolent remarks directed at a person of higher station

---

1 This is from a passage in the *Kung Tzu Chia Yu*. The full verse is: "Fish avoid streams with clear water; a man too judicious amasses no followers."

is rude. Extorting compensation actually represents a loss. It will have lasting repercussions on his reputation. Generally speaking, the filing of such petitions is triggered by greed to acquire profit. If a man is prepared to accept a loss from the outset, he cannot be beaten. In this sense, if you are patient (*kannin*) you will not lose. This man was not wise enough to realize this.

❀ ❀ ❀

27. Ishii Mataemon was once a warrior of laudable ability, but became somewhat irrational after taking ill. When discussing the arrangement of His Lordship's entourage of attendants, a man asked Mataemon about the position of poetry scribe. He replied, "Since becoming ill, I find myself unable to recall what is happening even in the present. Even if I do remember, how can I tell you lest it be a matter my master ordered me not to speak of? In any case, I cannot speak of something I have no recollection of."

❀ ❀ ❀

28. When fire broke out at a retainer's residence, in his capacity as the duty officer, inspector Yamamoto Gorōzaemon rushed to the scene to supervise the fire fighting. The keepers shut the gate, saying: "It's not this house that's on fire." His blood rising, Gorōzaemon threatened them by saying, "If it is your intention to prevent entry of a man who is here by order of His Lordship, then I will be compelled to cut you all down." They opened the gate as he drew his sword, and he saw that only a few of the retainer's men were trying to douse the fire.

❀ ❀ ❀

29. When I asked Yasaburō to brush a character, I emphasized the importance of 'determination': "Write each character without fear of tearing through the paper with your brush. The merits of the character can be decided by a calligraphy expert—do not be discouraged just because it does not go well."

❁ ❁ ❁

30. When Lord Mitsushige was still a boy and trying to read a book in the presence of the priest Kaion Oshō, he exclaimed: "Acolytes, come forth and listen. It is difficult to recite when there is no audience." Kaion was impressed, and told his young charges, "You should all have such an eager attitude for everything."

❁ ❁ ❁

31. Morning worship should commence with a show of reverence to one's lord, parents, the clan deity (*ujigami*), and guardian Buddha respectively.[1] Giving priority to your master will please your parents, and the gods will surely respond to your supplications. Samurai need not think of anything else other than serving their lord. As long as you are brimming with this desire, you will always be aware of him [and his needs]. Moreover, a woman should obey her husband as her master in the same way.

❁ ❁ ❁

32. Conventions teach that the *kanji* for "protocols of courtesy"[2] should be read as *date*, which means "elegance." Etiquette without elegance is substandard.

❁ ❁ ❁

33. It happened in spring of the third year of Shōtoku (1713). Discussions were convened regarding the rain ceremony at the Kinryū Shrine. An opinion was voiced at the administration headquarters: "The yearly event is a huge burden for all concerned. The festival should be carried out enthusiastically this year, but if the desired

---

1 Originally *ujigami* referred to a deified ancestor worshipped by descendants at a local family shrine, but by the Tokugawa period it had come to mean a local deity that protected all the inhabitants of a specific region.

2 時宜 = *jigi*, or bow.

effects are not forthcoming, then it should be stopped thereafter." Many orchestras, dance troupes, and *kyōgen* performers from 33 villages were summoned to participate. The rain ritual at the Kinryū Shrine is always miraculous in its efficacy, but not on this occasion. On the day, the drummers did not beat their drums as they had been taught, and the instructors ripped the drumsticks away from them, starting a fracas. There were sword fights and brawling in the lower area of the shrine, and some people were killed. Spectators also got into violent tussles and came away with injuries.

At the time, rumors abounded among the lower classes that the unrest was due to the wrath of the gods, provoked through the diabolical insincerity shown by the administrators. Sanjō-nishi Dainagon Sanenori[1] once remarked: "Unlucky events that occur during rituals to the deities are portents of calamity." Indeed, during the same year a number of officials at the domain headquarters were beheaded because of their deceptions, and many were killed in the tsunami that crashed into Terai. This was surely related with the lower precinct of the Kinryū Shrine being near the seashore. Also, there was the matter of Hara Jūrōzaemon killing a colleague in the palace.[2] Such misfortunes surely corroborate what Sanenori said.

❀ ❀ ❀

34. A certain priest is a man of rare talent in recent times. He is extremely tolerant. As such, he manages a big temple very well. The other day he said, "As I am too ill, I am sure to fail in my undertaking of overseeing this great temple. I am doing what I can to satisfy this responsibility, but when I am under the weather, I entrust all of the duties to my deputy and try to circumvent any kind of catastrophe."

Two generations earlier, the priest at this temple had been too strict, and nobody was prepared to follow him. The previous priest left everything up to his subordinates and was quite lazy. Since the

---

1 See Book 1-12.
2 Hara Jūrōzaemon killed Sagara Gentazaemon in the second citadel and was executed by decapitation in 1713.

current priest took charge, there are few complaints and his acolytes are obedient. He considers the big picture as well as the smaller details, and he leaves the staff alone to do their jobs. If he is asked a question, he explains with such clarity that there are no misunderstandings. This is why he has a good reputation for managing the temple successfully.

Once, there was another [Zen] monk who spouted shallow ideas with an air of authority. The priest summoned this man and said, "You misrepresent correct Buddhist Law. I must now beat you to death." The poor fellow was crippled after the beating he received. Still, the priest has many fine attributes. He uses illness as a front [to ensure his temple is run efficiently through delegation].

❀ ❀ ❀

35. The gaze of retainers today seems to be very low. Their eyes resemble those of crooks driven by covetousness and cunning. Even if a samurai seems to have spirit, this is merely a feigned exterior. A samurai is not a true retainer without placing himself in absolute servitude at the feet of his lord, thinking of himself as already dead, like a ghost, always mindful of his lord's wellbeing from the bottom of his heart, and thinking of sound solutions for the resolution of problems within the domain. This is the same for samurai who occupy stations both high and low. He must be completely unflinching in his resolve, even if it falls contrary to the bidding of the gods or Buddha.

❀ ❀ ❀

36. I once heard that the physician Matsugumasaki-no-Kyōan[1] said, "In the profession of medicine, treatments for men and women are meted out differently in accordance with positive and negative energy (*yin-yang*). The pulse of a man is different to that of a woman. Still, in the past five decades or so, the variance between the pulses

---

1 Attending physician to Nabeshima Motoshige.

between the sexes has become indistinguishable. Since noticing this, I have modified my treatment of eye ailments in men to comply with how I treat women. Male patients show little response to traditional male treatments. I have come to the realization that manly essence is absent in many of them, and they have become very feminine as a sign of the worsening times. This is an observation gleaned from medical treatment that I keep secretly to myself."

After hearing this, I realized how true it was; so many men now seem to have the pulse of a woman. There are few who can be thought of as a real man. This means that one man can surpass others by making just a small effort.

That manly courage has faded is evident when few men show enough nerve to behead a criminal with his hands bound behind his back. In the case of performing *kaishaku* for a man who is to commit *seppuku*, it's considered prudent or solicitous these days to decline the request. Four or five decades ago, when *matanuki*[1] was considered to be proof of manliness, no man dared show an unscathed thigh to others, so he would inflict cuts on himself. Such actions validated his valor and virility. A man's work was bloody indeed. Nowadays, however, such acts are condemned as foolish, and matters are resolved with a clever tongue, while difficult work is avoided altogether. This is a matter that young warriors should chew over thoroughly.

❀ ❀ ❀

37. There are retainers who still serve into their sixties and seventies. I, however, took up the tonsure when I was only 42 years of age; so, in retrospect, my career as a retainer was brief. I look back with a feeling of gratitude. When my lord passed, I resolved to die in a manner of speaking also, which is why I became a monk. I am sure I would be besieged by all manner of problems had I continued being

---

1 Opinions on what this means are divided. It could mean self-inflicted scars to resemble the aftermath of venereal disease, hence showing sexual experience as a mark of maturity. Or, it could indicate a practice in which young warriors secretly gathered and took turns at cutting each other's groin area as they vied to prove their level of personal courage.

a retainer. The last 14 years have instead been a time of peace and tranquillity, and immense contentment. Moreover, being acknowledged by others as 'a cut above the rest', I have received courteous treatment. I feel pangs of guilt when I reflect introspectively on what I have actually accomplished, and wonder if I ought not be punished in some way for the undue kindness I have had bestowed upon me.

❀ ❀ ❀

38. Once, a man was to accompany his master on his round of New Year greetings. "This time I am prepared. As we will be going to the countryside it is likely that we will be invited to partake in drinking, but I will try to refrain. If I say that I have given up drinking, people will assume it is because I am a bad drunk. Instead, I will say that it does not agree with me, and empty the cup two or three times. This way, people will not be so inclined to insist on making me drink. Also, when I bow, I will prostrate so deeply that my back hurts, and will not speak unless called upon to do so."

This is a commendable attitude. To think of such things in advance is the basis for excellence. Master Jōchō commented: "Indeed this is good preparation. Act in a way that people will think you may have become weakened through illness, and compared to the old days, that you have calmed down considerably. Your first words are so very important [in the way that you frame things]."

❀ ❀ ❀

39. The priest Tannen[1] said to me once: "I can't accept that all priests teach the complicated doctrine of *munen-mushin*[2] in order to reach an enlightened state. A mind 'free of thought' (*munen*) is one that is pure with 'correct thought' (*shōnen*)." Certainly, this is a salient point. I was also informed by the nobleman Sanenori[3] that "Following the

---

1 Tannen was the head priest of the Kōdenji Temple patronized by the Nabeshima clan, and Jōchō's teacher of Buddhism.
2 A mind free from obstructive thoughts, or "no-mind."
3 Sanjō-nishi Sanemori. See 1-15.

Way (*michi*) is to keep one's mind absolutely uncontaminated from evil, even in a single breath." It is not that there is no *nen* (thought). The point is to have correct thoughts without letting evil thoughts manifest. That being the case, the Way is one—but nobody is able to see the light, and understand this reasoning easily. It is only possible to reach a level of unadulterated purity after many years of diligent training.

❀ ❀ ❀

40. There is nothing so profound as the last part of a certain poem that asks, "How will you reply when your own heart asks questions?" This sentiment could even rival Buddhist sutra, and many know of it. Recently, erudite people put on pretences and feign wisdom—an act that makes them lower than ordinary men. At least ordinary men are forthright. If one asks this very question, there will be nowhere to hide from the truth. It is a penetrating "judge" of one's mind. Thus, it is prudent to avoid shameful behavior in anticipation of an introspective judgment of guilt.

❀ ❀ ❀

41. There is a doddering retainer whom I think may have gone somewhat senile.[1] He is often asked to lecture here and there, and it is said he is a passionate speaker. For the past several years, he has been preoccupied with helping others in their duties, and through his zest for service he has been very useful to the clan. Nevertheless, it is remarked that when people age and lose their marbles, they tend to become obsessed with the things they are accustomed to; so he is "service senile." Even if intentions are good, such deterioration of mental faculties is precarious. An old man in this state will seem dignified if he refrains from going out, and this is a far more respectable culmination of his life.

---

1 Possibly Ishida Ittei, a distinguished Confucian teacher of the Nabeshima domain.

❀ ❀ ❀

42. The Chinese character "*gen*" can also be read as "*maboroshi.*"[1] In India, sorcerers are referred to as "*genshutsushi*" ("illusionists"). Everyone in this world is like a puppet [controlled by other forces], which is why the character *gen* is fitting.

❀ ❀ ❀

43. When a betrothal was arranged, one of the bride's attendants voiced his opposition.[2] The following information requires serious consideration by young men. The attendant's disapproval surely had merit, and some saw it as the mark of a devoted retainer. Indeed, it can be assumed that the retainer felt compelled to express his disapproval and would have been happy to commit *seppuku* as a consequence. Nonetheless, consider this carefully. What he did was futile. If you believe that his action was heroic, then you are very much mistaken. He was unsuccessful in convincing his lord; and was no longer able to discharge his duties in raising the princess because of his forced retirement. Even when she took ill and died soon after, he was unable to be by her side—a most tragic fate for a faithful servant.

Men with impatient dispositions often make similar errors of judgment. Generally, a man who is not of a suitable high standing to speak his mind to his lord, but does so anyway, is disloyal. A man with a sincere heart will channel his ideas through a superior who holds an appropriate position. The superior will then explain the idea to the lord as if it was his own estimation, and so it will not fall on deaf ears. This is true loyalty. If the first senior man consulted is reluctant to cooperate, he can then confer with others in suitable positions, or

---

1 幻 = Vision, illusion, or dream.
2 Nabeshima Tsunashige's daughter, Mine, was engaged to be married to Uesugi Yoshi-nori to forge an alliance between the clans. The attendant was opposed to the mar-riage because of the Uesugi clan's "disgraceful" attitude in response to the celebrated storming of the Kira mansion by the 47 *Rōnin*. Yoshinori was the grandson of Kira Kōzukenosuke (1641–1702), the infamous antihero of the incident. Mine died the following year (1712), aged 14.

figure out another approach without revealing his act of loyalty. If discussing the idea with others proves fruitless, it can't be helped. Leave the matter for a while, and hopefully you can continue to seek a solution later. Goals can usually be achieved through persistence.

There are some men who wish to be called heroes, but as they think only of their own honor and reputations, they inevitably fail. They offer remonstrance thinking of it as a meritorious deed of service, but it leaves them open for condemnation, and then ruin. There are many examples of this. They fail because the root of their intentions is not sincere. A warrior who surrenders body and soul, thinking only of how to make things better for his lord, will always find the right course of action without making mistakes.

❊ ❊ ❊

44. It is testing to disavow things that run counter to moral principles (*gi*) and maintain righteousness. Many terrible blunders will be made through believing that the supreme principle is to uphold moral ideals at all times. Above the realm of moral principles is [divine] truth in the Way (*michi*). This is an exceedingly challenging concept to comprehend, and only extraordinary men can. When viewed from this highest plane of wisdom, righteousness or justice is but a trivial virtue. Such a notion cannot be truly understood without considerable study.

Still, there is a way in which this higher wisdom can be accessed, even if only partially, and that is through dialog with others. Even a man who has not realized this state of mind himself can observe others objectively. It is like watching a game of *go*[1] and anticipating eight moves ahead. There is no better way than to talk with others if you are keen to know your flaws. Listening to men and reading books helps complement your own good sense with the wisdom of the ancients.

❊ ❊ ❊

---

1 A traditional Japanese board game sometimes referred to as "Japanese chess."

45. A master swordsman relayed the following narrative in his old age: "Training over a lifetime involves various phases. Unskilled men at the lowest level will make little progress at the start of their training, and their ineptness is obvious to themselves and others. Men at this level are of no use. Those at the middle level are still unusable, but are aware of their deficiencies, and are able to identify defects in others. Men at the upper level have useful skills, are proud of their degree of proficiency, enjoy the praise, and empathize with those who lack ability. This level has worth.

"However, men who have traversed to an even higher stage of expertise in swordsmanship will pretend that they are unknowing, but those around them will sense that they have unmatched skill. This is probably the zenith of attainment for most men. Beyond this extends the ultimate realm that is impossible to describe in words. It becomes clear to the master that this realm is boundless and his skill can never be perfect. With this realization, the master, being fully conscious of his imperfections, is neither conceited nor contemptuous, but continues traveling the path."

Lord Yagyū[1] once said, "I do not know how to defeat others. All I know is the path to defeat myself. Today one must be better than yesterday, and tomorrow better than today. The pursuit of perfection is a lifelong quest that has no end."

❀ ❀ ❀

46. In his book of maxims, *O-Kabegaki* ("Wall writings"),[2] Lord Naoshige wrote: "Deliberate lightly when deciding on weighty matters." Ishida Ittei added a note to this axiom: "Be meticulous when deciding on affairs of minor importance." Important matters are few in number, and can be studied carefully in the course of daily affairs.

---

1 Yagyū Munenori (1571–1646) was one of the most influential swordsmen in the early Tokugawa period by virtue of his illustrious students, such as the second and third Tokugawa shoguns Hidetada (1579–1632) and Iemitsu (1604–1651), and many daimyo, including those in the Nabeshima clan.

2 A book of precepts written by the founder of the Nabeshima domain, Naoshige, which is made up of 21 articles.

From this, I infer that it is prudent to prepare for serious matters ahead of time so that they can be dealt with expediently. It is difficult to make quick decisions without planning in advance, and it is doubtful whether appropriate action can be taken. In this sense, the essence of Lord Naoshige's teaching, "Think lightly when deciding on weighty matters," is to envisage issues of critical importance well beforehand.

❁ ❁ ❁

47. When Lord Taku of Mimasaka, Ishida Ittei, and their study companions visited the priest Kōnan Oshō at Sōryūji Temple to discuss matters of learning, the priest commented: "It is commendable that you are learned fellows. But, if you do not know the Way, this relegates you to a level below ordinary people." Ittei countered, "Surely there is no other Way than that of sages and wise men."

Kōnan rejoined: "Someone who is knowledgeable, but who does not know the Way, is as flawed as a man who is supposed to be heading to the east but is actually moving westwards. The more you know, the further removed from the Way you become. If you learn the teachings of the sages of China through lectures and books, it does make you more knowledgeable; but you may become mistaken in thinking that you share the same wisdom, and conceitedly start looking down on ordinary people as if they are nothing more than insects. This is proof that you have veered far from the Way.

"Knowing the Way is to know your own faults. Discovering your imperfections with endless introspection and to remedy them by spending your life training body and mind (*shugyō*), that is the Way. The character for 'sage' (聖 = *sei*) can also be read as *hi-jiri*—this is because sages 'know' (*jiri*) their 'flaws' (*hi*). Buddha preached that one could master the Way through *chihibensha*—knowing your imperfections and quickly casting them off. If you vigilantly examine your own heart, it will become clear how many bad thoughts are invoked in your mind each day. You should never be contented with yourself."

Ittei advised that this is how to achieve salvation. But even so, the way a samurai should approach life is different again. If you don't believe, rather audaciously, that you are the singularly most gallant warrior in Japan, it will be difficult to exhibit true valor. The extent of one's courage is evident in one's confident attitude.

❀ ❀ ❀

48. In the book *Bushidō Kōshasho*,[1] there is a passage that says: "Some estimable warriors experienced in combat gain fame for meritorious feats they did not do." Such an observation in writing could be easily misinterpreted in the distant future. Misunderstanding can be avoided by simply including "can also" in the text so that it reads, "Some estimable warriors experienced in combat 'can also' gain fame for feats in battle that they did not do." Also, Shida Kichinosuke[2] said: "In cases where you must choose to live or die, it's better to live." This comment was made in jest by Shida, as he was actually a heroic fellow. Still, I worry that young samurai might not understand his comment properly [in the joking spirit it was made], and may end up saying something utterly shameful. Shida also said later: "If you wonder whether or not you should eat, don't eat. If you wonder whether you should live or die, it is better to die."

❀ ❀ ❀

49. After completing several years of service in Osaka, a Nabeshima clansman returned home and reported to the domain's administrative office, speaking the Kamigata dialect that he had picked up during his stay in the capital. The administrators were chagrined by his style of speech, and he was mocked. When a retainer is dispatched to Edo or the Kamigata region, it is important for him to try and stress his native dialect even more than he would at home.

　I think that when stationed in big cities for an extended period,

---

1　Also known by its other name of *Tōryū Gunpō Kōsha-sho*, this treatise was written in 1649 by Ogasawara Sakuun Katsuzō.
2　A former pageboy of Ryūzōji Masaie, lord of Saga from 1587–1590, preceding Nabeshima Naoshige.

it is natural to be colored by the spirit of the surroundings and start looking down upon the ways of one's birthplace as bucolic. To enviously praise the ways of another place upon hearing something that makes just a little sense is inane and absurd. That one's home is provincial and simplistic is precisely why it is worth treasuring. Copying the customs of other regions represents shallow imitation lacking authenticity.

Once, a man told the priest Shungaku[1] that he disliked the Hokke sect of Buddhism because of its "obstinacy." Shungaku rebuffed this comment by saying, "It is exactly because of the 'obstinacy' of our teachings that the sect is able to maintain its identity. If it wasn't mulish, it would be no different to the other sects." This was a sensible riposte.

50. A meeting was convened to deliberate on the promotion of a retainer. As the promotion was about to be declined because of past problems involving boozing, one of the council members spoke up in the clansman's defence by saying, "If those who have erred in the past are removed from contention for promotions, then this will prevent outstanding men from progressing. Any man guilty of slipping up will reflect on his mistakes, will be more judicious as a result, and will become a useful servant. I recommend that we promote him." Another council member inquired, "Are you prepared to take responsibility for this man if he is promoted?" He replied, "I will gladly be his guarantor." Others then asked him: "On what grounds do you vouch for him?" "I support him because he has already erred in the past. In my mind, a man who has no blemish on his record is more of a concern." With this endorsement, the clansman was promoted.

---

1 Shungaku Meiki was a Zen monk of the Rinzai sect, and served as the head monk of the Manjūji Temple in Saga. When he was accused of being a Christian and confined in 1687, Jōchō was appointed to guard duty.

51. When sentencing felons, Nakano Kazuma[1] stipulated that they be punished a degree lighter than what the crime merited. In his time, there was a secret vault of wisdom that only Kazuma possessed. Although there were always several men in attendance at such deliberations, nobody spoke until Kazuma had said his piece. Because of this, he was nicknamed "Lord Lid Opener" or "Lord Twenty-fifth Day."[2]

❀ ❀ ❀

52. It is an act of great loyalty to amend your lord's outlook on things lest he commit blunders. Generally speaking, it is best to help him understand clan lore and the trials and tribulations of his ancestors when he is still young. Education in such matters is very important.

❀ ❀ ❀

53. In the past, warriors often carried their swords upright and close to their bodies in the *otoshi-zashi* style, in which the weapon was inserted vertically into the sash. Now, few warriors give much consideration to the way they wear their swords. The Yagyū-ryū school of swordsmanship teaches to wear the sword sticking out horizontally. Recently, samurai do this not because they have learned the Yagyū style, or because they give particular thought as to why, but simply because they are imitating the school. Lords Naoshige and Katsushige adhered to the *otoshi-zashi* style. As those who had ability in swordsmanship preferred *otoshi-zashi*, this suggests that it was somewhat practical. If your sword protrudes out the front, an enemy may grasp hold of the handle when you least expect it. I hear that Lord Mitsushige took Lord Katsushige's advice in this matter.

❀ ❀ ❀

---

1 Jōchō became a member of Nakano Kazuma Toshiaki's unit when he was 23 years old.
2 Apparently this was in reference to the custom of opening *sake* barrels at the start of an event, or casks of *miso* (bean paste) after 25 days of fermenting. In other words, he was the starter of proceedings.

54. When His Lordships Mitsushige and Tsunashige were residing in Edo, Lord Mitsushige met with his retainers at the residence on the first day of the New Year. The young master Tsunashige was in the backroom near the entrance at the time. Lord Mitsushige asked, "Where is Shinano (Tsunashige)?" One of the pages replied, "The young prince is 'hiding.'" Without care, such awkward mistakes in speech can happen.[1]

❀　❀　❀

55. A samurai disgraced himself by not fighting back in a quarrel. To retaliate entails just frenetically throwing yourself at your adversary with the intention of being cut down. Being killed this way brings no shame. Thinking about how to win may result in missing the best opportunity to act. Or, being outnumbered, some men postpone reprisal to gather reinforcements, and eventually talk of calling the attack off altogether. Even if there are a thousand enemies in waiting, a warrior must have the grit to charge forth and cut through one after another. This can be unexpectedly successful.

The *rōnin* of the Asano clan were culpable for not immediately committing *seppuku* at the Sengakuji Temple [after the night raid on Lord Kira's mansion].[2] Moreover, it took too long to exact revenge after their master was killed by the enemy. What if [their intended victim] Lord Kira had died of illness in the interim? It would have been a disgrace. Warriors of the Kamigata region are clever and shrewd in finding ways of being showered in praise. Unlike our men who fought in the Nagasaki wrangle,[3] they are unable to override the shackles of rational judgment.

1　"Hiding" (*o-kakure*) was also used as a euphemism for the death of one's superior.

2　Lord Asano's grave was at the Sengakuji Temple. After the attack on Lord Kira's mansion, the 47 Asano retainers ran to the temple to inform their dead master of the successful vendetta.

3　This incident occurred in 1699 and involved samurai from the Fukabori-Nabeshima household and a servant of a Nagasaki town official. After being humiliated, the servant retaliated that evening by attacking the Fukabori-Nabeshima mansion with his companions, and meted out a beating to two Nabeshima samurai. They in turn retaliated the next morning by killing the official and his servants, and then committed *seppuku*.

The vendetta of the Soga brothers was also particularly long in its plotting. It was a pity that Jūrō Sukenari was unable to complete his objective at the time of a hunt as he was killed; but his brother Gorō's words [after Kudō Suketsune was slain] were magnificent.[1]

Normally I would not express such criticisms, but I will make an exception as it is an inquiry into the Way of the warrior. If you do not examine such matters beforehand, you will be unable to make appropriate calls when the time comes, and will be dishonored because of it. Listening to accounts from other people and reading are valuable ways of preparing for such a moment. In following the path of the warrior, one needs to be ready at all times by remembering these matters day and night, for one never knows what will happen, or when. You must anticipate all things at every moment of the day. Victory or defeat is all a matter of chance. Avoiding shame is a different matter. Simply be prepared to die. Even if you see no chance of prevailing, just attack. You do not need any superior wisdom or prowess to do this. A heroic warrior (*kusemono*) does not concern himself with victory or defeat. Without hesitating, he whips himself into a deadly fury (*shini-gurui*). This is when he understands; this is when he awakens from the dream.

❀ ❀ ❀

56. There is one thing that is damaging to a man in service, and that is to seek riches and honors. You will remain untarnished as long as you lead a meager lifestyle. There is a man I know who is very clever, but it was in his pedantic nature to always point out sloppy work.

Ten men who helped them were ordered to take their own lives, and nine others who turned up later were sent into exile.

1 This is referring to the *Soga Monogatari* ("Tale of the Soga Brothers"), a well-known medieval tale of revenge in which Kudō Suketsune was denied his inheritance by his uncle Itō Sukechika, and out of anger he had Sukechika's son slain in retribution. In 1193, 18 years after the murder, Sukechika's two sons killed Suketsune at a hunt near Mt. Fuji. The elder of the brothers, Soga Jūrō Sukenari, was killed, but his younger sibling, Soga Gorō Tokimune, was apprehended and brought before the shogun, Minamoto-no-Yoritomo. Yoritomo was impressed by his show of faithfulness and was prepared to pardon him, but Suketsune's son insisted on his execution.

This is something a first-rate vassal should not do. If you are unaware that the world is teeming with ineptitude from the beginning, you will develop a bitter countenance, and in turn others will eschew you. If you aren't acknowledged and trusted by others, you will not be able to demonstrate your true worth, no matter how outstanding a person you may actually be. Know that this is also a blemish on one's honor that invites ruin.

❉ ❉ ❉

57. There was a man who said: "That chap is bumptious. He bragged in front of so-and-so…" It was inappropriate for him to talk in such a way. He only did so because he wanted to be seen as a reliable hero, but it detracts from his worth. He appears to be immature. A samurai is respected first because of his proper manners. Scoffing at others in such an uncouth way is to be expected among men of low rank, such as spear-carriers (*yarimochi*) and foot soldiers (*chūgen*).

There are many people who live in houses or have utensils that are unbefitting of their status. It is not a bad thing, however, to use higher quality fans, tissue paper, writing paper, bedding, and so on.

❉ ❉ ❉

58. Once, a man was annoyed with his adopted son because of his apparent ineptness. On top of this, the adoptive father had become very short-tempered on account of a long illness, and insisted on tormenting the young man. The adopted son was unable to bear it any longer, and was on the verge of returning to his birth home. Burdened with this problem, the adoptive mother visited me for counsel. She said, "I am greatly troubled by this state of affairs, and although my husband must be suffering from his ailment, can you please advise him to show more tolerance." I declined, but she began to cry as she persisted in her request. Unable to turn her down any longer I finally agreed to help saying, "It is not the adoptive father I should be offering advice to, especially as he is ill. Please send your adopted son to me."

She returned home looking somewhat perplexed. The son came and I said: "Is not being born into the world as a human being indeed a matter of great fortune? Furthermore, there is no greater honor than being a samurai of the Nabeshima clan. A comparison of your circumstances with farmers and townsmen should leave you in no doubt of your good providence. It is gratifying to be born the eldest son destined to inherit the headship of your birth family. It is like an *udumbara* flower,[1] if you are not the first-born but are still lucky enough to be adopted to succeed the headship of another house, and are able to serve as a retainer to the lord. This is an extremely fortunate turn of circumstance. To turn one's back on such blessed conditions to resign one's post is blatant disloyalty; and to be disliked by one's [adoptive] parents is unfilial. It is disastrous in fact. Men bereft of loyalty or filial devotion have no place in the world. Think about this carefully when you return home.

"All that you have to do now to live up to your dutiful obligation of fidelity is to be loved by your father. Nevertheless, you are probably thinking that no matter how much you want to be viewed favorably, he will still be angry and unaccommodating. So, I will tell you how to make him more agreeable. You should shed tears of blood by praying as hard as you can to the *ujigami*,[2] so that your father will also hear your supplications. He will become fond of your countenance and other things about you. This is not for your own benefit, but to uphold the virtues of loyalty and filial devotion. Your hearts will connect with such sheer single-minded intent (*ichinen*). Go now, as I'm sure your father will see you in a new light. It is a wondrous how heaven, earth, and man are united. Particularly as your father is suffering from illness, he most likely has little time left. It is only a fleeting moment that you have left to be filial, so it will not be difficult to satisfy this onus with unreserved effort."

The young man was so moved by this splendid advice that he went home with tears in his eyes. I heard later that when the son

---

1 The *udumbara* flower (*udonge* in Japanese) holds great symbolism in Buddhism and is said to flower only once every 3,000 years. Hence, the reference here is to accentuate the fortuitousness of the adopted son's circumstances.
2 Family or clan deity.

arrived home, his adoptive father said, "It appears that you have been counseled well. Blessed be! Your demeanor is much improved." It seems that his irritability was appeased. There is indeed a marvelous truth that cannot be fathomed easily by human intellect. Through the advice he received, the son was able to be loyal and filial, and he visited again to express his gratitude. Pray to realize the true way, and your dreams will always come true. Heaven and earth are penetrated and bound together by such sentiment. The harder you pray with tears of blood, the more the gods will see fit to grant your wishes.

59. It is unwise to be fixated on a single point of completion. A man who has devoted himself to his studies and believes he has reached a consummate level will assume his training has finished, but this is erroneous. Devotion to the study of one's path—first acquiring the fundamentals, and then continuing to refine your knowledge and skills—is a lifelong pursuit with no end. Without becoming content with your level of accomplishment, think critically of everything, and spend your entire life traveling the path, asking, "How can I find the truth of the Way?" Never give up the quest. Continue to practice like this and you will uncover the Way.

60. The following articles are some of the teachings espoused by Yamamoto Jin'uemon:[1]

(1) If you can see in one direction, you can see in eight.[2]

(2) A man who fakes a smile is a coward, and a woman prurient.

(3) When speaking officially or just chatting with someone, you should always look him in the eye. A bow at the start is sufficient. It is dangerous to bow your head right down.[3]

---

1 Jōchō's father.

2 As long as you are careful in your observance, you will be able to perceive all things.

3 This axiom demonstrates the precarious world that samurai lived in, and how vigilance was required at all times.

(4) It is careless to insert your hands inside of your *hakama*.[1]

(5) Whenever I read a story written in *kana*[2] or other books [written in Chinese script], my father would then burn them. He would say, "Books and the like are read by courtiers, but members of the Nakano clan have a duty to train with wooden swords to develop military skills."[3]

(6) A man who is not in a *kumi* (military unit) and doesn't have a horse is not a samurai.

(7) A heroic warrior (*kusemono*) is one who can be relied upon.

(8) Rise at four every morning, cleanse yourself with water, shave your forehead (*sakayaki*), eat your morning meal at dawn, and retire to bed at dusk.

(9) A samurai should use a toothpick even though he has not eaten: a dog's skin inside, a tiger's hide outside.[4]

❀ ❀ ❀

61. How should one reply when asked, what is the most important thing to aspire to in one's training? Let me try to answer: "Pure will (*shōnen*) in every moment." Many neglect this attitude. When one is pure in heart, a vivacious expression appears on one's face. Something special manifests in one's heart when completely sincere in one's undertakings. If this is directed at one's lord, it is loyalty (*chū*), and filial piety (*kō*) to one's parents, or valor (*yū*) in war. It is applicable in all things. It is hard to find this special "thing," and it is even more difficult to hold on to when you have it. The only approach is to throw your heart into the moment, now.

---

1 *Hakama* are the traditional split-skirts worn by samurai. Inserting one's hands in the slits down the sides of the *hakama* would leave one vulnerable if attacked suddenly.

2 *Kana* refers to a syllabic writing system developed in Japan based on Chinese characters (*kanji*). The characters were used to express the sounds in the Japanese language rather than symbols for individual words.

3 Jōchō's father was born into the Nakano clan, but was later adopted by the Yamamoto family.

4 That way, even though a warrior suffers like a dog on the inside, his pain will never show on the outside. In other words, his outward appearance should show attentiveness and taste, but at the same time he must be frugal and "dogged" in his heart.

❀ ❀ ❀

62. In the past, *yori-oya* (military unit captains) and *kumiko* (unit members) were so intimate that nothing could come between them. In the time of Lord Mitsushige, there was a vacancy for the post of armored warrior among the elite guards (*o-umamawari*).[1] After deliberating, the chief retainers (*karō*) concluded that Mawatari Gendayū would be a perfect choice for promotion from his unit to fill the role, as he was considerably more competent than the other young warriors.

Mawatari Ichinojō, Gendayū's retired father, heard of this decision and hurried to the *yori-oya*, Nakano Kazuma,[2] early in the morning and said: "With due respect, this decision is out of the question. Apart from me, the unit consists only of men from your family. I was always unwavering in my intention to be a better retainer than any other, and told my son to be vigilant and rise above all others in your service. In spite of our wholehearted efforts, you decided to detach my son from your unit, which leaves us feeling dishonored. It is such a cruel turn of events. It is a black mark against my son's reputation, and humiliating to me in my retirement to the extent that we cannot show our faces. As such, we have decided to commit *seppuku*."

Kazuma said, "You have completely misinterpreted the situation. It is a great honor for your son Gendayū to be promoted to the elite horse guards. He was selected because the chief retainers acknowledged that he was a promising young warrior. You should both be overjoyed." Ichinojō continued to push his point. "During the deliberation, you should have spoken up for my son, and informed the chief retainers that he was as important as the other members of your family, and that you did not want to lose him. You released my son because you obviously do not consider him to be an integral part of your company, and I resent how you turned your back on him."

---

1 This particular rank entailed donning a *horo*, or cloth covering one's back to protect against arrows during battle.
2 Kazuma was also Jōchō's *yori-oya*.

Ichinojō seemed to be sincere in his grievance. Kazuma replied, "Dear me. You do make a good point. I will immediately inform the chief retainers that we will turn down the promotion." Ichinojō took his leave saying, "I would not have returned without your understanding." Kazuma went to the castle later that day and relayed the predicament to the chief retainers. "You just never know when someone's life will expire. I was delivered a terminal blow this very morning. It is all rather convoluted, but I request that Gendayū be excused from taking up the new position." As a result, the promotion was awarded to someone else.

❧ ❧ ❧

63. Until 50 or 60 years ago, every morning samurai would diligently groom themselves by bathing in the open air, shaving their foreheads (*sakayaki*), putting fragrant oil in their hair, cutting their fingernails and filing them with pumice stone, then polishing them with wood sorrel. Of course, military equipment was kept neat, dusted, and oiled to be free of rust. Although paying so much attention to personal appearance may seem vain, it is because of the samurai's resolve to die at any moment that he makes preparations so meticulously. If slain with an unkempt appearance, it shows a lack of forethought regarding his fate, and he will be scorned by his enemy as being unclean. This is why young and old alike should always pay attention to matters of personal grooming.

It may seem bothersome and time-consuming, but this is precisely the kind of care a samurai should take in his daily life. It is not as if he is too busy with other work. A warrior will never be shamed if he thus demonstrates his resolve to die in battle at any given instant, single-mindedly discharging his duties, and forging his martial spirit as if already deceased. Warriors these days do not contemplate such details even in their dreams, and spend their days indulging their own desires. When the time comes he will bring shame upon himself, but he will be unaware of his decadent behavior, and just do as he pleases in a boorish manner as he sinks into a swamp of vulgarity. This is a diabolical state of affairs. With a firm resolve to die, how can a warrior engage in such disgraceful behavior? This should be considered with earnest endeavor.

People have changed in the past 30 years. When young samurai congregate, they engage in vapid talk of money, about profit and loss, their household fiscal problems, taste in fashion, and idle talk of sex. I hear that they see no reason to assemble other than to indulge in such topics of conversation. Warrior customs are deteriorating beyond repair. In the old days, samurai, even in their twenties and thirties, did not harbor such contemptible thoughts, and never talked about such things. Even if an older man let slip an objectionable comment, he was quick to lament his mistake.

The existing state of affairs has emerged because society has become tawdry, and all that people think about are financial matters. If people refrain from indulging in extravagances beyond their station, then they can make do. Moreover, it is dumbfounding how young men who show thriftiness are praised. Men who are too miserly tend to lack a sense of duty or obligation (*giri*). Men lacking in *giri* are dirty cowards.

✿ ✿ ✿

64. Ishida Ittei said: "Even someone who is not particularly skilled with a brush, his ability to write characters will improve if he applies himself in copying a good model." In the same way, a man in service can also progress by copying the ways of an exemplary retainer. There are few examples worthy of emulation these days, so you should select from several to construct your own archetype. Choose one to imitate for their level of grace in protocols of propriety, another for his courage, one for his use of words, another man for his correct moral conduct, one for his sense of *giri* and honesty, and one who does not dilly-dally and is decisive. By taking the one good thing from different people and merging them together, you will be able to create an ideal standard for a retainer.[1]

---

1 Also see Book 2-47.

In the world of artistry or medicine, a disciple will often mimic his master's defects instead of his superior qualities. This is futile. There are some men who are very polite, but are dishonest. When modeling themselves on others, they risk acquiring his dishonest features instead of his meritorious traits if care is not taken. If you focus only on the good points of a man, then everybody can be a good model to learn from."

❀ ❀ ❀

65. When delivering important documents, letters, and notes, they should be kept in hand at all times on the road. Do not put them down even for an instant, and personally hand them over to the intended recipient.

❀ ❀ ❀

66. A man in service should never drop his guard at any time; he should always conduct himself with the same attentiveness as if he was in the presence of his lord, or in the public eye. It will seem as though the retainer is always slack if he is spotted relaxing during a break from duties. It is important to always be vigilant.

❀ ❀ ❀

67. There are times when it is best not to react too abruptly. For example, Jōchō mentioned the instance of moving residence.[1] Good opportunities will present themselves to those who show patience. All that is required is forbearance, and when the right moment comes, act swiftly without slackening. You may fail outright if you are tardy and think too much. Sometimes, however, it is best to act from the outset. Now and then it may be more advantageous just to

---

1 This is referring to Jōchō moving from his hermitage in Kurotsuchibaru to Daishōguma in 1713, as the former building was made into a mausoleum for worshiping Mitsushige's departed spirit.

vex and be a killjoy by taking your time. In such instances, what you say at that moment is very important. In any case, it is essential to get on with your work attentively and patiently.

❀ ❀ ❀

68. Many men are defeated by alcohol. This is a lamentable fact. Be attentive to how much you can imbibe without becoming drunk, and do not exceed your limit. Still, one will become intoxicated on occasion. When carousing, be constantly on the alert to deal with any unexpected occurrence. Drinking is a communal activity, so be very careful of your public appearance.

❀ ❀ ❀

69. Irrespective of rank, those who try to do things that are beyond their social station eventually commit depraved acts. They may even abscond if they are menials, so it is prudent to keep a close eye on them.

❀ ❀ ❀

70. Many misguidedly believe that they are outstanding samurai by virtue of their devotion to the martial arts, and because of the disciples they amass. It is sad that such men make bone-breaking efforts but amount to nothing more than a martial 'artist.' An art should be learned to the extent that you are 'proficient' in it. Generally speaking, a person talented in many things lacks refinement, and only retains perfunctory knowledge of important matters in their duties.

❀ ❀ ❀

71. Regardless of whether it is opportune or problematic, you will seem disconcerted if you withdraw in silence when your lord orders you to do something. Always prepare in advance to ensure you have a suitable reply. If you are appointed to some duty, and are so pleased that you feel great pride in this task, it will show on your face. I have seen this many times in the past, and it is quite unbecoming. Being aware of your shortcomings, you should think to yourself, "I was given this responsibility even though I am not particularly gifted. How can I serve my master in a way that is befitting of this position? This is quite a quandary and it makes me very apprehensive." Even though you do not say these words aloud, your trepidation will be apparent, and you will be seen as a man with a modest temperament. Conversely, a man who gets excited easily often acts in an unreasonable manner; he will come across as inexperienced and will eventually fail in the execution of his duties.

❀ ❀ ❀

72. Just as the priest Kōnan Oshō warned, acquiring knowledge is a good thing but in many cases it can also be perilous.[1] Looking at a man who has achieved something of merit, if he trains in order to know his own deficiencies he will evolve into a competent servant. Nonetheless, such a mind-set is difficult to realize. Many who study veer away from motivations of personal growth. Time and again they have a high opinion of themselves, and prefer to engage in splitting hairs.

❀ ❀ ❀

73. When visiting an acquaintance in some quandary with the purpose of reassuring him, your words should be carefully chosen. A man's true mind can be known through a single word. It is undignified for a samurai to be dispirited and downcast, for whatever reason. A warrior must be vivacious and ready to seize victory, otherwise he cannot discharge his duties. That's why a word of encouragement to bolster his spirit is of great consequence.[2]

❀ ❀ ❀

---

1 See Book 1-47.
2 See Book 2-57.

74. When Emperor Go-Daigo returned from exile in the Oki Islands, Akamatsu Enshin and Kusunoki Masashige went to greet him, and they received thanks for their troubles. In response, Enshin remained silent and prostrated on the ground, but Masashige courteously acknowledged the emperor's kind words. His response was very appropriate, and should be read in the original text.[1]

❀ ❀ ❀

75. Once when a man was chasing a menial who had absconded, he came across a palanquin with the door shut. He hurried to the palanquin, opened the door, and inquired, "Are you not so-and-so?" It turned out to be a case of mistaken identity, so the pursuer covered up his mistake by saying, "I have been waiting for my friend for such a long time. Please excuse my rude intrusion." The palanquin continued on its way.

❀ ❀ ❀

76. A few years ago, at an important deliberation, a man spoke his mind with the intention of killing the unit leader (*kumi-gashira*) if his voice wasn't heard. His view was agreed upon, but the ease with which acceptance was forthcoming prompted him to say, "This decision was made so hastily, it seems that there are few resolute men attending the lord, and dependability is lacking."

❀ ❀ ❀

77. On occasion, people stop by the administration office at busy times and thoughtlessly engage in chit-chat, unaware of the busy

---

1 The "original text" is referring to the war tale known as the *Taiheiki*. This story chronicles Emperor Go-Daigo's escape from the Oki Islands in 1333 after he was banished by the Kamakura shogunate for trying to keep the imperial succession in his direct family line. The civil strife that ensued was to bring the Kamakura shogunate to an end when two generals, Ashikaga Takauji and Nitta Yoshisada, decided to join the rebellious emperor.

atmosphere. Administration officers show a propensity to become angry and treat chatterboxes brusquely, but this is not good either. According to samurai protocol, the officer should remain calm and treat the man with due respect. Responding with scorn is the kind of vulgar attitude expected in servants of low station such as *chūgen*.

❀ ❀ ❀

78. You may seek to borrow items from others every now and again. But, it is akin to begging if you ask too often. If you can make do without asking people for favors, then it is better not to ask.

❀ ❀ ❀

79. There is a lesson to be learned from a downpour of rain. If you get caught in a sudden cloudburst, you will still get a drenching even though you try to keep dry by hurrying along and taking cover under overhangs of roofs. If you are prepared to get wet from the start, the result is still the same but it is no hardship. This attitude can be applied to all things.

❀ ❀ ❀

80. All artistic pursuits can be of use in some way, and are good if learned for the purpose of samuraihood and serving one's lord. Unfortunately though, many just end up becoming consumed in the art itself. Learning can be particularly perilous in this sense.

❀ ❀ ❀

81. In the Kingdom of Tang (China), there was a man who adored pictures of dragons. He had dragon motifs on his clothes, utensils, and other things. His profound love of dragons was felt by the dragon god, who sent a real dragon to appear before the man's window. The man was so surprised that he fainted. Some people like to talk big, but act in a way that doesn't match their words.

❀ ❀ ❀

82. When a distinguished spearman was on his deathbed, he summoned his best disciple and told him: "I have already conveyed to you the secret teachings of the school, so there is nothing left for me to pass on. If it is your desire to accept your own disciples, you must practice diligently with your bamboo sword (*shinai*) every day. Remember that the subtleties of winning duels cannot be grasped simply through the secret teachings." A master of linked verse (*renga*) also advised students: "Calm your minds and review books of poetry the day before a meeting." They were advocating the importance of becoming immersed in practice. A samurai should plunge headfirst into training for his professional duties.

❀ ❀ ❀

83. The middle path is generally the best way, but with regards to samurai engaged in martial affairs, this will not do. The samurai must strive to outdo others. In the practice of archery, it is taught that the left and right hands should be held at parallel height when drawing the bow across the chest. As there is a tendency to position the right arm higher than the left, if you consciously make the right lower than what you think it is, this will make both hands level. I was told by an old campaigner that if a samurai practices day and night to surpass the feats of distinguished warriors and claim the heads of celebrated enemies on the battlefield, then courage will swell from within. He will never become dispirited, and will thus be able to demonstrate indomitable valor. This should be a warrior's attitude at all times.

❀ ❀ ❀

84. Tetsuzan[1] once said in his old age, "Unlike sumo, I used to think that it was permissible to be held down when engaged in a grappling

---

1 Daiki Kenzaemon.

(*toride*)[1] contest as long as you break the hold and win in the end. I now realize that if someone were to break up the bout before reaching its conclusion, and you were pinned down at the time, then it would be counted as a defeat. Winning from the outset is the only way to attain victory in the end."

❀ ❀ ❀

85. There is a special way for rearing children in warrior families. From an early age, children must be taught to be brave, and not for a moment be threatened as a joke, or tricked in any way. Cowardly behavior learnt during boyhood will remain ingrained as a lifelong flaw. It is unwise for parents to make their children afraid of the sound of thunder, or of the dark, or to say things to frighten them. A boy is likely to become timid if scolded too severely when he is small. The parent must take care that the child does not develop any bad habits. A habit cannot be easily rectified once it has sunk in. Gradually make the boy aware of the proper way of communicating, etiquette and so on, and ensure he doesn't develop greedy tendencies. A normal boy will mature into a decent man if you nurture him properly with these and other points in mind.

Furthermore, if parents are not on good terms with each other, it is natural for the child to grow up deficient in a sense of filial devotion. Even birds and wild animals are affected by what they see and hear in their formative years. Moreover, the relationship between father and son can break down if the mother is foolish. If the mother pampers the boy, and sticks up for him when he is admonished by his father, the paternal relationship will deteriorate. Women have a shallow tendency to side with their children as they foresee that they will have only them to depend on in the future.

❀ ❀ ❀

---

1 Another term for *jūjutsu*.

86. A samurai wanting in steadfast resolve may be tripped up by others. Without proper attentiveness at a gathering, you may end up aimlessly listening to and nodding at something somebody says, even though you may hold a different view. Others will see this as an expression of agreement. That is why one must be heedful at all times when meeting with others.

Moreover, be mindful of being manipulated. Be clear in stating your opinion if you disagree with what is being said. It is easy to make a terrible mistake even in seemingly trivial matters, so be on your guard. It is prudent to avoid becoming overly friendly with someone with questionable scruples, lest you are duped into his nefarious scheme. It takes years of experience not to be deceived.

❀ ❀ ❀

87. A man believed he was owed a generous reward after serving his lord diligently for many years. His friends were quick to offer their congratulations when he received a much-anticipated letter from his lord, but he was to be disappointed. To everybody's surprise, all he was awarded was a small increase in stipend. They continued to rejoice as this was still a welcome reward, but he looked surprisingly dejected. Full of woe he lamented: "I feel so embarrassed, and find it hard to face you all. I suppose I was of little consequence to my lord after all. I will retire from service and become a recluse." His close friends consoled him, and persuaded him not to retire.

Yet, his attitude clearly demonstrates that his heart was not really in service. His main motivation was self-aggrandizement. It goes without saying that when you receive a reward, or even in the case of demotion from samurai to foot soldier (*ashigaru*), or if you are ordered to commit *seppuku* for a crime you did not commit, a hereditary retainer unflinchingly accepts his fate. Saying he was too ashamed to show his face proves that he was an egoist only concerned with his own standing. All warriors should bear this in mind, although it will be beyond comprehension for conceited rogues.

❀ ❀ ❀

88. To say "Mastery in the arts is helpful" only applies to samurai of other provinces. To the Nabeshima samurai, accomplishment in an art can actually be ruinous. A specialist in an art is an 'artist.' He is not a samurai. Aim to be referred to as "that samurai." Only when you concede that even a smidgen of ability in an art is detrimental will your talents actually be of use [in your duties]. Be aware of this.[1]

❀ ❀ ❀

89. Be sure to look at yourself in the mirror when fixing your appearance. This is a secret tip. People look slovenly because they do not check themselves in a mirror. Correct your diction at home when rehearsing how to speak in public. When engaged in writing exercises, compose a draft, even if it is only a letter of one line. Each of these skills requires poise and dedication. Also, Ryōzan[2] said Kamigata people are told when writing letters to imagine that the characters will be hung on the wall as a scroll by the recipient.[3]

❀ ❀ ❀

90. It is said: "When you make a mistake, never hesitate to correct it." A wrongdoing can be rectified immediately if you are quick to address the problem. It will look worse if you try to cover it up, and you will suffer more. If you utter "forbidden words" that upset others, explain your indiscretion; your profanity will be forgiven, and there will be no need to feel penitent. Do not yield if somebody insists on taking you to task. Be prepared to stake your life and rebuff them by resolutely saying, "It was a mistake to say those words, which is why I felt obliged to explain myself. If you are not satisfied with my apology, then there is little more I can do to convince you. It could be said that you have not been listening to what I had to say. All of us are sometimes guilty of slips of the tongue." Such a

---

1 See Book 1-70.
2 A priest who taught Jōchō poetry.
3 See Book 1-107 and Book 2-43.

situation can become quite serious, so never speak of others, or divulge secrets carelessly. Likewise, be mindful of where you are and who is around you when you are chatting.

91. It is important to brush characters correctly and neatly, but concentrating on this alone will make your writing appear too rigid and lacking in something. Class is a quality that transcends conventional standards for good form. This can be said of all things.[1]

92. A man once said: "People think that nothing could be worse than being a *rōnin*; and, that if dismissed from duty, it must crush the spirit and lead to a loss of incentive. Yet, when I was a *rōnin*, I found it was not at all that bad. It was different than what I expected, and to be honest, I wouldn't mind being a *rōnin* again."[2] This was well said. With regards to the way of death, if you are prepared to die at any time, you will be able to meet your release from life with equanimity. As calamities are usually not as bad as anticipated beforehand, it is foolhardy to feel anxiety about tribulations not yet endured. Just accept that the worst possible fate for a man in service is to become a *rōnin*, or death by *seppuku*. Then nothing will faze you.

---

1 Initially the student calligrapher must master the basic forms, a stage known as *shin* (真 = essence). When the basic form becomes second nature, that is, an embodiment of the student, individual style can be infused (*gyō* 行 = running style). Following further intensive practice, the student creates a distinctive cursive style which in the final stage is referred to as "grass-writing" (草 = *sō*). This cursive style abbreviates and links the characters, resulting in a curvilinear, highly artistic form of writing.

2 There were many situations in which a samurai could become a *rōnin*, either from his own volition, or through severance from duty for a transgression, the death of his lord, or other reasons. The Nabeshima domain was distinctive in that even if a warrior was dismissed, the possibility was left open for reinstatement at a later time. It was more like home detention.

93. You are a coward if you harbor a fear of failure when conducting your duties. There will be times when a retainer makes mistakes. Nevertheless, it is shameful to go astray in private matters outside the realm of your official responsibilities. Ask yourself, "How can I serve to the best of my ability given my shortcomings?"

❀ ❀ ❀

94. As the saying goes, "There is nothing like illness to discern the hearts of others." Those who are usually affable but drift away when you are down with an illness or are enduring hardship are not nice fellows. You should be considerate to a suffering man, and pay the poor chap a visit, or send gifts to cheer him up. Never spurn a person who has shown you favor in the past. This is how you can fathom the measure of a man. Many in this world seek comfort when they are in need, but don't give their benefactors a second thought afterwards.

❀ ❀ ❀

95. The vicissitudes a man experiences during his life cannot be attributed to matters of good and evil in his deportment. Changes in fortune occur naturally; verdicts of good and evil depend on the worldly judgment of men. Still, notions of "good" bringing providence and "bad" begetting ruin are useful precepts for moral instruction.

❀ ❀ ❀

96. If a servant did something wrong, former Yamamoto Jin'uemon[1] would keep him in his employ for the rest of the year without saying a word, and then release him at the end of the year without a fuss.

❀ ❀ ❀

---

1 Jōchō's father. In the text he is referred to as Yamamoto Zen-Jin'uemon Shigezumi. The prefix "Zen" translates as "former," or "senior." Jōchō inherited the same name from his father in his youth.

97. At the time of Nabeshima Jirōemon's *seppuku*, an opinion was expressed about the four-staged process for deciding the offender's culpability.[1] When considering punishment, not paying attention to how people perceive the offense may lead to the lord's honor being compromised. It would have been appropriate to ignore the wrongdoing in this case, regardless of His Lordship's call for chastisement, for it is his reputation that would be tarnished. Next, when the offense was officially investigated, it would have been reasonable to accept the culprit's pretext. Then, when the council gathered to deliberate on the wrongdoing, somebody should have mentioned the fact that his ancestor had performed remarkable feats of valor for the clan; namely, his grandfather Nabeshima Daizen Masayuki's exploit in defeating Amakusa Shirō and acquiring his banner during the Shimabara Uprising.[2] With this, it should have been recommended that the offender not be punished. Only after all of these avenues had been exhausted, and the offense was still deemed unforgivable, should a punishment have been agreed upon.

❀ ❀ ❀

98. When Morōoka Hiko'uemon was summoned, he was told to sign an oath to the deities that his testimony was true.[3] "A samurai's word is harder than metal. Once I have decided something, not even the gods can change it." Consequently, he did not have to make an oath. He was 26 years old when this came to pass. (This particular inquiry

---

1   Nabeshima Jirōemon committed *seppuku* in 1693 for the crime of urinating in front of his lord.

2   The Shimabara Uprising was a peasant rebellion that erupted on December 11, 1637 in the overtaxed Shimabara domain (modern-day Nagasaki) and spread to the Amakusa Islands (Kumamoto Prefecture). The Tokugawa shogunate saw the uprising as being inspired by Christianity, and it turned out to be an important factor in the decision to cease all unauthorized contact with the West. The uprising ended on April 12, 1638 with the slaughter of 37,000 men, women, and children who followed the rebellion leader, Amakusa Shirō (1621?–1638), at the hands of a huge army summoned from various domains by the shogunate.

3   Hikoemon was a *rōnin* from 1685, but was reinstated to service soon after. See Book 2-26.

concerned the border dispute over the Benzai peak.)[1]

❀ ❀ ❀

99. Regarding seconding (*kaishaku*) for Nakano Shōgen at his *seppuku*.[2] The inspectors (*o-metsuke*) were Nabeshima Jūdayu and Ishii Saburōdayu. Confirming "It has been witnessed," Saburōdayu erected a folding screen (*byōbu*) around the body.[3]

❀ ❀ ❀

100. Regarding the procedure for Yamamura Miki's *seppuku*; details of the circumstances of both Miki and Yasuke;[4] what was said to Nakano Kazuma when his possessions were inspected; the witness arrived and a greeting was made; Miki's wife becoming ill and summoning a doctor; asking what Yamamura Miki's final statement was.[5]

❀ ❀ ❀

101. It pays to be wary of retainers hired from different provinces. They often reveal tendencies to showcase their capabilities for excellent service, and do things to enhance their reputation to benefit their descendants. Their children usually inherit this trait. Hereditary retainers are predisposed to serve their lord selflessly, and read-

---

1 A border dispute with the Fukuoka domain in 1692–1693.

2 Yamamoto Jōchō served as Shōgen's second (*kaishaku*) by beheading him as he committed *seppuku*. The two were related.

3 In Sagara Tōru's modern rendition of *Hagakure* based on the Nakano Book, there is an extra dictum: "When Hikoemon was in his Lord's presence, he is said to have answered inquiries about Nakano Shōgen." This is not in the Kōhaku Book lineage, which this translation is based on. Such discrepancies are not uncommon in the many *Hagakure* versions in circulation. From this point, the *Hagakure* texts I am using for reference in this translation fall out of alignment by one, but I decided not to include the dictum in the main text.

4 Yasuke was Mitsushige's son. Yamamura Miki was a shrine custodian.

5 This section is difficult to follow, but seems to be a summation of the main points Jōchō may have discussed with Tashiro Tsuramoto regarding events leading to the death of Yamamura Miki in 1690.

ily take the blame for his faults. This was exemplified by a certain retainer[1] through remonstrating with his lord when there was discord between the three branch families.[2] This is the attitude of a hereditary retainer.[3]

102. Ishida Ittei said, "If you wish for something strongly enough, it will eventually come to pass. We didn't have any *matsutake* mushrooms in our province. People who tasted *matsutake* in the Kamigata region wished for them to grow in the northern mountains of our domain, and now there is an abundance of them in Kitayama for the taking. From now on, I wish for cypress trees to grow in our mountains. This is in my list of predictions simply because people desire it. Make wishes for the times ahead, and they will come true."

103. It is crucial for a general to be able to judge a man's character by his facial expression. The scroll that Kusunoki Masashige handed

---

1 Nakano Shōgen.

2 This incident involved conflict between the three sub-fiefdoms within the Saga domain. The Ogi domain was established by Nabeshima Motoshige (1602–1654, Katsushige's eldest son) in 1617 (73,000 *koku*). The Hasunoike domain was established by Nabeshima Naozumi (1616–1669, Katsushige's son) in 1639 (52,000 *koku*). The Kashima domain was created in 1642 with Nabeshima Naomoto (1622–1709, Katsushige's son) as the first lord (20,000 *koku*). All three branch families were autonomously governed within the Saga domain, and as daimyo, each branch head of the Nabeshima clan was expected to reside in Edo under the *sankin-kōtai* system. Around 1678, one of the sub-branches presented the bakufu with an unauthorized gift that was viewed by the main branch of the Nabeshima clan as a slight on their authority. Until this time, the three branches were clearly subsidiary through the paternal link, but by the time Mitsushige became the lord of the Saga domain, it was decided that their position within the hierarchy be re-established. The discord was brought to an end around 1683 with the creation of a memorandum officially defining the positions and expectations of the three branches in the Saga domain.

3 "Hereditary" is designated as *fudai* in the text, and is used to distinguish those who were born into a samurai family of the Nabeshima domain, as opposed to outsiders who had their roots in other regions. *Hagakure* often draws such distinctions, and demonstrates elitist sentiment towards the former and distrust of outsiders in the lord's service.

over to Masatsura in Minatogawa is said to have been covered with pictures of eyes and nothing else.[1] There is a secret way of interpreting a man's countenance [though his eyes and expression].

❀ ❀ ❀

104. When something extraordinary happens, it is foolish to call it "mysterious" and claim that it is a harbinger of future catastrophes. Lunar and solar eclipses, comets, banner clouds, falling stars, snow in the sixth month, and lightning in the twelfth month are phenomena that occur every 50 or 100 years. They transpire because of transitions in the balance of *yin* and *yang*. If the sun rising in the east and setting in the west did not happen every day, then this would also be considered a mystery. It is no different. Bad things seem to happen whenever strange phenomena occur simply because people think of peculiarities such as banner clouds as ill omens. In their hearts they wait for something calamitous to happen, which actually augurs disaster. There are oral teachings for coping with mysterious events.

❀ ❀ ❀

105. The story of Chōryō[2] receiving Kōsekikō's[3] text on military strategy,[4] or Yoshitsune being bestowed the [sword] teachings of the Tengū, were stories concocted to legitimize the creation of new martial art schools.

❀ ❀ ❀

---

1 Kusunoki Masashige was a warrior chieftain from Kawachi Province that is now part of modern-day Osaka Prefecture. He committed suicide after backing Emperor Go-Daigo in the Kemmu Restoration (1333–1336). He was defeated by Ashikaga Takauji in the spring of 1336 on the banks of the Minatogawa River.
2 Zhang Liang.
3 Huang Shigong.
4 "The Three Strategies" 三略 = *San Lu*.

106. When close attendants to Lord Mitsushige were allocated to garrisons in two groups in Nagasaki,[1] Master Jōchō saw the documentation in which his name was listed in the second group [which would be deployed later]. He declared to the official, "I cannot comply with this order when it will keep me away from His Lordship in battle. Bear witness as I swear an oath to the God of War (Yumiya Hachiman) that I cannot possibly attach my seal of acceptance to this order. I suspect this directive was made because I am a scribe; and if you think me impudent and decide to dismiss me from my post, then so be it. If it is determined that I should commit *seppuku*, then I will willingly comply." He then left. His stance was reviewed later, and amendments were made to the assignments. He told me that a young warrior should be strong-headed. Consider this well.

107. Constantly check yourself in the mirror when learning how to groom your appearance. I was allowed to grow my forelocks when I was 13. I did not appear for duties for almost a year until my hair had grown long enough to satisfy that hairstyle properly. Family members commented, "He looks excessively erudite, so he is bound to slip up someday. The lord especially despises men who look as though they are too clever." So, I decided to change the way my face looked. I scrutinised my face in the mirror, and tried to adjust it. When I resumed my duties a year later, everyone said I looked feeble and sickly. I believe the extensive efforts I made to be the foundation for service. You will never be trusted with a face that looks too discerning. Without composure and resolve you will appear to lack grace. Ideally, one should be reverent, refined, and poised.

---

1 The shogunate assigned the Nabeshima domain to oversee the port of Nagasaki in 1642. The incident talked about here happened in 1683 when Jōchō was 25 years old.

108. When faced with an emergency at a time when you are unable to confer with others, you will find a solution simply by considering your predicament in accordance with the "Four Oaths." Nothing more is needed than this.

❀ ❀ ❀

109. It can be counter-productive if the *o-metsuke*[1] (domain inspector) does not see things with a broad perspective. This position is created to ensure efficient governance of the domain. The lord is not able to see all that goes on in his fief. The *o-metsuke* is appointed to gather accurate information on matters pertaining to the lord's deportment, right and wrongdoings of the higher retainers, the appropriateness of legal process, rumors in the community, the joys and sorrows of the lower classes, and to improve the domain's administrative procedures.

As such, the original objective of this post is to investigate malfeasance among those in positions of authority. Unfortunately, *o-metsuke* officials seem hellbent on investigating mischief in the lower classes and reporting trivial incidents to the lord, which is more damaging to the domain. There are a few commoners who engage in evildoing, but this is not going to adversely affect the domain. Furthermore, those responsible for investigating criminal matters are obliged to listen to the defenses of the accused in order to try and assist them. Ultimately, this is also for the benefit of the lord.

❀ ❀ ❀

110. There are various ways to admonish one's lord. Offering heartfelt rebuke should be done in a way so that others are not aware. Your thoughts must be expressed prudently so as to not infuriate your master as you help him mend his weak points. This was appar-

---

1 The position of *o-metsuke* was directly beneath that of *karō* (chief retainer) but was sanctioned to operate as an independent authority reporting on affairs in the domain.

ent in the loyalty of Hosokawa Yoriyuki.[1] Once, the lord wanted to make a detour during a journey. Upon hearing this, an elder proclaimed, "I will sacrifice my life to persuade him not to. We are already behind schedule, so another diversion will just not do." He then faced the others and said, "I bid ye all farewell." He prepared himself for his impending death by bathing in cold water, put on a *shiro-katabira* (light white hemp garment),[2] and requested an audience with the lord. Not long after, he returned with an air of importance and said, "I am glad to report that our lord listened to my reasoning. I am also overjoyed that I am able to see you all again." This performance was intended only to expose the foibles of the lord, and champion his own sense of loyalty and valor. Men employed from outside the domain often stage such acts of pretension.

❀ ❀ ❀

111. A calculating man is a coward. This is because he considers everything from the perspective of loss and gain, and his mind never deviates from this track. To him, death is a loss, and life is a gain. He is afraid of death, which is why he is a disgrace. Moreover, erudite men conceal their cowardice and avarice through their wit and glibness. Their cloak of deception tricks others into overestimating them.

❀ ❀ ❀

112. Since it was decreed that *oibara*[3] was no longer lawful, there

---

1 Hosokawa Yoriyuki (1329–1392) was a celebrated councilor to Ashikaga Yoshimitsu (1358–1394), the third shogun of the Muromachi bakufu (1333–1573).

2 Symbolic of his preparation to die if ordered to do so.

3 *Junshi*, the act of self-immolation following one's lord in death, was variously called *oibara* ("disembowelment to follow") or *tomobara* ("disembowelment to accompany"). Criticisms of the practice became prominent in the early years of the Tokugawa period, and in 1663 the shogun Ietsuna verbally outlawed *junshi*. This was preceded by Nabeshima Mitsushige who forbade *junshi* in the Nabeshima domain on the seventh day of the seventh month, 1661. The custom was formerly made illegal nationally when a clause was added to the *Buke Shohatto* ("Laws for Military Houses") during the fifth shogun Tsunayoshi's rule (1680–1709).

have been no retainers prepared to martyr their lives for their lord. Also, since it was declared that even an infant may inherit the household, this has removed any incentive for service [to the lord]. Young pages are no longer appointed, and samurai customs have become lax. My lord's overly compassionate measures actually did more harm to his retainers than good. It is not too late to reinstate child pages into service. At the age of 15 or 16, young men have already removed the hair on their foreheads [with their coming of age], but lack prudence as they engage in superfluous discussions on drinking and food, and say and do things that they shouldn't without reflecting on their ways. They become preoccupied with frivolous amusements, so do not make good retainers. Those who have had experience as a pageboy will be familiar with a range of duties, having observed them from a young age, and will make useful retainers. Soejima Hachi'uemon was 42, and Nabeshima Kanbei 40 when they came of age.[1]

❀ ❀ ❀

113. "Bushido is to enter a 'death frenzy' (*shini-gurui*). Even dozens of men cannot kill a man in a frenzied state already determined to die." Lord Naoshige said this. One cannot accomplish great exploits in a normal frame of mind. Just become insane and desperate to die. In the Way of the warrior, contemplating matters too deeply will cause you to fall behind others. Don't think of loyalty or filial piety, just enter a frenzy to perish in *shidō*.[2] Loyalty and filial piety will manifest as a matter of course in the death frenzy.

❀ ❀ ❀

---

1 The *genpuku* coming of age ceremony was a rite of passage in which boys assumed adult attire, hairstyle, and an adult name. It was usually for boys falling between the ages of 10 and 16, depending on the family. In this instance, we can see that there were exceptions to the rule. They were obviously preferred attendants of the lord.
2 *Shidō* was a common Tokugawa period term for warrior ethics influenced predominantly by neo-Confucian thought.

114. Shida Kichinosuke said: "If it won't damage your reputation whether you live or die, then you should live." This is an oxymoron. He also said: "When you wonder if you should go or not, don't go." And: "When you wonder if you should eat or not, it is better not to eat. When you wonder if you should die or not, it is better to die."[1]

❀ ❀ ❀

115. It is not sufficient just to remain calm in the event of catastrophe or emergency. When challenged by adversity, charge onwards with courage and jubilation. This is rising to a higher level. It is like the saying, "The more water there is, the higher the boat rises." Muraoka talked of this before he changed his name [through promotion].[2]

❀ ❀ ❀

116. Ittei said: "It is spineless to think you cannot outdo a maestro after watching or listening to him. A maestro is also but a human being, as are you. If you consider in what way you are inferior and make your mind up to study the art, then you are ready to master it, too. Confucios was a sage when he set his heart on studying at the age of 15. He did not become a sage due to his later studies." A Buddhist teaching states: "When you have a spiritual awakening [to study Buddhism], it is because correct Buddha teachings have already infiltrated your mind with your decision to become a monk."

❀ ❀ ❀

117. Samurai should be heedful of everything, and detest falling even a little behind his rivals. Pay particular attention to your words lest you utter nonsense like "I am a coward," "I will run if things get nasty," "I'm afraid," or "It hurts." Under no circumstances should such aberrations of speech pass your lips in jest, in your sleep, or when

---

1 See Book 1-48.
2 Muraoka Gohei Kiyosada was a *toshiyori-yaku* (elder) of the Nabeshima domain.

you are babbling incoherently during illness. Percipient men in earshot will see straight through to your core. Beware.

❀ ❀ ❀

118. A samurai with a strong martial spirit and an unwavering resolve will be called upon first when the time comes. This is because his qualities are evident in his daily deportment and each of his comments, and this will give rise to various opportunities. Above all, words spoken on any occasion are consequential. There is no need to reveal all that is on your mind. Your qualities will be apparent through your daily actions.

❀ ❀ ❀

119. When in training to be a retainer, I never sat with crossed legs inside or outside. Nor did I ever open my mouth. When I had to speak, I endeavored to express my thoughts in one word rather than ten. Warriors such as Yamasaki Kurando were of a similar disposition.[1]

❀ ❀ ❀

120. It is said that you can do one last thing even when your head has been cut off. This is known by the exploits of Nitta Yoshisada[2] and Ōno Dōken.[3] Why would you be inferior to them? Mitani Jokyū[4] said, "I will live on for another for two or three days even after dying from illness."

❀ ❀ ❀

---

1 Yamasaki Kurando was a *toshiyori-yaku* (elder councilor) of the Nabeshima domain.

2 Nitta Yoshisada (1301–1338) was a renowned warrior of the late Kamakura (1185–1333) and early Muromachi (1333–1568) periods. He is said to have cut off his own head, buried it, and then prostrated himself over his own grave before dying.

3 Ōno Dōken Harutane (?–1615), the third of three brothers (Harunaga, Harufusa, and Harutane), served as a chief retainer in the entourage of Toyotomi Hideyoshi. After being burned at the stake, he was somehow able to "come back to life" and kill the inspector as one last act of defiance.

4 A retainer of Nabeshima Mitsushige, who became a monk in 1700 when Mitsushige died.

121. An ancient saying goes: "Think, and decide in seven breaths." Lord Takanobu[1] commented: "One's judgement will diminish with prolonged deliberation." Lord Naoshige[2] said: "Matters decided at a leisurely pace will turn out badly seven times out of ten. Military affairs must be executed expeditiously." Decisions will also be difficult to make when one's heart is adrift. With an unperturbed, invigorated, and dignified state of mind, resolutions can be made within seven breaths. This is when one's mind is steadfast and clear.

❀ ❀ ❀

122. A man who can reason over trifles will become conceited, and will take pleasure in being described as 'odd.' He will start boasting that he was born with a personality that doesn't fit well with contemporary society, and be convinced that nobody else is above him. He will surely meet with divine retribution. Regardless of what abilities a man may possess, he will be of little use if rejected by others. People don't slight those who are eager to help and serve well, and who readily exhibit humility to their associates.

❀ ❀ ❀

123. If you are not high-ranking enough to remonstrate with your lord, requesting that a senior official correct his mistakes instead is a mark of prodigious loyalty. This requires maintaining affable relations with those above you. It is just an act of flattery, however, if you do it for your own gain. But it is not kowtowing if you are acting to support the clan. This is achievable if that is what you wish for.

❀ ❀ ❀

124. It is an act of loyalty to educate others to become better retainers. Therefore, those with the will to learn should be given instruc-

---

1 Ryūzōji Takanobu was lord of Saga before the Nabeshima clan's rise to power.
2 The first Nabeshima daimyo of Saga.

tion. Nothing is more joyous than passing on knowledge to be vicariously useful in service through others.

125. Broken relations between retired and incumbent lords, father and son, older and younger brothers, derive from avarice. The fact that there is no such thing as bad blood between the lord and his followers [in this clan] is proof of this.

126. A man who is successful when he is too young will not be useful for long. Even though he may be gifted at birth, young men lack maturity in terms of disposition and ability, and will not receive the confidence of others. Success is best secured from around the age of 50. It is actually propitious if people believe that your success is late in coming. Also, even if his house is waning because of some blunder, a man with willpower can quickly overcome any setback because it was not triggered by selfish desires.

127. It is preposterous to feel crestfallen when dismissed from duty. It was customarily said at the time of Lord Katsushige: "You won't make a true man of service unless you have experienced being a *rōnin* seven times. Fall down seven times, and get up eight (*nana-korobi-yaoki*)." A man of the caliber of Naridomi Hyōgo was a *rōnin* seven times.[1] It should be thought of as being like a self-righting doll. The lord may dismiss you from his service as a test.

---

1 Naridomi Hyōgo was known for his work in land development and flood control in the Nabeshima domain.

128. An illness will become graver depending on your state of mind. Born when my father was 70 years of age, I was a shadow of a child with a frail constitution. Because I had great ambitions to serve my lord into my old age, I made every effort to become strong and retain my health, and never became ill. I chose abstinence, and received treatment with moxa.[1] Through my experiences, there are some things of which I am certain. It is said that a *mamushi* will return to its original form even after being burnt seven times.[2] My greatest hope is that when I die, if I am to be reincarnated seven times, each time is as a samurai of the Nabeshima clan to realize my purpose of faithful and valuable service. I wish this from the bottom of my heart.

❀ ❀ ❀

129. As Lord Naoshige supposed, samurai with ambitions [to serve with excellence] stay on good terms with their colleagues. I was always well-mannered to all people, from samurai to low-ranked *ashigaru*. This forms the basis for soliciting help should the need arise. All I would need to say is, "It's for His Lordship's benefit, so please rally with me." My allies would be sure to offer assistance without a moment's delay. This amounts to the lord having numerous worthy retainers, and contributes to the prosperity of the clan.

❀ ❀ ❀

130. The following verse is found in the book *Yoshitsune Gunka*.[3] "A general must communicate well with his men. In normal times, but even more so in times of emergency, if a unit captain says to his subordinates, 'You have done very well, but let us enter the fray one more time, for you are strong!' they will sacrifice life and limb for the

---

1 A traditional East Asian medical treatment in which mugwort herb is applied on the skin at precise points and then ignited to enhance the flow of energy through the body to adjust any physical irregularities.

2 *Mamushi* is a small, venomous snake found widely throughout Japan.

3 A collection of military poems attributed to Minamoto-no-Yoshitsune. This passage is quoted from the first verse.

cause. It is important for a leader to offer a word of encouragement to his men."

❀ ❀ ❀

131. Yamamoto Jin'uemon often said, "It is essential for a samurai to have men of talent under him. No matter how eager you are to serve your lord, you cannot fight a war alone. If in need of money you can borrow it; but good retainers cannot be assembled on a whim. You need to take good care the ones you have. To engage good men you shouldn't feed only yourself, but share your rice with them. They will follow you gladly. It was widely recognized that nobody with the same stipend as me had retainers that could match the caliber of my men. They were envious of the subordinates I commanded. Of the servants who I nurtured, many went on to serve as attendants to the lord, or were given the rank of *teakiyari*."[1] When Jin'uemon was appointed as a *kumi-gashira* (captain) in command of his own unit, he was directed by his lord: "Choose any men you wish to join your unit, Jin'uemon." Extra rice was allotted to pay their stipends. All who were selected for the *kumi* were Jin'uemon's retainers. When Lord Katsushige worshipped at the moon-waiting festival, he decided to send some servants to fetch [holy] salt water from the shrine in Terai. He said, "Send the men from Jin'uemon's unit. They will draw the deepest water." He served with utmost sincerity, relishing the trust his lord had for him.

❀ ❀ ❀

132. Jin'uemon said: "Exceptional warriors (*kusemono*) are dependable men. Dependable men are exceptional warriors. I know this through considerable experience. Dependable men can be relied upon to keep away when things are going well, but will come to your aid without fail when you are in need. A man of such temperament

---

1 A position falling between the lower (*kachi*) and middle-ranked (*hirashi*) warriors.

is most certainly a *kusemono*."[1]

❀ ❀ ❀

133. A man's son was to be reinstated by his master [after a period as a *rōnin*]. When the samurai was to be interviewed by the lord, his father advised him: "When you bow to him, think to yourself, 'How privileged I am. I was hidden from view before, so could it be a divine blessing to be reemployed as his servant? There is nothing more providential than this opportunity. As I have this chance, I will throw my whole body and life into service.' He will be impressed by your attitude, and you will be able to serve him well." He added, "When you are beckoned before the lord, refrain from looking at things in the palace, be determined not to talk, don't move from where you are seated, and even when spoken to, reply in one word rather than ten. This way, you will be judged as a man of steadfast character. Your inner thoughts will be exposed if you glance around and chat incessantly, and you will appear to be a fool. This is what constitutes an unwavering mind. The more familiar you become with the surroundings, the more you should take heed of this."

❀ ❀ ❀

134. A man who possesses a little wisdom will criticize the times. This begets misfortune as he digs a hole for himself. A man who is prudent with his words will be useful in prosperous times, and will avoid falling foul of the law when times are bad.

❀ ❀ ❀

135. Written oaths to the deities (*jinmon*) contain mysterious powers.[2]

❀ ❀ ❀

---

1 See Book 1-60.
2 See Book 1-98.

136. "If I was to offer my opinion to the lord, it would just make him obstinate and do more harm, so it is better not to intervene. Even if it is unreasonable, the matter is better left." Saying such things is just an excuse. Your lord may acknowledge your admonishment if you offer it at the risk of your life. The lord's ire is roused because opinions are only made in a half-hearted manner. And, sensing his anger, so many would-be petitioners stop in mid-sentence and withdraw.

One year, Sagara Kyūma presented a strong point of view that enraged his lord, so he was ordered to commit *seppuku*. Ikuno Oribe[1] and Yamasaki Kurando informed him of the lord's command, to which Kyūma stated, "*Seppuku* is my intention. However, there is one more thing I need to say; the matter will not be resolved, even after my death. As both of you are good friends, I implore you to convey this message for me." They both informed the lord of Kyūma's words. I hear it made the lord even angrier, but surprisingly, he issued a stay on Kyūma's impending *seppuku*. He acknowledged what Kyūma had said and pardoned him.

Also, when Nakano Kazuma was an elder (*toshiyori*) of the clan, Hamuro Seizaemon,[2] Ōsumi Godayu, Ezoe Jinbei, Ishii Genzaemon, and Ishii Hachirōzaemon were ordered to commit *seppuku* to atone for their disobedience.[3] Kazuma went to Lord Tsunashige and pleaded, "Please pardon these men." Lord Tsunashige was maddened and retorted, "They have been ordered to commit *seppuku* as a result of an inquest. For what reason do you make such an appeal?" Kazuma replied, "There is no reason, Sire." When Lord Tsunashige chided him for insolently making such a request for "no reason," Kazuma retreated. He then came forth again saying, "My Lord, I beseech you to pardon these men." He was admonished yet again, retreated, and then approached once more. Kazuma made his plea seven times. Lord Tsunashige said, "With no plausible reason, you insist on making this supplication seven times. Because of your persistence, I somehow feel obliged to grant your request." He

---

1 A chief retainer (*karō*).
2 Hamuro Seizaemon held the high position of *chakuza*, one rank below *karō*.
3 See Book 1-168.

changed his mind, and the men were spared. I have witnessed many such incidents.

❀ ❀ ❀

137. The best way to outdo your colleagues is to ask for their advice about your own ideas. Most men conclude matters based on their own opinions, which prevents them from rising to a higher level. Consulting with experts is the best way to advance. A certain person sought my advice about writing an official document. Although better at writing such documents than I, he demonstrated his superiority through a willingness to solicit remedial help.

❀ ❀ ❀

138. There is no point in one's training[1] in which one reaches the end. The instant you think you have finished, you have already strayed from the path. Realize that nothing you do is perfect until you have taken your last breath; then, when you are dead, you will be seen as having completed the Way. Purity without excess, and focusing single-mindedly on one thing is difficult to achieve during one's lifetime. If the purity of your training is diluted, then it cannot be called the proper Way. Strive to follow the Way of service and samuraihood as your singular pursuit.

❀ ❀ ❀

139. It is ruinous to pursue two Ways. The warrior needs only train in bushido—the Way of the samurai—and seek nothing else. The character for all Ways, '道', is the same. Nevertheless, one cannot master the Way of the warrior while simultaneously becoming immersed in the teachings of Shintō[2] and Buddha. If one understands

---

1 The word used repeatedly throughout the text for training is "*shugyō*" (修行).
2 Some variant texts refer to *judō* (儒道—the Way of Confucius) instead of Shintō (神道—the Way of the *kami*, or deities).

this, then learning about the other Ways [for reference only] will serve to improve your training in the pursuit of bushido.

140. It is said that, "The method in which verses are linked with apposite word endings is very important when composing poems." Similarly, each and every word should be from the heart.

141. Any word a samurai utters is of great consequence. His courage is divulged by a single word. In times of peace, it is a man's words that make known his valor. In times of turmoil, words convey either strength or cowardice. A samurai's word is a flower of his heart. The weight of one's words cannot be expressed in words.

142. A samurai should not, in the slightest degree, say or do something faintheartedly. Never forget this. The depth of one's heart is discernible even through something seemingly inconsequential.

143. Nothing is impossible. With single-minded resolve (*ichinen*), heaven and earth can be moved as one pleases. There is nothing that cannot be achieved. A man's fecklessness prevents him from making up his mind. "Effortlessly moving heaven and earth"[1] can be accomplished through sheer single-minded determination.[2]

---

1 A phrase from a poem in the *Kokin-shū* ("Collection of Japanese Poems from Ancient and Modern Times"), a compilation completed in 905.
2 See Book 1-58.

144. My father Jin'uemon always said: "You won't break your back by bowing too deeply. The concluding polite phrase of a letter should not be abbreviated."[1] These days, people do not bow deeply enough, so they look sloppy, and their posture is poor, too. It is best to show respect at all times. If you must sit for an extended period of time at some gathering, bow politely at the beginning, and then again at the end, while acting as the occasion requires in between. If you regulate your politeness in accordance with others present, it will often be substandard. These days, people are rude and fidgety.

❀ ❀ ❀

145. Another axiom Jin'uemon always repeated was: "Even when a samurai has had nothing to eat, he should still use a toothpick [as if he had already dined]. Wear a dog's skin inside, a tiger's hide outside." A samurai should show taste in his outward appearance, but be frugal on the inside. Most warriors have it the wrong way round.[2]

❀ ❀ ❀

146. Warriors extolled as being highly skilled in the arts come across as being imprudent. To become accomplished in an art necessitates a preoccupation with that activity to the detriment of all else. Such a samurai is of no value in service.[3]

❀ ❀ ❀

147. A sage or wise lord will always acknowledge remonstrance from his retainers. In such cases, a retainer does his utmost to advise on an array of topics, and tries to be held dear. This contributes to the stability of the clan. A treasurable samurai is one who interacts affably with his peers, and seeks advice from men about various

---

1 See Book 11-42.
2 See Book 1-60.
3 See Book 1-70.

matters. A warrior who reflects on his faults and spends his life training with all of his might will become a treasure to the clan.

❀ ❀ ❀

148. Everything you do until the age of 40 should be executed with
all of your energy. It is preferable for a samurai approaching the age
of 50 to moderate his behavior.

❀ ❀ ❀

149. Be sure to engage with somebody fully as you converse. Regardless of how inspiring your comments may be, they will be ineffectual
if the other person is not following you.

❀ ❀ ❀

150. Be on familiar terms with close attendants of the lord. This is
obsequious if only for your own gratification, but if your intentions
are to serve, it opens up a channel to pass on useful advice to your
lord. The outlook is be bleak if the attendant is bereft of loyal con-
sciousness. Do everything with the best intentions for the lord.[1]

❀ ❀ ❀

151. When someone gives an opinion, even a seemingly inconsequential one, listen carefully with good grace. Otherwise, they will
desist from relaying to you what they have overheard or observed.
Ingratiate yourself with your colleagues so they can convey their
estimations with ease, as this buoy your cause.

❀ ❀ ❀

---

1 See Book 1-124.

152. The manner and timing in which reproach is delivered to your lord is important. If you rebuke him with the intention of "rendering him contrite," it is likely that your criticisms will be ignored completely, and may even cause more harm.

Tell him "It is acceptable to enjoy amusements if retainers are inspired to serve well, and the commoners can live peacefully. Everybody will want to discharge their duties diligently, and the domain will be governed peacefully. I hope that is not such a bothersome request." The lord should be pleased with your petition.

If admonishment and opinions are not communicated carefully with a spirit of accord, it will amount to nothing. Insensitive protests will cause umbrage, and even simple problems will not be resolved.

❈　❈　❈

153. There are many who like to impart moral lessons in the world today, but few who choose to listen. Moreover, fewer still are those who actually abide by the precepts. No one ventures to teach morality to a man in his thirties. Without advice, he does as he pleases and continues with his foolish antics, and wastes his life in a downward spiral of nefariousness. Be conversant with wise men, and seek lessons in morality from them.

❈　❈　❈

154. A samurai who does not care much for his reputation tends to be contrary, is conceited, and good-for-nothing. He is inferior to a samurai who craves glory, and is thus completely unusable.

❈　❈　❈

155. A well-known adage states: "Great talent takes time to mature" (*daiki-bansei*). An undertaking of consequence takes 20 or 30 years to achieve. In service as well, if a man hurries to achieve something meritorious, he will speak of business that is not his concern. Although he may be described as a promising young man, he will become arrogant and rude, and act with an air of smugness as if he was already accomplished. Turning into a frivolous panderer, others will point their fingers in disdain behind his back. A man must train hard and garner the support of his superiors, otherwise his existence will be superfluous.

❀ ❀ ❀

156. Whatever the duty may be, understand well the importance of your position, imagining that each day is your last on the job. You will never fail if you execute your responsibilities with single-minded devotion, imagining that you are performing directly under the lord's watchful eye. It is said: "Achieve your greatest aspirations of service through your official position." First, make that position yours.

❀ ❀ ❀

157. For someone whose position is attained through hereditary succession (*fudai*), rejecting a post because you don't like it, or withdrawing from service for some reason, is an insult to the lord. It is akin to treason. Samurai from other provinces construe it as a matter of pride to resign if they harbor any grievances. It is incumbent of *fudai*[1] samurai [in the Nabeshima clan], to undertake any duty assigned to him by the lord, irrespective of whether it is to his liking or not. If there is something you dislike about the mandate, you have recourse to lobby for a change [instead of quitting].

❀ ❀ ❀

158. In the *Kusunoki Masashige Hyōgo-ki* it states that: "Even if surrender is used as a ploy, or it is beneficial to the lord, it is an unforgivable course of action for a samurai." A faithful retainer must embody this attitude.

---

1 *Fudai* refers to a samurai who is born into a family which has served the clan for generations.

❀ ❀ ❀

159. A retainer should adore serving his lord. It is a timorous coward who winces at an important task and withdraws because of the danger. If you meet with failure in your mission despite your best efforts, it will be lauded as an honorable death.

❀ ❀ ❀

160. A samurai who opts only for the duties he likes, or gauges the mood of his lord or unit captain to serve his own best interests, will get his comeuppance in the most unbecoming way after a single failure, even if his designs had been successful ten times before. This is because he lacks a sense of unyielding loyalty, and is motivated only by selfish and evil desires.

❀ ❀ ❀

161. If you are properly prepared for when your role in bushido requires performing *kaishaku* for a family or unit member, or arresting an outlaw, your outstanding deportment and determination will be noticed. In matters of military prowess, train with all of your might to never be surpassed by others, and think to yourself, "My valor is beyond compare."

❀ ❀ ❀

162. An old-timer said that in battle, when you are recklessly determined to "not be outdone by others" and aim to "charge the enemy line," you will not fall behind, your spirit will be intrepid, and you will exhibit fearlessness. What's more, if you are killed in the fray, be sure that your corpse falls in the direction of the enemy.

❀ ❀ ❀

163. Tranquillity will prevail when people act in accord and leave outcomes to divine mandate (*tendō*). Unless your hearts are one, you can't perform loyal service, even if you have an impressive record. Not being on good terms with your peers, avoiding gatherings, and passing tetchy remarks are signs of narrow-minded folly. Keeping in mind what could happen should a catastrophe bear down upon you, pleasantly extend courtesies to others without prejudice whenever you meet, even if you find them to be irksome. All things in this world are transient and there is no way of foretelling what will happen next. It would be a pity to die while people embrace ill feelings towards you.

Still, no matter how much you are told to get along with others, it is unseemly to resort to lies and wispy flattery motivated by self-interest. To maintain friendly relationships, put your colleagues first and avoid any antagonism, and always act politely and with an air of humility for the good of others. All encounters will be like meeting for the first time, and the rapport will be easy to maintain. This is the same for married couples as well. If you remain as thoughtful as when you met for the first time, there will be no reason for you to quarrel.

🌼 🌼 🌼

164. Try to view things from a higher position than others. If matters are pondered from the same level, disagreements will erupt and nothing will be seen with clarity. Once, a man had his stipend rescinded and people gossiped about it. He rebuffed them by saying, "It wasn't a major incident that led to this, so I am upset at being so ill-fated." Also, "My lord's conviviality is a false kindness to manipulate people, so I am not particularly grateful to receive his favor." He was told, "Well then, you are not suited to retainership. Men with a will to serve their lord from the bottom of their hearts are contented even to be deceived by him."

🌼 🌼 🌼

165. A certain priest is very capable and has a magnificent handle on various problems.[1] There are no other monks in Japan who can challenge him. It is not because he is so brilliant. There are just no monks who can perceive the fundaments of matters as well as he does.

❀ ❀ ❀

166. Alas, there are no worthy men. Few pay attention to useful stories passed down from the great men of old, let alone engage in rigorous training to better themselves. Recently, I have had conversations with several people here and there. They withhold opinions through fear of ridicule if they reveal what is really on their minds.

❀ ❀ ❀

167. It seems that the elderly reveal their true leanings as they become senile. They can regulate their own behavior when they still have vitality, but their true colors show as their energy dwindles, and they humiliate themselves. There are many ways in which this manifests. Nobody over the age of 60 is devoid of senility. Believing you are not senile is a good indication that you actually are.

Ittei became quite argumentative in his old age. Determined to carry the clan on his own, he traveled hither and thither, calling on prominent families in his decrepit state to convince others of his cause. Many politely feigned interest in Ittei's rants, but in hindsight it was because he was losing his marbles. He provided me with a pertinent lesson. Feeling timeworn, I decided not to visit the temple after the thirteenth anniversary of Lord Mitsushige's passing, and refrain from going out any more. One needs to have a clear view of what lies ahead.

❀ ❀ ❀

168. As with everything new, unexpected liabilities arise even if it seems like a magnificent idea. Before departing for Edo one year,

---

1   See Book 1-34.

some attendants and elder councilors discussed a proposition to take some of the low-ranked *teakiyari* reserve warriors employed by the bodyguards (*umamawari*). More men skilled in Noh would be needed for the performance scheduled to commemorate the new shogun's appointment.[1] Besides, it would give the lord an opportunity to become acquainted with the men. And so it was decided. A few experienced retainers, however, opposed the idea outright, predicting that bad things were sure to happen. A quarrel soon erupted. Five *o-heyatsuki* room attendants, including Hamuro[2] and Ōsumi, were relieved of their position. Twenty inspectors (*kiwameyaku*)[3] were appointed to accompany the *teakiyari*, and keep the lord informed of daily occurrences. So many appalling things happened that they could hardly keep up.

❧ ❧ ❧

169. As long as you have a firm understanding of the situation, the "branches and leaves" (details) are of small consequence, and minor hitches will not matter so much. Nevertheless, branches and leaves should not be entirely overlooked, as a small detail may cause perpetual frustration.

❧ ❧ ❧

170. According to the priest at the Ryūtaiji Temple, "In the Kamigata region a diviner once said it is futile for a man, even if he is a priest, to find success before 40. He is likely to make mistakes thereafter. Confucius was not the only man to be 'liberated from the shackles of confusion at 40.' Both wise and foolish men accrue enough life experience by the time they are 40 not to be perplexed any longer. After reaching 40, all men know their limitations, and how realistic their aspirations are."

❧ ❧ ❧

---

1 Tsunayoshi became the fifth Tokugawa shogun in 1681.
2 See Book 1-136.
3 See Book 1-109.

171. In war, dying for one's lord in battle is a greater feat of merit than taking an enemy head. This was epitomized by the actions of Satō Tsugunobu.[1]

❀ ❀ ❀

172. I kept a diary when I was young, and called it "A Record of Regrets."[2] In it, I logged the mistakes that I made each day. Not a day passed when I didn't commit 20 or 30 gaffes. There was no end to what I had to document because of my incessant blundering, so I eventually stopped. Now, when I reflect on each day before retiring, there is not one that is free of slip-ups in word and action. Indeed, it seems that a perfect day is impossible to pull off. Men who wriggle their way through life relying on their talents will fail to grasp this.

❀ ❀ ❀

173. Shikibu said, "Read books from your gut. Your voice will falter if you read only with your mouth."[3]

❀ ❀ ❀

174. Conceit and haughtiness are perilous during times of good fortune. One must redouble efforts to maintain a sense of humility. Those who revel when times are good will wither in adversity.

❀ ❀ ❀

175. An old saying advises that, when searching for a loyal retainer, look in the house of a filial son. He embodies the virtue of faithful

---

1 Satō Tsugunobu was a retainer of Minamoto-no-Yoshitsune. He allegedly sacrificed his life by acting as a human shield, protecting his lord from incoming arrows at the Battle of Yashima in 1185.

2 *Zannen-ki.*

3 It is not clear who this was, but is possibly Nakano Shikibu. See Book 1-180.

devotion. Many become remorseful only after their parents have gone. Warriors apply themselves in serving their lord well, but so few fulfill their filial duties to their parents.

True loyalty and filial piety is known under an unreasonable master or irrational parents. If they are indulgent, even a stranger will be deferential to them. It is said "The green hues of conifer trees are revealed in the hoar frost." The monk Gensei would secretly visit a fishmonger at dawn and hide fish under his robe as he rushed to his mother's side.[1] He was a wonderfully faithful son.

❀ ❀ ❀

176. Ittei said, "When practicing calligraphy, make the paper, brush, and ink as one." But, they are so inclined to be separate.

❀ ❀ ❀

177. His Lordship (Mitsushige) took a scroll from a case. The fragrance of dried cloves wafted forth as he opened the lid.

❀ ❀ ❀

178. "Tolerance" is another word for "great compassion." In a sacred verse it states, "If viewed with an eye of compassion, nobody can be despised. All the more should a sinner be pitied." There is no limit to the breadth and depth of compassion. It is ubiquitous. The reason why people still revere the sages of the three ancient kingdoms[2] is because of the vastness and extent of their compassion. We must do our best for the benefit of our parents, neighbors, and descendants. This is "great compassion."

Wisdom and courage based on compassion are genuine virtues.

---

1 Gensei (1623–1668) was a Kyoto monk of the Nichiren sect who was famous for his skill in the arts. The filial duty indicated in this story is demonstrated by the lengths he went to give his mother tasty morsels to eat, even though partaking of animal flesh and even fish ran counter to Nichiren's ideals as a strict vegetarian.

2 Japan, China, and India.

Punishment is an act of compassion, as is service. A compassionate mind will help others in a way that is righteous and knows no bounds. Anything done for personal gain is trivial and small-minded, and will lead to malevolence.

I have long been cognizant of what constitutes valor and wisdom, but have only recently come to grasp the meaning of compassion. It was Lord Tokugawa Ieyasu who said: "If I love my retainers and the people as my children, they in turn will love me as their father. A peaceful realm is based entirely on compassion."

In the same way, *kumi-gashira* (unit captains) are also called "*yorioya*" (parents) and unit members called "*kumiko*" (children). The bond that binds them is predicated on the same compassion which unites parent and child.

Lord Naoshige taught, "A man who seeks to render others contrite will get as good as he gives."[1] This precept underlies the importance of compassion. He also said "There is reason beyond logic," which is also analogous to compassion. He declared passionately that we should all savor the boundless profundity of what this means.

❀ ❀ ❀

179. The priest Tannen said, "A retainer who is too clever will never make it; but by the same token, there is no chance of stupid people succeeding, either."

❀ ❀ ❀

180. Shikibu had an opinion [regarding *shudō*, or homosexual relationships]:[2] "One is likely to trigger a lifetime of shame through

---

1 This is one of the dictums contained in the text *Naoshige-kō O-kabegaki*, a collection of teachings by Nabeshima Naoshige. See Book 1-46.

2 Male homosexuality has a long and well-documented history in Japan, but became taboo with the introduction of Western moral ideals after the Meiji Restoration of 1868. Widespread in Buddhist and court circles from as early as the Heian period, homosexuality was also accepted by warriors throughout the Kamakura (1185–1333) and Muromachi (1333–1568) periods. In the Tokugawa period, *shudō* ("the Way of the young") was an important factor in the culture of the military and religious

a *shudō* relationship in one's youth. Care is needed. There is nobody to teach young men about the perils of *shudō*. I will tell you the basic knowledge required. 'A wife does not serve two husbands.' Be true to only one man in your lifetime. Otherwise you are the same as a male prostitute, and equivalent to a whore of a woman. This is abominable conduct for a samurai."

In Ihara Saikaku's well-known prose it says: "A young man before his coming-of-age ceremony (*genpuku*) without an older male lover is like a woman without a husband."[1] Some men will try and coerce you. If you wish to ascertain the affectionate intentions of an older man, you should first test the association for five years to see if he is true; only then should you assent to a *shudō* relationship.

A man guilty of wantonness is unable to commit, and will likely abandon you. The bond is one of total devotion and mutual sacrifice, so knowing his character is crucial. If something seems awry, stand strong and tell him that there are some complications, and that your reluctance to commit right away is unavoidable. If the man complains and asks what you mean by "complications," tell him you can't reveal that for as long as you live. If he persists, get angry with him; and if he still doesn't relinquish, smite him down with your sword.

The elder man in the relationship must be certain of his younger lover's devotion before advancing. His affectionate yearnings will not go unrewarded after devoting himself to the relationship for five years. Under no circumstances should you be duplicitous. Only then can a samurai be called an adherent of bushido.

❀ ❀ ❀

181. Hoshino Ryōtetsu is the expert on *shudō* in Saga. Although he

---

elites. *Shudō* as explained here in *Hagakure* is akin to relationships of pederasty (not paedophilia)—i.e., a relationship between a man and a pubescent boy outside his immediate family—and was considered a pure form of love in which ideals of loyalty and devotion were practiced. Lords would often engage in pederasty with young pages or junior retainers, but the practice was also seen among all of the warrior ranks.

1 Ihara Saikaku's (1642–1693) *Kōshoku Ishidai Otoko* (*The Life of an Amorous Man*, 1682) and *Nanshoku Okagami* (*The Great Mirror of Male Love*, 1687).

amassed many followers, he divulged his knowledge individually. Edayoshi Saburōzaemon was taught about the basic theory of *shudō*. As Edayoshi was leaving for Edo with his lord, Ryōtetsu asked him of his thoughts on *shudō* from the younger man's perspective. Edayoshi responded by saying that "The elder partner should be loved, and not loved." Ryōtetsu was pleased. "Yes! It took such a long time to nurture this understanding in you."

Some years later, somebody asked Edayoshi what he meant by his comment. He explained: "The essential point in *shudō* is preparation to forfeit your life for the sake of your lover. Otherwise you risk humiliation. On the other hand, though, this means that you would be unable to surrender your life in the service of your lord. Through this contradiction, I came to realize that in *shudō*, you should love your partner, but not love him at the same time."

❀ ❀ ❀

182. Master Nakashima Sanza was a page to Lord Ryūzōji Masaie. He died onboard a boat, and his grave is located in the Kamōin Temple in Takao, Saga. He is the ancestor of Nakashima Jingozaemon. A certain man was enamored with Sanza but lamented how the feeling was not mutual, so he wrote a poem: "After the seventh hour (four o'clock in the afternoon), one hungers for the young master like the evening meal." Sanza is even said to have recited it in the presence of his lord.

Sanza was described as the most beautiful boy that ever lived. Even Lord Katsushige is said to have been smitten with him. Once when Lord Katsushige was in the castle, Sanza walked by and his leg brushed against Katsushige's knee. Sanza immediately moved back and placed his hand on his lord's knee, apologizing profusely.

One night, Sanza appeared at Hyakutake Jirōbei's house in Tsujinodō, announcing that he must see him. Taken aback, Jirōbei ran outside to meet him. Jirōbei said, "I am afraid to be seen with you. You are His Lordship's beloved attendant. You must leave immediately." Sanza explained, "I was forced to slay three men with my sword. I thought of committing *seppuku* immediately, but I am reluctant to atone for my transgression without explaining my actions first. I know we are not close, but I believe you to be reliable, and request your company until it is time."

Upon hearing this plea, Jirōbei made up his mind. "I am elated that you think of me as a trustworthy samurai. You can rely on me. Let us depart without further ado, as we have no time to waste." He escorted Sanza dressed as he was. Taking Sanza by the hand, and sometimes carrying him on his back, first he headed in the direction of Chikuzen, then to Todoki. They reached the mountains by dawn, which is where they hid. Sanza said, "I must confess, what I said to you earlier was a lie. I was testing your character." With this confession they made a lover's pact.

For two years prior to this event, Jirōbei waited on the bridge every day as Sanza made his way to the castle and back.

❀ ❀ ❀

183. Ittei said, "If I were to describe in a word what it means to do 'good' as a samurai, it is to withstand hardship. To not endure suffering is sinful."

❀ ❀ ❀

184. A man of stature should speak with brevity. When Nabeshima Ichiun visited Master Nichimon[1] on a chore, the only thing that Nichimon uttered was, "Pass on my regards to Tango-no-Kami (Nabeshima Mitsushige)."

❀ ❀ ❀

185. More than with wisdom and discretion, a man under 40 should attend to his duties with tenacity. Depending on his status, a man may well go unnoticed after 40 without strength of mind.

❀ ❀ ❀

---

1 It is unclear who Nichimon was, but he was possibly a Buddhist priest.

186. Unit captains should show kindness to their men. Nakano Kazuma held an important post, and had little time to pay his subordinates courtesy calls. Nevertheless, if one of them became ill or was in a quandary of some sort, he would be sure to visit on his way home from the castle. For this reason, his men held him in high esteem.

❀ ❀ ❀

187. A certain man traveling to Edo sent detailed letters home from his lodgings. Most people overlook such matters when they are busy, so he surpasses them for his thoughtfulness.

❀ ❀ ❀

188. According to an old retainer: "A samurai should be excessively obstinate. Anything done in moderation will fall short of your goals. If you feel that you are doing more than is needed, it will be just right."

❀ ❀ ❀

189. Do not hesitate once you have decided to cut a man down. Bypass any thoughts of postponing for alternative options premised on the excuse that diving in headfirst will likely fail. You will miss your chance, and will not accomplish your mission. In the Way of the warrior, be ready to leap headlong into the fray without a second thought.

A man went to a sutra reading at the Jissōin Temple in Kawakami. His page became intoxicated on the boat ride and started a fight with the ferryman. When the page climbed up the bank and drew his sword, the ferryman struck him on the head with an oar, and the others converged with their oars at the ready. While these events were transpiring, his master walked by as if nothing was happening. This prompted another page to run to the ferrymen and apologize for his colleague's behavior. He ushered him away from the scene while trying to mollify him. That evening, they say the drunken page had his swords confiscated.[1]

First, the master was amiss for not scolding the page, nor did he try to pacify the ferryman. Even though the incident was sparked by the drunken page's belligerent behavior, an apology was unnecessary as the ferryman, a commoner, struck a samurai on the head.[2] The master should have approached the ferryman as if he was going to make amends, and then cut him and his page down together. The master was sadly remiss.

190. The degree of determination shown by old warriors is unfathomable. It was decreed, "Men aged between 13 and 60 must go to the front." Because of this, older men concealed their true age [so that they might be deployed too].

191. A certain person recorded in his memoirs: "Those in close attendance to the lord need to be careful of their conduct as people are disposed to judge a master's character by the deportment of his aides. Furthermore, cautioning your master should be done without delay. If you defer because he appears to be in a foul mood, he may inadvertently slip up because of your hesitation.

Also, it is iniquitous to speak ill of an offender. If you can attach reason to his actions and gradually cast him in a positive light, his reinstatement to service will be all the quicker. Paying no attention to a man enjoying good fortune will not augur problems; but you should do your utmost to assist a friend who has fallen on hard times to get him back on his feet. This is the moral code (*giri*) of the samurai."

---

1 In other words, the page was relinquished of his status and released from service.
2 Striking a samurai on the head was considered to be extremely insulting.

192. Since taking up an official post, not only does a certain man refuse to receive any gifts, but concerned that his servants may secretly hide the gifts, he sometimes sought written confirmation from the senders proving they had been given back. As he spurns all people who try to ingratiate themselves and ask for mediation or special favors, he has earned a reputation for being the most upstanding administrator in Saga, shining in his duties like rays of the sun.

Actually, he is quite infantile in my opinion. Of course, it is better than being greedy, but he is not inspired by pure intent. It is merely pretence to elevate his standing. Few people are as principled as this anymore, so he has become the talk of the town. It is easy to become famous with a little effort, but not so to purge yourself of avarice, and remain inconspicuous.

❈ ❈ ❈

193. Make up your mind to boldly advance without hesitation whenever your honor as a samurai is at stake, otherwise you will not fix the problem. When you consult with others, they may be flippant, or less than candid with you. It suffices to rely on your own good judgment. In any case, just give yourself over to insanity and sacrifice yourself to the task. That's all you need to do. If you attempt to solve problems through careful manoeuvring, doubts will creep in and paralyze your mind, and you will fail miserably. Often it is the case that associates who have your best interests at heart unintentionally impede your success. This happened to me when I requested to take the holy orders.[1]

❈ ❈ ❈

194. When I went to see my adopted son Gon'nojō in the New Year this spring,[2] he told me: "I have been on sabbatical since the end of last year, and as I have free time until the eighth month, I plan to

---

1 See Book 1-9.
2 The year is possibly 1715. Gon'nojō died in Edo of illness that year at the age of 38.

write characters from the sutras on stones."[1] I offered him my thoughts. "Nay, now is the time when you have the least free time. It cannot be rewarding for you to return to your duties in the ninth month. What is more gratifying than being summoned back to service earlier than expected? For this reason, now you should be busier than ever. Your ambitions will be realized if you are determined to be recalled to service during your time off, and work your fingers to the bone without stopping.

I speak from experience. When I was 12, I was permitted to grow my forelocks to wear my hair in a topknot [as a sign of maturity], so I confined myself to my quarters and did not attend until I was 14. When I turned 14, I became eager to serve when I saw Lord Mitsushige and Tsunashige's return procession from Edo.[2] I paid homage at the Kosenomiya Shrine so that I could commence my service from the first day of the fifth month that year. The most miraculous thing happened on the very last day of the fourth month when I received a directive to start service on the first day of the following month.

After this, it became my strongest desire to attend the young prince, and I waited attentively, day and night, for the right opportunity to make my request. Then, one evening it was announced: "Master Tsunashige is here, and bids all pages to come forth to his chamber."[3] I went immediately, to which the young prince said repeatedly, "You came so quickly, and nobody else has. Thank you for coming." To this day, I cannot forget my feelings of thankfulness for his kind words. If you will something strongly enough, it will come to pass. Much to our bewilderment and delight, it so happened that Gon'nojō was beckoned back to service before his scheduled return.

---

1 In this religious practice, stones inscribed with the characters were then buried in the ground to bring good fortune. It was also done to placate ancestral spirits.
2 The Tokugawa shogunate instigated a system known as *sankin-kōtai* in which daimyo lords, family members, and an entourage of servants were obligated to reside for alternate years in Edo to attend the shogun. The system was devised as a means to maintain control over the more than 260 provincial lords located throughout Japan. They were required to divide their time equally between the capital and their domains in what was essentially a form of "hostageship." Jōchō is referring to his lord's return from *sankin-kōtai* tenure obligations.
3 Nabeshima Tsunashige. Jōchō was 20 years old at the time.

From a young age, I was nothing more than a run-of-the-mill servant, and there were times when I was envious of successes enjoyed by my colleagues. Still, I came to believe that no one cherished the lord more than I. This one thing brought me solace, and I was able to forget my lowly rank and mediocre ability by devoting myself to his service. As I foresaw, when Lord Mitsushige passed, I was the only one who upheld the honor of his good name.[1]

195. "A retainer who is too perceptive is bad"—a famous comment by Yamasaki Kurando.[2] Preoccupation with concerns of whether someone is loyal or disloyal, just or unjust, appropriate or inappropriate as a retainer, and scrutinizing matters from the perspective of right and wrong, good and evil, is not a desirable attitude. It will suffice to simply relish the role of service, and esteem your lord above all else. This makes for a top-notch retainer.

Serving with too much gusto, or cherishing your lord excessively may lead to mistakes; but it will bring to fruition the goal in one's heart. It is said that excessiveness in anything is harmful, but service is surely the exception. In this case, failure through overzealous attention to duty is nothing short of honorable.

It is lamentable that men who are governed only by reason often become fixated on trifling matters, and end up squandering their lives. A lifetime is but a fleeting moment. It is best to surge headlong into it. It is unhelpful to be sidetracked by this and that.[3] The ultimate way for a retainer is to discard redundant concerns, and just be devoted to serving his lord. Quibbling conceitedly about matters of loyalty (*chū*) and morality (*gi*) is unpardonable.

---

1 Jōchō is referring to his action of renouncing the mundane world to take the tonsure and become a lay priest. This action was taken in lieu of self-immolation, which had been outlawed.
2 A clan elder (*toshiyori*). See Book 2-61.
3 See Book 1-139.

196. Lord Naoshige declared, "An ancestor's good or evil doings are defined by the manner of his descendants."[1] There are ways in which progeny should comport themselves so that an ancestor's good deeds are revealed, not the bad. This is an act of homage to one's forefathers.

❀ ❀ ❀

197. It is a shallow state of affairs that suitors for adoption [through marriage] are decided on wealth rather than family pedigree. Justification by claiming, "Although admittedly improper, it is unavoidable as ends need to be met," is sinful. Such excuses represent an abandonment of one's scruples.

❀ ❀ ❀

198. A certain samurai commented, "What a shame so-and-so died at such a young age." To which I replied, "It is indeed a pity [as he was a valued man]." He bemoaned: "The end of the world is nigh, and due consideration to social rectitude (*giri*) has fallen by the wayside." I consoled him by saying, "When things can get no worse, they will then change for the better. Conditions will unequivocally improve in time." In this way, it is important to be a step ahead of others in your ripostes.

At the time of Nakano Shōgen's *seppuku*,[2] unit members gathered at the residence of Lord Ōki Zen-Hyōbu[3] and talked disparagingly of Shōgen. Hyōbu, the unit captain, scolded his men saying, "Nobody should talk ill of the dead, particularly if the man was sentenced to death for a felony; and as fellow warriors, we are obligated to seek compassionate things to say. In 20 years from now, Shōgen may be

---

1 This statement is found in Naoshige's *Naoshige-kō O-kabegaki*.
2 See Book 1-16.
3 Ōki Hyōbu Norikiyo (1568–1651) was an elder councilor (*toshiyori*) of the Nabeshima domain who became famous for his exploits during the Shimabara Rebellion. (See Book 1-97). The prefix "Zen" (former) indicates that his position and name was inherited by his son.

celebrated as having been a man who demonstrated great loyalty." These were fitting words by a seasoned veteran.

❖ ❖ ❖

199. Furukawa Rokurōzaemon[1] said: "There isn't a lord anywhere who doesn't wish for consummate subordinates. Even warriors of humble standing like me yearn for good servants, so it must be more so for men of status. Therefore, a samurai who is eager to be useful will quickly find his way into service of a lord, as their aspirations are compatible. If a man desires something for a long time, he will jump at the chance when it is offered to him on a plate. I have come to see that men waste their lives oblivious to the opportunities before them, only to rue missed chances later in life. Young men should always be on the lookout."

This statement resonated in my ears, and I remember it well. In essence, leave specifics aside and simply aspire to serve one's master without reservation. Samurai are not necessarily devoid of this spirit, but stumbling in the face of various obstacles, they sadly end up achieving little over the course of their lives.

Some self-effacing men belittle themselves, thinking 'I cannot possibly be useful to my master.' In truth, cloddish men whose eagerness to serve is strong are ultimately more valuable. Conversely, having insight and talent can be a hindrance in service.

Rustic samurai with low status tend to hold chief retainers (*karō*) and elders (*toshiyori*) in great esteem. They keep a respectable distance believing them to be magnificent men with mysterious powers beyond the comprehension of ordinary folk. Once on friendly terms, however, it becomes apparent that they are just the same, except for their profound sense of devotion to their duties and master.

You don't need any special wisdom to be an effective servant. Even people of humble station like us can aspire to be "valuable to the lord, the clan, and the farmers who reside in the domain." The challenge is in thinking earnestly about being of value in service.

---

1 An inspector (*o-metsuke*) in the Nabeshima clan.

❀ ❀ ❀

200. Come what may, never become conceited when enjoying a period of good fortune. You will be in great jeopardy without displaying twice as much caution as usual.

❀ ❀ ❀

201. It is good to display resplendent armor and weapons, but enough on hand is all that is required. Fukahori Inosuke's[1] [modest] armor is a good example. Men of high status with many vassals need to set funds aside to maintain military readiness. Okabe Kunai[2] prepared the same number of bags as men in his unit. He wrote their names on the bags, and placed a suitable sum of war funds in each. This arrangement shows thoughtfulness.

Lower ranks can rely on their unit captain for assistance if they are unable to procure funds when duty calls. For this reason, it is essential to be committed to your unit captain.

Men who attend the lord and are always at his side need not concern themselves with organizing war funds. A certain warrior accompanied Lord Taku Zusho on deployment during the summer siege of Osaka Castle[3] with 12-*monme* of refined silver.[4] All you need to do is depart for your destination immediately. I think such [generous] assistance is not necessary.

❀ ❀ ❀

202. Often, various theories abound when studying events that happened in the past, and some facts cannot be determined. Certain particulars should just be accepted as inexplicable. Lord Sanjō-nishi

---

1 An elder councilor (*toshiyori*) to Nabeshima Shigemasa.
2 A notable unit captain and elder.
3 The winter campaign of 1614 was the first assault by Tokugawa Ieyasu's forces to eliminate Toyotomi Hideyoshi's son, Hideyori. Osaka Castle fell in the summer campaign on June 3, 1615, thereby removing the last serious threat to Tokugawa hegemony.
4 1 *monme* = 0.13 oz. (3.75 grams). The inference is that it was quite a significant sum.

Sanenori[1] once said, "There are some things that you gradually come to understand. There are some things that you realize with effort. Then, there are other matters that you will never be able to comprehend at all. This is curious indeed." His observation is profound. It is folly to assume that everything in our mysterious world can be understood by the human mind. Things which can be fathomed with relative ease, however, are invariably shallow.

---

1 See Book 1-33.

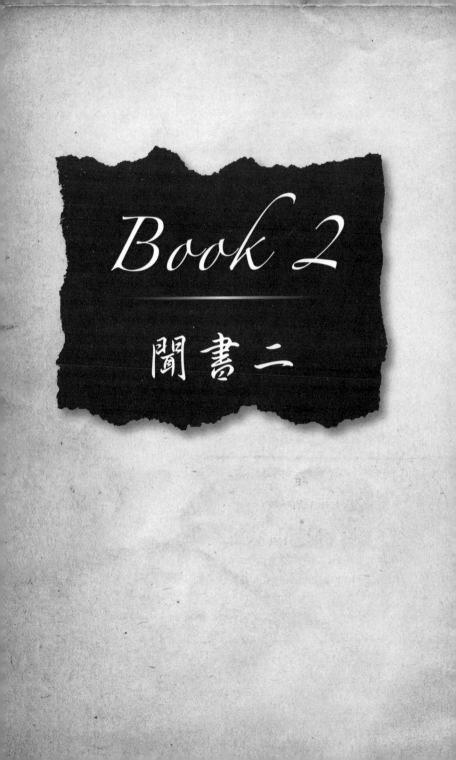

Book 2

闇書二

1. Upon inquiring, "What is off limits for a man in service?" I was told: "Drinking too much, boasting, and extravagance. There is little need for concern in times of misfortune; however, take heed when riding a wave of prosperity. Look around you. People become arrogant and conceited when enjoying success. It is most unbecoming. Therefore, a man who has not endured hardship will lack resilience at his core. It is best to experience adversity when one is young. Of little use is a man who is weak and feeble in stressful times."

❋ ❋ ❋

2. Upon asking, "What is the philosophy of the Kakuzō-ryū school?" I was told: "A sandal carrier for [Nabeshima] Kiun[1] named Kakuzō was a man of considerable dexterity. A skilled student of swordsmanship, he was taught grappling (*torite*) by Kiun and after mastering the techniques, he called his art the 'Kakuzō style' and taught the techniques to others. The *kata* of this school are still practiced today. Referred to as *kumiuchi* or *yawara*,[2] it is not a particularly famous style of combat such as that authorized by the shogunate. My style is not a particularly refined school either, but is effective in its simplicity like sandal carrier Kakuzō's, and so I call it 'my Kakuzō-ryū.'"

He (Jōchō) also said: "At a recent gathering I declared that the highest form of devotion is 'secret love' (*shinobu-koi*).[3] If one's feeling of love is confessed it becomes diluted. The original intention of love is to take it with you to the grave. There is a poem that goes, 'Observe when I am dead, my internal burning love for you, from the smoke ascending from my body.'"[4] When I suggested that this was analogous to the highest form of love, they all concurred, and thereupon we called ourselves the 'smoke blokes.'"

---

1 A retainer of Nabeshima Motoshige, a son of the first lord of the Nabeshima domain, Katsushige.
2 A term for *jūjutsu*, or the art of unarmed combat. *Torite* or *toride* are also other names for the grappling arts.
3 See Book 2-34. This is in reference to love between males.
4 An allusion to cremation after death.

❁ ❁ ❁

3. Lord Taku Mimasaka[1] often treated his men in a callous and irrational manner in his twilight years. When questioned about his sudden change in demeanor, he replied: "I am doing this for the sake of my son Nagato, so that he will be able to puff up his pillow and rest easily after I am gone." Thus, if the master behaves cruelly before he retires, even though he was kind-hearted before, it will help his successor foster strong bonds of loyalty in his men as they eagerly await his accession. I hear that this was a secret discussion.

❁ ❁ ❁

4. When you encounter another fellow, quickly fathom his character and greet him accordingly. When dealing with a man who is argumentative and uncompromising, it is best to take an amicable stance without rousing ire. Win him over using higher reason, trying not to generate antipathy afterwards. It is all a matter of attitude and wording. I heard this from somebody who talked with a monk.

❁ ❁ ❁

5. The priest Ryōi Oshō,[2] who retired from the Daijōji Temple in the province of Kaga, resided at the Sōjuan hermitage in Kitayama before moving from Kaga. When cleaning duties were conducted at the Sōjuan, Gyōjaku Oshō[3] took care of the upper room in the meditation hall. Also, Setsumon Oshō, now retired at the Ten'yuji Temple, took a *yukata*[4] to Kaion Oshō. He refused to accept it, saying that it was too pristine and didn't suit him, and that he wanted

---

1 A chief retainer of Nabeshima Katsushige.
2 Ryōi was the eleventh priest at the Kōdenji Temple who guided Jōchō in taking his Buddhist vows. They resided together at the Sōanji hermitage after Mitsushige's death. He became the head priest of the Daijōji Temple in 1709, and moved back to the Sōjuan in 1714.
3 Gyōjaku became the head priest of the Kōdenji Temple after Ryōi.
4 An unlined cotton summer *kimono*.

Setsumon's old clothes instead. The upper hall was newly constructed before Suigan Oshō[1] moved into Sōjuan. Ryōi plastered the walls himself to welcome Suigan with the room fully ready. Such an undertaking meets with Buddha's biddings. The hermitage where Ryōi stayed in Kitayama Kurotsuchibaru after his retirement was called Chōyōken. Following an agreement made on the nineteenth day of the fourth month, second year of Shōtoku (1712) to succeed the temple, it was renamed to Sōjuan.[2]

❖ ❖ ❖

6. "Dreams are a prophetic reflection of one's nature. Sometimes I dream of being slain or committing *seppuku*. My heart becomes ever more gallant as I experience being killed in my dreams." His dream on the twenty-seventh day of the fifth month was like this.[3]

❖ ❖ ❖

7. To summarize the essence of samuraihood, first and foremost the warrior must be devoted body and soul to his lord. In addition, he must internalize the virtues of wisdom (*chi*), compassion (*jin*), and courage (*yū*). Although it may seem impossible to embody these three virtues, it really is easy. To nurture wisdom simply requires listening to others. Immeasurable knowledge comes from this. Compassion is for the sake of others. It is opting to do good things for other people rather than through selfish motives. Courage is found through "gritting one's teeth." That is to say, gritting one's teeth and charging forth without concern for the consequences. There is no higher mind-set than this.

External matters requiring attention are one's appearance, manner of speech, and handwriting. These are routine affairs which can be refined through daily training. Most of all, one should try to

---

1 The sixteenth priest of the Kōdenji Temple.
2 See Book 2-55 and Book 2-87.
3 1713.

generate a sense of calm inner-strength. Once these things have been realized, study the lore of the Nabeshima domain. After this, you may enjoy learning the arts as diversionary pursuits. All things considered, loyal service is quite straightforward. These days, those thought of as exceptional retainers are men who are attentive to the three external details.

❀ ❀ ❀

8. According to a certain monk: "If you attempt to cross a river without checking the depth, you will be swept away and drown before reaching the opposite bank, and thereby fail to accomplish your mission. Similarly, you will be ineffective if you serve indiscriminately without being cognizant of the changing times or the lord's preferences, and it may cause your ruin. It is loathsome to act only to curry your master's favor. The best course of action is to first take a step back, understand the depths and shallows of various matters, and avoid provoking indignation in your master."

❀ ❀ ❀

9. The late Jin'uemon was skilled at making straw sandals. When he was a unit captain, he would always ask, "Can you make straw sandals? If you can't, it is like having no feet." When walking a distance in excess of 1-*ri* (2.44 miles) with his men, he would give them food in a bag so that they could head straight to battle from wherever they happened to be. If each man starts with 1-*shō* (1.8 litres) of provisions, the rest will be attainable later. This is why he had made a supply of light-yellow cotton sacks.

When Toyotomi Hideyoshi came to Hizen-Nagoya [during the Korea campaign], he walked along the northern Takagi-Jōdō road with his long and short swords in vermillion scabbards, wearing half-soled straw sandals (*ashinaka*).[1] When Tokugawa Ieyasu presented

---

1 This is in reference to Toyotomi Hideyoshi's invasions of Korea (1592 and 1597). Hideyoshi built a fortress in Hizen-Nagoya. Note that this is a location in Saga, not the city of Nagoya in modern day Aichi Prefecture.

his cavalry to Toyotomi Hideyoshi, Naruse Shōkichi[1] attached some scarlet sandals to Ieyasu's scabbard. Spare sandals are requisite when preparing for battle. If dispatched for guard duties in Nagasaki now, tens of thousands of straw sandals would be needed for all ranks. Supplies of ready-to-wear ones would be exhausted. This is why it is prudent to learn how to make them yourself. Incidentally, when walking in grass fields, mountain trails, or wading through rivers, straw sandals have a tendency to slip, so it is advisable to wear *ashinaka* in such terrains.

❀ ❀ ❀

10. You will not be adversely affected by inclement weather or catch a cold if you keep a few bags of cloves handy. One year, when the late Kazuma[2] traveled back to the domain on horseback in the midst of a cold snap, his health was not affected in the slightest despite his old age [because he knew about the remedial quality of cloves]. He taught me this. Also, hemorrhaging after falling from a horse can be stopped by drinking extract from the droppings of a gray horse.

❀ ❀ ❀

11. A 'yes man' will withdraw when something happens. You must have strength of will.

❀ ❀ ❀

12. Shower praise on one's lord though he may be reticent and mediocre, and ensure that he can execute his duties without blundering. This will help cultivate his confidence. If he is an unyielding or intelligent leader, it is an act of "great loyalty" to be a thorn in his side to the extent that, before implementing his designs, he respects you

---

1 Lord of Inuyama Castle in the Owari domain, in the northwest of modern day Aichi Prefecture. He was a vassal of Tokugawa Ieyasu.
2 See Book 1-51.

enough to contemplate "What would my pesky retainer think?" Without such retainers, the lord will pay no attention to his men, thinking that his domain is full of panderers who cajole him to gain favor. He will then become conceited.

Irrespective of high or low station, it doesn't bode well if a man becomes arrogant, notwithstanding of his past meritorious deeds. Nobody takes notice of this anymore. Men such as Kyūma[1] and Kichiuemon[2] paid attention to these points, and were acknowledged by their lord. It is said that Kichiuemon advised his lord (Tsunashige) on various matters when he was ill and even after he retired from service. He was eternally grateful for this.

Some samurai do not hold such high aspirations. They are predisposed to think it is impossible to occupy a position to offer counsel. From my own experience, I can say that becoming your lord's confidant after a decade of bone-breaking toil is indeed achievable. Meek is any man who does not aim to be the most treasured attendant in the domain, of the likes of Nobukata[3] and Takatomo.[4] A retainer will not be able to serve, however, if he is alienated from his lord. This point is important, but many don't get it. Make him take notice little by little.

❀ ❀ ❀

13. Hurrying to one's post in the event of a fire is not just for the purpose of extinguishing it. Enemies or conspirators may commit arson to cause confusion and incite conflict, and so vigilance is needed to prevent such occurrences. Thus, not making haste when there is a fire is reckless. Remember this. For the same reason, the gates should always be guarded during a fire.

Assigning sentries at Buddhist memorial services is also a pre-

---

1 Sagara Kyūma.
2 Harada Kichiuemon was a celebrated retainer of the first three lords.
3 Itagaki Nobukata (1489–1548) was a retainer of the Takeda clan who served both Nobutora and Shingen, becoming one of Shingen's famed "24 generals."
4 Akimoto Takatomo (1682–1699) was a "junior elder" (*waka-doshiyori*) of Tokugawa Tsunayoshi, the fifth Tokugawa shogun.

ventative measure for emergencies. As the proverb goes, "There is more bad than good in this world" (*sunzen-shakuma*), and evil will always manifest at a Buddhist service. Should something unexpected erupt, such as a fight or quarrel, quell it without delay so that it does not interrupt the service. That is why guards should be assigned. Although aware of this, people are often careless on the day, and too slow in reacting. Lord Suke'uemon urged that we investigate actual incidents and how to cope with them.[1]

❀ ❀ ❀

14. Remonstrating with, or giving advice to one's lord after something untoward has already happened will be meaningless, and likely lead to harmful rumor-mongering. It is like taking medicine after becoming sick. You will not fall victim to serious ailments if you take care of yourself beforehand, rather than resorting to treatment after you contract an illness. Advising your lord before he conjures up bad ideas has the same effect as taking precautions against disease.

❀ ❀ ❀

15. Undoubtedly, those seen as promising attendants will receive an appointment, and will be able to serve as they yearn to do. This is because those in high positions spend time searching for faithful servants to recruit to meet his needs. For example: a master who has a penchant for Noh will look for a man with these skills, and will hire someone who is accomplished at playing musical instruments, such as flutes and drums, even if he is a farmer or townsman.

Over and above such "Noh actors," lords who aspire to improve the domain will need effective retainers. Men skilled in whatever it is that the lord is fond of will come out of the woodwork in the hope of being employed. So, it's incumbent on the lord to keep an eye out for men with fidelity who can serve the domain at large. History shows that not all those who hail from the ranks of families with high status

---

1 Tokunaga Suke'uemon was Tashiro Tsuramoto's uncle on his mother's side.

prove to be useful. In every generation there are capable warriors of humble lineage who achieve success and serve their lords well.

❀ ❀ ❀

16. After discovering that his lord (Mitsushige) transferred the family's Buddhist mortuary tablets from the Sakyamuni Hall to another place, a certain retainer asked me "Should I set him straight?" I told him to abstain from taking such action. "It would be justifiable, as nobody else other than you has noticed. But there is no need to caution him. If you successfully persuade him to return the tablets, your reputation will soar when people come to know of your accomplishment. If he rejects your advice, they will gossip about his inappropriate deeds, whereas your standing will continue to rise. A retainer should take vicarious atonement for his lord's errors. If the matter is left unaddressed, others will not notice and it will not be talked about by idle tongues. An opportune moment will present itself later to urge him to return the tablets to the rightful place without making a commotion." News of the lord's blunders will spread quickly. The right timing for counsel will reveal itself if you are patient.

Often it happens that the lord's mistakes and wrongdoings are exposed to the world by his inner circle. Never disparage your lord openly. Some mistakenly think it is acceptable to criticize the lord's transgressions within your inner-circle of relatives such as parents, children, brothers, and intimate friends. Eventually, this damaging information will be leaked to people in the domain, to neighboring provinces, and then throughout the country.

Also, a master will earn a bad reputation in the community if he doesn't treat his servants and others in close proximity with respect. Be particularly circumspect around your immediate family.

❀ ❀ ❀

17. All that matters is having single-minded purpose (*ichinen*), in the here and now. Life is an ongoing succession of 'one will' at a time, each and every moment. A man who realizes this truth need not hurry to do, or seek, anything else anymore. Just live in the present with single-minded purpose. People forget this important truth, and keep seeking other things to accomplish.

Having the resolve to stay the course comes only with years of dedicated training. If you are enlightened to this mind-set just once, it will always be with you, even if you are not conscious of it every-day. Your life will become simple and clear if you are unwavering in purpose, knowing that 'now' is the time to act. Loyalty is a virtue born of this state of mind.

❀ ❀ ❀

18. Current trends cannot be stopped in the flow of time. The world continues to degenerate because we are nearing the end of times. The year is not comprised only of the two pleasant seasons of spring and summer. The same can be said of each day. Thus, any longing for the "good old days" of a hundred years ago is futile. It is more judicious to adapt and improve the ways of the present. Men who hold a nostalgic view of the past are misguided in their outlook because they are blind to the reality of the present. Conversely, those who revel in the present, but loathe the customs and traditions of yesteryear, can't differentiate between core principles and insignificant details.

❀ ❀ ❀

19. A retainer with a will to serve, who plans and trains to this end, can become pompous and forget the basic tenets of service. A retainer just needs to eagerly attend his master without reasoning why, and delight in the humdrum of serving.

❀ ❀ ❀

20. It is best to return to the starting point and serve accordingly. But still, this approach will be pointless at the very beginning before you have learned the basics. Devise plans and train for service, and when you have reached a certain level, discard all your strategies and be faithful to the absolute fundamentals.[1]

❀ ❀ ❀

21. You need nothing more than to maintain a pure mind, and stay vigilant as you execute your duties. Just live for each moment with single-minded purpose.

❀ ❀ ❀

22. There is a special way to make bookmarks. Cut strips of paper into the shape of a sword tip, apply a thin layer of adhesive on the edge, and paste to the back of the page. Fold both edges in from each side when enveloping a condolence message or other sympathy notes. For normal letters, each edge is folded around from the left.

❀ ❀ ❀

23. "Since olden times, men celebrated as valiant warriors were characteristically uncouth. Being roughnecks, they were spirited and bold." Unsure of what this means, I asked Jōchō for further explanation. "Since they were spirited, they were habitually rough-and-ready. Warriors are not as spirited as they used to be, and are not nearly as unruly. There is less zeal, but it must be said that men now show better decorum. Courage, however, is a different matter. Although warriors today are not as vigorous, and could even be described as docile, this is not to say that they cannot work themselves into the same deadly frenzy when executing their duties.[2] This mind-set has nothing to do with high-spiritedness."

❀ ❀ ❀

---

1 In the Koyama and Yamamoto copies of *Hagakure*, these two sections (19 and 20) are joined as one.
2 *Shini-gurui.*

24. I remarked, "There are various things to bear in mind when serving one's master, but one can't perform conscientiously without preparation." I was told in reply by Jōchō, "This is not the case. Just perform your duties using the powers of judgment you were endowed with at birth. Simply abide by the rules that Lord Katsushige formulated.[1] It's as easy as that. Working for the benefit of fellow retainers and those below you counts as valuable service. Imprudent administrators devise new strategies to assist the lord, but care not for the plight of the lower ranks. This stinks of disloyalty because all members of the clan belong to the lord. All that is required from the lord is compassion for his men. At times, even crucifixion can be an act of compassion."

❀ ❀ ❀

25. Gon'nojō came to inquire about preparing for guard duties at the Nagasaki garrison. Jōchō said, "I served in close proximity to my lord, so my situation is different than yours. Back then, everyone wondered what to prepare when setting off. I only took my pillow, for I knew I only needed to accompany my lord. I would be provided with armor and weapons, money, and provisions. I was allowed to procure equipment from the storeroom. I just asked His Lordship whenever I needed something, and in no way could officials object. This is how I prepared. I also wrote down instructions for directing the coolies and wagon horses and so on, but my real place was beside my lord."

❀ ❀ ❀

26. I was not perturbed in the slightest by troubled finances or the like during my tenure of service. If I needed food, I could contact the lord's staff, or even the lord himself, to ask for assistance, just as Ezoe Hyōbuzaemon had done.[2]

---

1 This is referring to *Torinoko-chō*, a rulebook written by Nabeshima Katsushige.
2 Ezoe Hyōbuzaemon was one of 13 loyal retainers who committed *seppuku* following the death of Nabeshima Noashige in 1618.

One year when I came back from Kyoto and then had to return again to resume my mission, I made a request to the elders for assistance. "Due to the length of my sojourn in Kyoto, my household budget has come under considerable strain.[1] I humbly request your favorable treatment in this matter. It would not look good if I had to borrow money before departing. I ask this favor not out of self-indulgence, but because the fulfillment of my duties in Kyoto necessitates it." The councilors conveyed my request to the lord, who responded by kindly affording me some money.

At another time when I was not feeling well, the physician prescribed a course of ginseng. I couldn't afford such an expensive item, but hearing of my predicament, Moro'oka Hikouemon[2] said: "As you are such a diligent servant, you will be given as much ginseng as you need to recover." Once a retainer has given himself wholeheartedly to his master, he need not be troubled by such affairs. Things become difficult when you isolate yourself.

❀ ❀ ❀

27. Uchida Shōemon said, "Lord Naoshige's military strategy was exceptional. He never told his men anything in advance, but was precise and made flawless decisions when it was called for at the front." His chief retainers asked him questions about his tactics in his dying hour, but he never divulged his secret.

❀ ❀ ❀

28. Lord Tokugawa Ieyasu's forces were overpowered in a certain battle. In the aftermath, people talked of the feats of his men with great admiration. "Ieyasu is truly a courageous general. Not one of his warriors was slain with his back to the enemy. They all fell forwards." A warrior's attitude is revealed even after his death, so take care not to bring disgrace to your name.[3]

---

1 This was in 1698 and 1699. Jōchō was sent to Kyoto a number of times.
2 See Book 1-98.
3 See Book 1-162.

❈ ❈ ❈

29. Somebody said: "It is fortuitous there are no wars anymore." This is a terribly imprudent thing for a samurai to declare! Life is short. It's a warrior's calling to experience battle at least one time. Dying in one's futon is an insufferable waste, and not the end a samurai should hope for. The ancients were particularly aggrieved by the unfortunate fate of perishing on a sleeping mat. I think there is no better end than to die in battle."

Be sure to refute a comment such as this. You may think it pointless, as the proclaimer might be a pretentious old man "putting on airs." If, however, a thoughtful man overhears the banter, he will think that you are agreeing. Therefore, it is best to respond, but in a way that won't cause offense. For example, you could judge the mood and say: "That is not necessarily true. The reason why people today lack spirit is because there is peace throughout the realm. They would surely be pluckier as the situation dictates. I don't expect that the men of old were that different from warriors now. Even if they were, that was then. Samurai today are merely in tune with the state of the world, where everything is mediocre compared to before—but that doesn't mean that they are inferior." Expressing your opinion is crucial to avoid misunderstanding.

❈ ❈ ❈

30. As Yasuda Ukyō declared regarding one's attitude when putting *saké* cups away, "The end is important." The same can be said about one's life. When your guests leave, hopefully there is a reluctance to bid farewell. If not, it is a sign of disinterest, and all the good memories forged through the discussions in the day and night will fade away. When interacting with guests, it is important that you don't tire of each other's company. Act as if you haven't seen each other for some time. This can be achieved with just a little mindfulness.

❈ ❈ ❈

31. Master Jōchō said, "Irrespective of the undertaking, sincerity is of the essence. Even so, your attitude in service differs depending on the circumstances, such as whether you serve in close proximity to your lord or not, your high or low social status, if you come from a long-serving family, or are a recent member of staff, etc.

"For those who attend the lord directly, there is nothing more objectionable than being too intrusive. The lord will not take kindly to this. Show restraint in front of your lord. It is preferable if he thinks of you as slightly inadequate, but will have to suffice as there is nobody else to fill the role." Naturally, you should try to assist your superiors as well as your associates in their duties. At times when there is a shortage of hands through illness, some complication, or a change of post, you should work hard to fill the breaches. This is the correct attitude for men following the way of service.

You will understand if loyalty is your foundation. Success gained too early in life will not endure. There are many examples of this extending way back in time. I started serving my lord from childhood, but I never said anything forceful [beyond my station]. There is a profound reason for this."

❀ ❀ ❀

32. It is said that the body receives life from emptiness. The phrase *shikisoku-zekū* ("form is emptiness") means "existence where there is nothing." That all things derive from emptiness is expressed by the phrase, *kūsoku-zeshiki* ("emptiness is form"). I was taught not to think of these as separate.[1]

❀ ❀ ❀

33. You should be proud and claim to be the best in the land when it comes to courage and *shudō* (male love). When training in the Way each day, know your faults and learn to shed them. You will not

---

1 These phrases are quoted from the *Hannya Shingyō*, or Heart Sutra, originating in Mahāyāna Buddhism.

make headway unless you purge yourself of limitations.

❊ ❊ ❊

34. Love in its supreme form is "secret love" (*shinobu-koi*). "Observe when I am dead, my internal burning love for you, from the smoke ascending from my body."[1] Love confessed when still alive is contrived, but the profundity of love taken to the grave knows no bounds. What if the object of one's affection inquires, "Can it be that you have feelings for me?" Reply without hesitation: "That is the furthest thing from my mind!" Dying without ever confessing is supreme love. Is love not torturous? When speaking of this matter recently, my colleagues agreed with me, and our brotherhood became known as "Smoke Blokes." This [spirit of *shinobu-koi*] should be the attitude in all things. Particularly so in the relationship of fealty between lord and vassal.

Also, serving when out of sight of others should be done with the same prudence as when in the public eye. If you can't suppress lewd thoughts or ideas when you are on your own, you appear to others as lacking grace. Feigned discretion will actually bring one's shortcomings to light.

❊ ❊ ❊

35. Shōan is fond of *renga*,[2] and Sohō is partial to *haikai*.[3] This reveals a difference in character. I believe that we need to aim high even in our pastimes. Master Jōchō said that he has a penchant for *kyōka*[4] over *renga*. (Personal note: *Koshiore* ["My Humble Poem"] is not an expression samurai should use.)[5]

---

1 See Book 2-2.
2 *Renga* is a genre of Japanese collaborative poetry which consists of at least two stanzas, but usually many more.
3 Humorous or vulgar *renga* poetry.
4 *Kyōka* is a form of "humorous *tanka*," a genre of classical Japanese poetry. *Tanka* consist of five units usually with the pattern of 5-7-5-7-7.
5 This is a comment added by Tashiro Tsuramoto. *Koshiore* was a common phrase used as a show of humility when introducing one's poetry. The inference is that warriors

❀ ❀ ❀

36. It is interesting indeed that Lord Kenshin said, "I never think about winning. All I think of is not missing the opportunity."[1] This is very perceptive. A retainer should also realize that if he misses his chance he will be unable to articulate his point effectively. As such, a samurai must never be guilty of paltriness in every action and greeting he makes.

❀ ❀ ❀

37. Treating one's condition after becoming ill is not at all smart. Just as Buddhist monks argue peripheral matters, it seems that physicians don't cite the importance of preventative measures before the onset of disease. I speak from experience. To maintain my health and well-being, I did not indulge in eating and drinking, or engage in sexual intercourse, and I applied moxa each day. Being born when my father was advanced in age,[2] I was diagnosed as being "deficient in water."[3] When I was young, doctors said: "He won't make it past the age of 20 because of his weak constitution." I thought, "Being blessed to have entered this world, it would be a pity to die without properly serving my master. I must try to live a long, salubrious life." I abstained from having sex for seven years, I didn't fall ill, and am still very much alive. I have never really needed medicine before; although there were times when I felt under the weather, I was able to power through.

In spite of being born with fragile constitutions, people these days are too lascivious and end up dying young. It is diabolical. I would proffer to physicians that if people who are sickly suppress their

---

need not show humility in such cases.

1 Uesugi Kenshin (1530–1578) was a warlord who ruled Echigo province during the War-ring States period. He was highly respected for his strategic and administrative ability. His rivalry with Takeda Shingen became legendary, and although mortal enemies, they both harbored an intense respect for each other.

2 Jōchō's father was 70 years old when he was born.

3 An expression that implies a short lifespan.

sexual desires for six months, or a year or two, they will recuperate without need of any special treatment. Most young men are weak-willed. It is woeful that they lack willpower to control their carnal urges [for the sake of their wellbeing].

❀ ❀ ❀

38. Be wary of talking indiscriminately about matters such as literature, morality, or old customs in front of noblemen and elders. It is unpleasant to be forced to listen to such ramblings.

❀ ❀ ❀

39. In the Kamigata region, people carry multi-layered picnic boxes with them for enjoying the cherry blossoms. They are only used for one day, and having served their purpose, people just stamp on the boxes and discard them as they leave. It is indeed a capital conception. The end is important for all things.

❀ ❀ ❀

40. A warrior should not be immodest regarding his valor, and be prepared to enter a frenzied (*shini-gurui*) state when faced with death. All aspects of his attitude, language, and demeanor in daily life should be pure, precise, and prudent. He should be content with his tasks, and consult with others about how best to fulfill his role. He should confer about important matters with men not directly involved. A lifelong position in service requires that one work for the benefit of others. Don't become ensnared in financial concerns.

❀ ❀ ❀

41. When Master Jōchō was asked, "Some people don't seem to care when their colleague is promoted ahead of them, and carry on as usual. Conversely, others may find the situation disappointing, and after making their feelings known, they resign from service with a chip on his shoulder. What are your thoughts on this?" He simply replied, "It depends entirely on the time and circumstances."

❀ ❀ ❀

42. As the saying goes: "The more water there is, the higher the boat rises."[1] A competent man, or one engrossed in a pursuit he enjoys, will relish the challenge of surmounting difficulties. There is a huge difference between these men, and those who feel as though they are drowning when the going gets tough.

❀ ❀ ❀

43. The monk Ryōzan Oshō[2] said: "I learned a good lesson from the Kamigata region. Whatever you write on paper will remain in the world; and so, even if it is just a letter, you should write carefully, imagining that it will be hung on the wall of the recipient's home. Many people write 'shamelessly.'"[3]

❀ ❀ ❀

44. A man in service exceeds his peers through superior deportment, manner of speech, and his handwriting.[4] Correct deportment forms the base of elegance. Manners maketh the man, and impeccable behavior is impressive to behold. These days, only those who are accomplished at reading and writing will find success, but they neglect the basic things in terms of their manners.

❀ ❀ ❀

45. While walking together along the path, Master Jōchō proclaimed,

---

1 See Book 1-115.
2 Jōchō's teacher of *waka* verse.
3 This sentence employs a play on words. *Haji wo kaku* can mean "to write the character for 'shame'" and to "bring shame."
4 See Book 2-7.

"Are men not like masterfully controlled puppets? It is magnificent craftsmanship that allows us to walk, jump, prance, and speak even though there are no strings attached. We may be guests at next year's Bon festival.[1] We forget it is an ephemeral world in which we live."

❋ ❋ ❋

46. One of Lord Yagyū's[2] teachings states: "It is unsightly to exhibit fear upon encountering an ox on the road. Oxen don't jab people with their horns from their regular posture. They angle their horns at the target, and then move in to thrust. You need not be afraid when passing an ox as long as it does not assume a fighting stance." Samurai should also be mindful of such particulars.

In my opinion,[3] I have seen horses rear with their forelegs in the air many times, but they are not really jumping. They pull their front legs up, stretch them out, but are only stamping the ground. You will not be kicked as long as you keep your distance. And, you will not be struck even if the horse changes its step towards you.

❋ ❋ ❋

47. Master Jōchō said, "Men in service need good examples to follow, but, alas, there don't seem to be any worthy role models of late. Men like Ishii Kurōuemon are exemplary when it comes to manner and speech.[4] Muraoka Gohei is a paragon of sincerity and loyalty.[5] I cannot think of anyone after Harada Kichiuemon as providing a better model for eloquent speech.[6] But there are no others who set an example. Combine the attributes of various men and they probably still won't amount to an first-class man of a bygone era. Of

---

1 The Bon festival is a Japanese Buddhist custom to honor and appease the spirits of dead ancestors. Thus, the inference here is that human beings can die at any time.
2 Yagyū Munenori. See Book 1-45.
3 Probably Tashiro Tsuramoto's opinion, although it is not clearly stipulated.
4 See Book 1-11.
5 Clan elder.
6 Some versions of *Hagakure* refer to writing rather than speech. See Book 2-12.

course, consummate retainers must have been atypical in the past as well. Young men can easily outshine others with a little effort, but still they are remiss."

❊ ❊ ❊

48. Master Jōchō relayed the following to his adopted son, Gon'nojō. "Now is the time; the time is now. He who thinks of the present and the critical moment as separate will never react in a timely fashion when disaster strikes. What if you are suddenly summoned to an audience with your lord and asked to give your thoughts on a particular matter? If you are at a loss, and struggle for words, this shows that you don't get the notion that 'now' is always the time to act.

"To see the critical moment and the present as one and the same requires diligent training in one's private hours. If unexpectedly called upon to do so, a retainer must be able to explain matters before his lord or advisors, or to officials in the Edo Palace, or even to the shogun himself. This is true even if one occupies a lowly station, and the odds of being called upon are virtually non-existent. This attitude is applicable for all things. Everything should be considered from this perspective—from wielding a spear on the battlefield, to administrative duties. Thought of in such a way, it becomes glaringly obvious how negligent and unprepared one usually is."

❊ ❊ ❊

49. Mistakes in protocol made at governmental offices can be dismissed as errors through ineptitude or a lack of experience. Then again, how can excuses be made by those who fell short of the mark in this shameful incident?[1] Master Yoshitada[2] would always say, "A samurai doesn't need to be anything other than a valiant and trust-

---

1 Probably referring to an incident that happened on the fourteenth day, seventh month in the third year of Shōtoku (1713), in which Hara Jūrōzaemon killed Sagara Gentazaemon as preparations were being made in the kitchen for the Bon festival. This episode is recorded in Book 11-104.

2 Yamamoto Jin'uemon Yoshitada. Jōchō's father.

worthy hero." He professed this with this kind of situation in mind.

If you become vexed, your luck as a warrior will dry up; if you are unable to serve when needed owing to a bad reputation, then you belong nowhere. Instead of living in disgrace and spending the rest of your life in the doldrums, you are better off just cutting open your stomach. If you aren't inclined to give up your life, and choose to keep making excuses about *seppuku* being a "meaningless death," you may live five more years, one or two decades at most. Nonetheless, your peers will disparage you, and you will live on in ignominy. This dishonor will continue after your death, and your descendants will inherit your shameful reputation. They will suffer humiliation just because they are related to you, even though they are innocent of wrongdoing. You will also bring disgrace to the memory of your ancestors, and the family name will be irreparably besmirched.

It is a crime to have no serious purpose, living idly and giving little consideration to what a warrior should be, even in your dreams. The man who was suddenly cut down in this incident had no ability, or his luck had run out. The one who dealt the fatal blow did so because there was no other recourse. He cannot be criticized as he also put his life on the line. It is inappropriate for a samurai to be short-tempered, but two men who face off in combat cannot be accused of being cowards. Nevertheless, those survivors at the scene of the aforementioned incident are smeared in shame. They are not worthy of being called samurai.

Realize that "the time is now," come up with a plan to meet any situation in a flash, and carve it in your heart. There is a saying: "It is curious how people aimlessly negotiate their way through life." The Way of the warrior entails a rehearsal of death morning after morning, picturing one's life ending here or there, and imagining the most wonderful way of dying. Decide adamantly that one's heart is in death. This is all a samurai needs to concern himself with. It is demanding but totally achievable. Nothing is impossible.

Also, the power and timing of words is important in military affairs. As with the aforementioned incident, ideally the culprit should have been convinced to stop through negotiation. If this was not possible, cutting him down would be admissible. If he managed to break away, then the pursuers could have shouted at him: "Fleeing is futile, for we will hunt you down. Only a coward runs away!" Thus, depending on the circumstances, you can rely on the power of words to resolve any problem.

The man who slew the culprit is to be admired for being "perceptive and of good judgment." In dealing with the problem, he demonstrated that "now" is always the "critical moment." This is also the case with the duty of *yokoza-no-yari*—the bodyguard who swiftly takes up his spear to protect his master in a crisis. One must be prepared at all times, no matter what.

There are many things that should be considered in anticipation of emergencies. If there is a slaying inside the lord's residence and the culprit cannot be restrained, he must be cut down lest he continue flailing his sword while advancing closer to the lord's room. Of course, you may be blamed for being an accomplice, or accused of embracing a personal grudge at the ensuing interrogation. Simply explain: "All I could think of at the time was to exterminate him. I had no time to mull over the consequences."

❀ ❀ ❀

50. A man can achieve much as long as he prepares himself daily. A recent happening provides testament of this. Mitani Yozaemon concluded his orders exhibiting true valor. He must have invoked the divine favor of the god of war.[1]

❀ ❀ ❀

51. Master Genshin was asked, "I have heard that if you are attacked by someone in the [shogun's] palace, it will work in your favor to

---

1 This is referring to the execution of 80 adherents of Christianity in 1658 in the village of Ōmura. The anti-Christian inquisition was one of the most pronounced elements of the Tokugawa bakufu's policy of national seclusion. Christians were forced to apostatize, and those who refused to denounce their faith were tortured until they recanted, or were executed. According to Book 6-201, Mitani Yozaemon was suddenly ordered to decapitate three of the unfortunate captives, and did so exhibiting "unparalleled skill."

keep calm and simply report the incident to the inspector (*o-met-suke*) without retaliating, even if you are at fault. I wonder if it's worth enduring the shame, thinking that you may be better off for it later on." The master responded: "This is where skill with words is indispensable. You can take the other fellow to the inspector, or you could go on your own and explain the situation. Say 'Although the humiliation is difficult to bear, as the incident took place at my master's palace, I prioritized his feelings, and chose to endure the shame [through not taking immediate action], and hope for your understanding as I explain the details of the affair.' If nothing happens, you can kill the other man because you are already dead."

❀ ❀ ❀

52. I said, "My attitude towards warriorhood and service is evolving. Even when I believe that I have at last learned the ideal way to act as a retainer, after a while I discover that my estimation was in fact perilous and deficient, and I am forced to reconsider. If I had kept a record of my changing opinions since my youth, it would exceed one or two-hundred times. It is never ending. I wish I could come to understand the supreme level." The master replied, "The process of rethinking one's stance is important. When you think you have discovered the secret, this is already a mistake. Know that your study will last for as long as you are breathing."

❀ ❀ ❀

53. You can achieve one more action of consequence even if your head is suddenly removed with the flash of a sword. The last moment of Nitta Yoshisada's life is a fine example of this.[1] You will collapse if you are weak in spirit. Ōno Dōken performed his last meritorious feat of service more recently. Single-minded determination and belief will allow you to accomplish your mission, even in death. If you

---

1 According to *Taiheiki*, Nitta Yoshisada achieved the remarkable feat of cutting off his own head, burying it in the ground, and then dying straddled over his grave!

become like a ghost or rancorous spirit to accomplish a feat of bravery, you won't die just because your head has been lopped off.[1]

❀ ❀ ❀

54. A person said, "I always wondered why eminent men could make sage remarks, but the reason occurred to me one day. Lower-class men are too busy being selfish and thinking lewd thoughts, so their hearts are polluted. They are incapable of eliciting a wise opinion and don't have the inclination to compose poetry. Noble people of high stature are void of impurity in their hearts to start with, and are inherently able to formulate sage ideas through their chasteness."

❀ ❀ ❀

55. Details of a wild dream on the night of the third day of the eighth month, in the third year of Shōtoku (1713).

❀ ❀ ❀

56. Nobles and low-born men, old or young, enlightened or shackled, are all destined to die. We all perish eventually. Nobody is ignorant of this fact. Here though, people rely on their trump card. Although knowing that death is inevitable, they put these thoughts aside in the belief that others will succumb first, and think that their own death is a while off. Is this not vain? It is meaningless, and like playing a game in a dream world. It is ill-advised to keep your head in the sand as death creeps at one's feet; so prepare, and embrace your imminent death.

❀ ❀ ❀

57. If one is insensitive when sympathizing with a man who is plagued by misery by blurting lame comments like "How sorry I feel

---

1 See Book 1-120.

for you," he will become even more despondent and unable to see reason. Instead, it is better to cheer him up by nonchalantly implying it is not serious at all. Say, "Actually, this is quite propitious old chap. It could have been much worse!" With such reassurance, the unfortunate man will see things differently. As we live in an ephemeral world, feelings of sorrow or joy need not be embraced for long.

❈ ❈ ❈

58. Wicked people will latch on to a scandal, and gleefully convey the details to others. They will cast aspersions such as "So-and-so committed a crime. He was interrogated and put under house arrest." They will make sure that the rumor is spread, and that the victim of the vexatious fabrication also hears it. The victim will think that some actual past digression has been revealed, and lock himself inside his house, feigning illness. The scandalmonger will not relent, and assert: "He wouldn't be staying inside his house unless was sickened with guilt. He should be investigated." Men in positions of authority who catch wind of the rumors will be obliged to unearth some wrongdoing. The fibber will take delight when the victim loses his presence of mind as the orchestrated litany of lies is no longer doubted by others, and he will make sure to benefit in some way.

Things like this happened frequently. For example, the time when a statue of Benzaiten was brought to Saga,[1] the "mother drinking party incident,"[2] and the time when the two monks (Nihōshi) refused to take the post of *tōnin*[3] in Edo.[4] Details of each incident can be given verbally. Some wicked men of this breed can be seen among

---

1 Benzaiten is the Japanese name for the Hindu goddess Saraswati. The goddess is worshipped in Shinto as the *kami* Ichikishima-Hime-no-Mikoto, and in Tendai Buddhism as Ugaijin. Jōchō brought a statue of Benzaiten carved by a Buddhist priest back to Mount Sefuri in Saga in 1697.

2 In 1706, Nabeshima Yugie invited Ishii Den'emon, an elder councilor (*toshiyori*), and others to a bawdy drinking party attended by his mother when Lord Nabeshima Tsunashige was in Nagasaki. Ishii Den'emon was dismissed from his post, and Yugie was placed under house arrest as a result. This story is recorded in Book 7-23.

3 The post of administrative facilitator for the clan based in Edo.

4 There is no other information about this particular incident.

the many retainers of our clan. Discretion is advised.

❀ ❀ ❀

59. When a young man yawned in the presence of Master Jōchō, he was told: "Yawning is impolite. Yawns and sneezes can always be stifled if your mind is set on it. Yawns or sneezes happen when you are not alert and your mind is wandering. If you can't help but yawn, hide it with your hand. Sneezes can be suppressed by pressing your forehead. There are people who can drink, but few who are good at entertaining. Care should be taken when drinking as it is done in front of others. These minor details should be taken to heart by those in service, and samurai should be trained properly in each aspect of etiquette when they are young. I have itemized 100 articles concerning behavior that samurai should learn. These matters should be discussed further, and more added to the list."[1]

❀ ❀ ❀

60. Nabeshima Kaga-no-Kami Naoyoshi[2] reportedly stated: "It is best to follow the customs of the Nabeshima domain when it comes to fastening the *obi* (sash) or *kami-shimo* (formal attire)." These protocols were established by Lord Naoyoshi. No other domain requires that samurai tie their *obi* with the end tucked in after making the knot. It is a particularly elegant look.

❀ ❀ ❀

61. Yamasaki Kurando[3] said, "An overly perceptive retainer is harmful." This is a golden maxim. The best retainer is one who is passionate about service as his true calling. If not, he might assiduously

---

1 This is referring to Jōchō's *Sōan Zatsudan Oboegaki*. A remaining copy of this document consists of 107 articles.
2 Nabeshima Naoyoshi (1622–1689) was the second daimyo of the Nabeshima Ogi subdomain.
3 See Book 1-195.

argue about right and wrong, and lamenting how the world is eva-
nescent, he will prefer the life of a recluse, renouncing a society rot-
ten to the core with its bustling cities of sin. He studies the teachings
of Buddha to detach himself from the perpetual uncertainties of life
and death. He toys with arts such as poetry and other genteel pursuits, thinking all these things are praiseworthy. He desires a lifestyle
of equanimity and comfort. This is acceptable for a hermit, or for
one who has taken holy orders and lives beyond the mundane world.
It is totally inappropriate, however, for one who shoulders the burden
of duty. A retainer who opts for this is a coward. In his pursuit of a
carefree existence, he is shirking the taxing responsibilities that come
with practicing the Way of the warrior.

One just needs to observe the actions of unlearned men devoted
only to serving their masters, or those who struggle to look after
their families. The way they discharge their day-to-day chores
throughout their lives is truly magnificent. A retainer who insists
on practicing Zen, or composing poetry, or collecting stylish objects,
and dressing in outlandish attire is want to squander his stipend,
and will eventually fall to pieces. He will not resemble a layman or
monk, nor a nobleman, or hermit. He is just an ugly sight to behold.

Some are of the opinion that men should be free to engage in
cultural diversions in their spare time, after completing their daily
chores. In this sense, such activities will not obstruct one's work. Yet,
a retainer should have no leeway to think of such things if he is fully
focused on his profession. A samurai with spare time on his hands
is obviously not working hard enough.

The words of the veteran Kurando regarding this matter are
weighty. When he was an elder councilor, many of his colleagues
enjoyed composing *haiku* poems at the palace. He never participated
in these gatherings, however, and would bid the other vassals farewell
by saying, "Please take pleasure in your *haiku* now that your duties
have finished for the day." He spent many hours enjoying *haiku* after
retirement.

❀ ❀ ❀

62. A retainer need only keep one thing in mind. He will become distracted through his fixation with reasoning or nurturing artistic talents. It will make him rather agitated. Having an artistic talent as the basis for one's service is of a lower level. A samurai who is not gifted with superior acumen, or cannot boast a particular artistic flair or bold nature, and deems himself useless and thus resigned to dwell in the backwaters, should take solace in being his lord's one and only worthy retainer. Regardless of whether his lord shows him kindness, or no consideration at all, or if he doesn't even recognize the man, he shouldn't care in the slightest. He still feels indebted to his lord day and night, and serves so devotedly that it brings tears to his eyes.

This is easy to achieve. Nobody alive doesn't innately possess this capacity. Few are unaware of it, but there are hardly any who choose to live in accordance with this ideal. It is simply a matter of attitude. If a man makes up his mind to do so, then he can be a remarkable retainer.

This sentiment is comparable to love. The more unsympathetically a man is treated, the stronger his love becomes. When he finally sees his lover, he does not hesitate forgoing his life for him. Secret love (*shinobu-koi*) is indeed a fine standard. It is deepest when bottled tight in his heart and not confessed for his entire life, determined to take it to the grave. He feels great happiness when he realizes he has been deceived by his lover's pretense. He yearns for him all the more. The master-follower relationship is similar. The true meaning of service can be appreciated in this way. The basic spirit of fealty transcends judgments of right and wrong. (Personal note: The similarities seen in male love and the bonds of fealty between lord and vassal were outlined by Sōgi.)[1]

❊ ❊ ❊

63. Serve reticently and diligently when you are in close attendance of your lord. By spending many years attending with this attitude, you will become useful to your lord before he realizes it in due course.

---

1 A master of linked verse (1421–1502).

This is the ideal approach because a close aide is like one of the lord's family members. Conversely, a samurai who is not a close attendant cannot afford to serve in this way, as he will fall behind. He must work extra hard and try to be noticed by his superiors.

❀ ❀ ❀

64. Being devoid of any special talents, and not having had an opportunity to fight in battle, I was not a particularly good servant. Nonetheless, from a young age my feelings for my lord ran deep, and I simply made up my mind to be his 'one and only' retainer. I was his most valiant warrior. This determination permeated right into the marrow of my bones. As such, no intelligent or competent man of the highest pedigree could make light of me. On the contrary, I have been afforded so much tender solicitude by other retainers, it is somewhat flustering.

All I did was value my lord above all else. Come what may, I was resolved in my heart to throw myself into a frenzied state (*shinigurui*) to die for him. Only now will I venture to admit that my single-minded faith was strong enough to shift Heaven and earth, and it has been acclaimed as such by other members of the clan. I am overcome with gratitude for recognition of my fidelity by my lord's son and senior advisors.[1]

For a hereditary vassal, venerating one's lord is a given, regardless if one is serving near or from afar. An increase in stipend or a gift of gold and silver from one's lord is received with due appreciation; but more treasured than monetary rewards is a single kind word, which is enough to elicit the will to cut one's belly [upon his passing].

When the Nabeshima retainers residing in the Edo estate were consigned fire duties,[2] I was allocated the task of preserving documents. Yet, my lord saw the roster and requested, "As he is a young man, he will serve at my side," in case of a fire. I knew at that point that I would gladly sacrifice my life for him. When we were stationed

---

1 Nabeshima Tsunashige, son of Mitsushige.
2 This was in 1685 when Jōchō was 27 years old.

in Osaka together,[1] my lord once gave me his sleeping garments and bedding. He said: "As I am unable to increase your stipend for your assistance in my diversions, please take these as a token of my gratitude. You need not express thanks to the elder councilors for this gift from me." These kind words filled me with happiness and I thought, had it been in the old days [before the prohibition of *junshi*], I would eagerly follow him in death on this futon wearing these garments.

❊ ❊ ❊

65. Before being reinstated to a previous post after a period away, it is better to seem a little blunted. It is ideal to have an attitude that is settled and calm. The more grateful one feels to the clan and its retainers for their consideration, the weightier one's sense of obligation becomes. When aware of this, you will realize that becoming a *rōnin* is no great imposition. The pact of loyalty between master and servant is our insurance. Don't waver in the slightest even if Buddha, Confucius, or the Sun Goddess, Amaterasu Ōmikami appear and preach the pitfalls of such a bond. A samurai need not do any more than entrust his life to his master, even if he is sent to hell, or suffers divine retribution for his blind devotion. Unless you are heedful, you may be accused of flouting the divine mandate of the deities and Buddha. But then, even the gods and Buddha would never dismiss such staunch faithfulness as mistaken.

❊ ❊ ❊

66. I accompanied Master Jōchō when visiting his friend. After chatting for a while, we were about to leave when the host said, "Please stay a little longer. I would have liked to enjoy your company until the evening, but I have a prior engagement with some other guests." We left without delay. Master Jōchō said, "With such an empty invitation, it feels as though he wanted rid of us because we were in the way."

---

1 In 1696, when Jōchō was 38 years old.

❀ ❀ ❀

67. It is always handy to carry some powdered rouge to fix your complexion when you are sobering up, or awakening from sleep in the morning. Apply the rouge to put the color back in your cheeks.

❀ ❀ ❀

68. Never again will a man as wise as Sagara Kyūma appear on the scene. One could sense his wisdom just by laying eyes on him, but it became clearly evident the more you got to know him. Prince Mitsushige was enthralled by poetry. His grandfather, Lord Katsushige, warned him about his obsession, and ordered his elder councilors to home detention [for not discouraging him].[1] Those attending Mitsushige were summarily scolded. Kyūma was still in his youth and was Mitsushige's playfellow. He reputedly declared: "Nobody knows the character of Tanshū[2] better than I. He is an extraordinarily smart young master, but simultaneously short tempered and aggressive. Nothing can supplant poetry to assuage his temper. Poetry may actually help prolong the clan's existence for many more generations."

Kyūma maintained this opinion throughout his years of loyal service. Later on, Lord Katsushige said: "When I scolded Tango-no-Kami's[3] servants, nobody uttered a single word in his defence. They are fools. There was a young man in the back who, judging by appearances, looked to be quite capable." (Note: This version of events differs to other accounts I have heard, and requires verification.)

❀ ❀ ❀

69. I tend to view new methods with suspicion, even if they are thought to be for the better.[4] A member of Nakano Matabei's former

---

1 Baba Ichinosuke and Fukushima Gorōzaemon.
2 Nabeshima Mitsushige.
3 Yet another name for Nabeshima Mitsushige.
4 This comment is made in reference to the rearranging of *ashigaru* units in 1695. *Ashigaru* foot soldiers were low level combatants.

unit said: "Our captain labored to appoint and train 25 skilled archers.[1] In spite of this, the unit was disbanded, and ten of the best 25 archers were incorporated into Sawano's unit.[2] The ten selected men amazed their new superiors because of their high level of expertise. We thought we could repay the debt of obligation to our former master through our outstanding skills. Still, the rest of us were dismayed at being reassigned to a firearms division. We broke our bows and vowed never to pick up a musket. One man was to be consigned to lead a 1-*koku ashigaru* unit, but everybody refused to go.[3] I told them that 'Although unmatched in archery, I am too old, and it would be rude to disobey a direct order from our lord, so I will volunteer to go.' This is why I am no longer able to take up my bow and arrow."

He relayed this sorrowfully and with tears in his eyes. It is lamentable that such things go undetected by those in positions of authority, and the rank and file suffer as a result. Thankfully, the clan is first-rate so the men's dissatisfaction will eventually dissipate because of our undying appreciation. Naoshige thought it especially important that harmony be maintained.

A poll was taken to canvass who deserved credit for the victory at the battle in Arima.[4] An inspector (*o-metsuke*) was assigned to each unit, but no one could agree. How can anyone determine who did what in the thick of battle? If the inspectors were not eminent warriors themselves, their verdicts would not be readily accepted. When Ishii Yashichizaemon began discussing the Shimabara Uprising in the meeting room of the Edo mansion, Kadota Ichirōzaemon happened to be there and said: "If anyone here arrived at the place of battle before me, speak now." Ishii replied, "Perhaps your point of attack was different to the others." In this way, countless acts of valor went unnoticed to the chagrin of many.

---

1 Jōchō's uncle. He was archery instructor and the captain of an *ashigaru* unit. He died in 1695.
2 Sawano Shin'uemon. Captain of a unit of archers.
3 Perhaps referring to a unit captained by a samurai receiving a stipend of one *koku* of rice. A *koku* of rice or grain equals about 180.39 liters (5.12 US bushels), which was supposedly enough to feed one person for a year.
4 During the Shimabara Uprising of 1637–1638.

❀ ❀ ❀

70. One day, a man visiting an inn complained that his *kōgai* had gone missing.[1] His companion tried to appease him, and then escorted him away so that the host would not hear about it. The thief was discovered and punished. It would have been abysmal had the host been subjected to humiliation without checking all avenues first. Carefully consider the fittings (*koshirae*) on your sword, where you place them, and what to do in case you lose them.

❀ ❀ ❀

71. There are occasions when you get carried away chatting incessantly on account of your jubilant mood. As you ramble on enthusiastically, people will detect that you are being offhand and untruthful. When this happens, it is best to face up to the truth and confess. Then truthfulness will manifest in your heart, too. Even when exchanging casual greetings, it is wise to assess the situation and talk in a manner not to cause offense. If somebody mocks the Way of the warrior, or criticizes the clan, tersely counter him without conviviality, and put the heathen firmly in his place. Be prepared for this at all times.

❀ ❀ ❀

72. With any matter requiring consultation, first discuss the content beforehand with someone you trust. Only then should concerned parties be gathered, and the matter opened for deliberation. Not taking precautions ahead of time will invite contempt. Also, with regards to problems requiring urgent attention, opinions should be solicited in private from people not directly involved, or recluses who have renounced the mundane world. These men will see the issue objectively without bias. If you seek advice from a colleague in the same unit, he will assess your plight according to his own interests, which

---

1 *Kōgai* were small hairpins inserted in the scabbard of Japanese swords.

serves no purpose at all. (The Nihōshi affair conveyed verbally.)[1]

73. Even though it is normal for men who excel in the arts to see others as rivals, Hyōdo Sachū[2] bestowed his title of "Master of Linked Verse" (*renga*) on Yamaguchi Shōchin.[3] This act of humility was admirable.

74. The priest Tannen[4] hung a wind-chime in the temple saying, "I'm not dangling it there to enjoy the sounds. I put it up to know how strong and which way the wind is blowing in order to prevent fires. Fire is the main threat when charged with managing a big temple." He walked around the precinct on nights when strong winds blew. For his entire life, he never let his smouldering *hibachi*[5] go out, and he always kept a lantern and lighting stick at the ready by his pillow. He said, "People panic during emergencies, and there is nobody who can make a light quickly."

75. If you differentiate between public space and your private quarters, or being on the battlefield or on a *tatami* mat, you will not be able to respond in timely fashion as the exigency of a crisis may require. Be Argus-eyed at all times. Inability to demonstrate valor even on a *tatami* mat in your house means that you cannot be relied on in battle.

---

1 See Book 2-58.
2 A priest at the Yoga Shrine in Saga.
3 A townsman of the Rokuzachō district in Saga.
4 See Book 1-39.
5 Brazier.

76. The extent of one's courage or cowardice cannot be measured in ordinary times. All is revealed when something happens. (Two stories regarding missions conveyed verbally.)[1]

❀ ❀ ❀

77. You won't be able to serve effectively if your master doesn't see you. How you are rated depends entirely on your faithful attitude. When Lord Mitsushige was angry, he would shower criticism on the object of his wrath, but I was never censured at all for as long as I was his attendant. The young prince [Tsunashige] often said to me, "You look like the type of fellow who will desert his master one day." I assumed he was speaking from the heart, but he never once doubted my counsel after Lord Mitsushige died.

❀ ❀ ❀

78. Master Jōchō said, "Even now, I cannot help but weep when I reflect on how I am still ready to be the first to respond, and be the most useful servant should a catastrophe strike. I have discarded everything and am in need of nothing as I live in these hills as a hermit. I consider myself already dead. Still, I have felt this keenness to act in the very marrow of my bones since I was a lad. No matter how much I try purging it from my heart, I still believe I'm the only one who can save the day. I have to wonder if the chief retainers and other vassals feel as deeply for the lord as I do."

When he talked of this, Jōchō was teary-eyed and his voice trembled, and he could barely force his words out. "Every time I think of my abiding devotion, I break down like this. Be it the middle of the night or during the day, or when I'm alone or with guests, I just can't help it." I have witnessed Jōchō shed tears on several occasions when talking wistfully about this topic.

❀ ❀ ❀

---

1 Probably referring to Jōchō's two sojourns in Kyoto in 1686 and 1696.

79. Upon meeting Ittei one day, I said, "The clan will not fall until the end of time. This is because each time I die, I will be reborn to protect and serve the clan all by myself." Master Ittei said, chuckling: "What a bold declaration." This is when I was either 24 or 25. Ittei then told Takumoto Oshō "I just met with an extraordinary fellow who the clan can surely rely on. He's not in the least bit inferior to the great men of old." This anecdote was relayed to me by a certain priest who overheard the conversation.

❀ ❀ ❀

80. The priest Tannen preached: "Always pledge your heart to the clan deity (*ujigami*). This will bring you luck. The *ujigami* is like your parent."

❀ ❀ ❀

81. The former [Yamamoto] Jin'uemon always used to say, "It is unacceptable for men of Saga not to pray to our ancestor Lord Nippō.[1] Some men prayed to him even when he was still alive so that their dreams may come true. They were never disappointed."

❀ ❀ ❀

82. Although deities shun impurity, I still prayed to them every day, entreating them for providence in battle should I have to fight soaked in blood, striding over rows of corpses. I thought it could not be helped if a god spurned me on account of bloody defilement, but I offered prayers notwithstanding in the hope that there were gods who would not mind.

❀ ❀ ❀

83. One timely word is vital in times of calamity or disaster. A timely

---

1 Another name for Nabeshima Naoshige.

word is also needed in times of good fortune. When exchanging greetings in the street, again, a timely word is important. Think carefully before speaking. A word has the power to make people brace themselves if it is fitting for the occasion. I remember having such experiences. Always keep this in the back of your mind, and be ready to say the right thing as each situation dictates. It is terribly difficult to explain, but it ultimately depends on your heart. A man with no sentiment in his heart will never understand.

❀ ❀ ❀

84. A monk happened by when Master Jōchō was chatting at some-body's house. Jōchō was sitting in the seat of honor, but moved to the lower position as he greeted the monk, and then continued as usual. This was in accordance with old protocols of etiquette.

❀ ❀ ❀

85. Gon'nojō (Jōchō's adopted son) was appointed as an auxiliary captain of a unit to be deployed to the Nagasaki garrison. Master Jōchō wrote a memo of important considerations for his reference. Included in his advice were tenets such as: "Make plans to depart as quickly as possible; show lodgings to the coolies; assemble the men, treat them to a meal, and greet them with care. One careless word will lessen their estimation of you as a leader." He also wrote: "If your will to serve is genuine, you will be appointed as the permanent captain next time."[1]

❀ ❀ ❀

86. A man's life is very short, so it is best to do what he enjoys most. It is foolhardy indeed to waste your life in this world between dreams, doing things you don't enjoy as you endure the suffering. I take care when expressing such an opinion. I keep it to myself, lest young

---

1 See Book 2-25.

samurai hear it and adopt wrong ideas to their detriment. That aside, I like to sleep. Accordingly, I intend to confine myself to my quarters and spend more time napping.

🌸 🌸 🌸

87. About a dream on the twenty-eighth night of the twelfth month, in the third year of Shōtoku (1713). As my willpower strengthens, the content of my dreams is gradually transforming. Dreams are a representation of your actual state of mind. Dreams can guide you in your training.

🌸 🌸 🌸

88. Repentance is like pouring spilled water back into a container. I pitied the person who belatedly confessed to his crime of pilfering somebody's *kōgai*.[1] If only he had repented quicker, residue of his crime would have vanished for good.

🌸 🌸 🌸

89. Those with a little understanding of things presume to know their own strengths and shortcomings. Because they identify themselves with people whom they deem to be of an even higher level of attainment, they believe they can determine the "limit" of their own lofty caliber, and with false modesty they label this as a fault. This eventually metastasizes into conceit. The priest Kaion Oshō remarked that it is difficult to genuinely discern your own virtues and faults.[2]

🌸 🌸 🌸

90. A quick glance at a man's appearance will reveal the measure of

1 See Book 2-70.
2 See Book 2-5.

his dignity. There is dignity in humility. There is dignity in calmness. There is dignity is reticence. There is dignity in proper comportment. There is dignity in graciousness. There is dignity in clenched teeth and piercing eyes. All of these features manifest externally, but their substance emanates from attentiveness and purity of mind.

❀ ❀ ❀

91. "Greed," "rage," and "folly" are fittingly apportioned categories of depraved comportment. Ill-fated occurrences in the world can always be attributed to one of these corruptions. On the other hand, auspicious events are linked to the virtues of "wisdom," "compassion," or "bravery."

❀ ❀ ❀

92. [Yamamoto] Gorōzaemon[1] said: "Fundamental conditions for retainers don't change, but the circumstances do, depending on the era. With their lordships Naoshige and Katsushige, all things big and small were well-defined—there was nothing they didn't know, so no mistakes were made as long as their instructions were followed. If there was anything you didn't understand, you only had to ask and they would teach you. They were convivial masters to serve. When it comes to lords lacking the requisite knowledge, retainers need to be resourceful and plan carefully to facilitate his effective governance. This can be rather taxing."

❀ ❀ ❀

93. Kazuma (Toshiaki)[2] once said: "Some believe that using old utensils in a tea ceremony is dirty. New ones are cleaner. By contrast, there are those who maintain that older utensils should be used as they are not as garish as new ones. Both of these views are mistaken.

---

1 Jōchō's nephew.
2 Nakano Kazuma Toshiaki. See Book 1-51.

In the case of an old utensil, although it may have been used by people in the lower classes in the past, it eventually comes into the possession of a man of high station because of its desirable quality. This trait is to be valued."

The same can be said of retainers. A man of humble beginnings who has come to occupy a position of importance, will have earned his promotion because of his merits. As such, it is a grave mistake to think, "I am disinclined to work with such-and-such a man because of his lowly background." Or, "He was merely a foot soldier until recently, so it is premature to make him a captain." As a humble man embodies the qualities needed to elevate himself to a position of respect, he should be afforded more kudos than a man who inherits his status through birth.

❀ ❀ ❀

94. When I was a child, I was often sent on errands by my father, the former Jin'uemon, to the bridge in Tōjin-machi to feel the town wind on my face, and become accustomed to the townsfolk. From the age of five, I was asked to go to places on behalf of my father, and from the age of seven I was sent to visit the ancestral graves in the temple wearing *musha-waraji* straw sandals to make me more robust.

❀ ❀ ❀

95. Important tasks cannot be accomplished without an element of moderation between the lord, his chief retainers, and elder councilors. It is impossible to function properly in a laissez-faire environment. A retainer should appreciate this.

❀ ❀ ❀

96. Don't be ignorant of the clan, its inner workings, and the historical roots of your province. Depending on the situation, however, excessive knowledge may prove to be a hindrance. Discretion is mandatory. Knowing too much about everyday goings on may also be a burden. Mention of the dispute between Ishii Shingozaemon and Yamamoto.[1] (Details conveyed verbally.)

❀ ❀ ❀

97. The monk Shungaku[2] remarked: "It is written that 'Forcefully bellow STOP, and the power of two men will emanate from within.' This is inspiring stuff. Something unable to be settled there and then will probably never be changed. When it is too demanding to straighten out matters with the power of one, it can be achieved by the strength of two. Nothing is reconciled through postponement. Another interesting tenet I read was, 'Break through an iron wall with a roar and a step from the left foot.'[3] Trample any problems underfoot from the first step from the left. Hideyoshi was the only man in the history of Japan with this kind of vitality and ability to seize the moment."

❀ ❀ ❀

98. A certain person is brazen, bright and competent in service. Recently, I informed him that his erudite nature was written all over his face, and it appeared to have no depth. When I asked him if he could conceal three or four things out of ten, he said "no." He is capable of managing official dealings with the government with some blandishment, but he doesn't have the quality of character to deal with important business related to the lord or clan governance. He is similar to you-know-who. They think cleverness and wit is all that's needed to muddle through.

But, there is nothing more disagreeable than canniness or wit. People keep him at arm's length, and avoid becoming intimate. On the other hand, an obtuse-looking man who is sincere in character turned out to be an excellent retainer.

---

1 It is uncertain what dispute is being referred to here. Ishii Shingozaemon was an attendant to Nabeshima Tsunashige.
2 See Book 1-49.
3 "Left foot" here implies "quick march." Basically, the phrase means to seize the opportunity and act expediently.

❈ ❈ ❈

99. It is damaging to cajole one's lord. A man who is promoted because he is a relative through marriage, or because of the lord's nepotism, will never be able to speak his mind. In spite of years of devoted service, his peers will likely talk of him disparagingly as "His Lordship's darling," and his illustrious record will amount to little. It is easier to serve without the fetters of favoritism.

❈ ❈ ❈

100. When someone blathers incessantly, it is probably an indication that something else is on his mind. He continues prattling on and on in an attempt to conceal it. If you keep listening, it will strike a chord of doubt in your mind.

❈ ❈ ❈

101. If you concur with everything brought up at a formal discussion or when chit-chatting, and just dally in the conversation, you will be unable to see higher reason. When somebody describes an object as black, think to yourself, "It can't be black, but could be white. There must be a reason for it to be white." Endeavoring to attach a reason to something will help you educe a higher logic. You will be incapable of exceeding others without making efforts like this.

If it is something that can be said on the spot, do so in a way that won't cause offense. If he cannot be told, keep conversing without causing ire, and craft a logical response in your mind. This is how to develop sounder logic than others. Points concerning a man who severed ties with another (relayed verbally).[1] This approach is different to "conjecturing," "forestalling," or "holding reservations."

❈ ❈ ❈

---

1 Possibly the dissolution of an adoption.

102. Master Jōchō offered his estimation to a samurai. "It is good that you exceed your contemporaries in terms of moral conduct and discretion, but always seek further improvement. It would be a shame if you stay as you are now. Your penchant for the arts, however, shows that your aspirations are lower than what is expected for a samurai. That is, if you excel in whatever art, you will serve your master using that talent instead of shining as a warrior like generations of your ancestors. In essence, this means you are little more than an entertainer; which is why I tell people that excellence in an art is cause for ruin as a samurai. Of course, that wouldn't be so bad for a lower ranked warrior. I am urging you to step up so that you are regarded as a true samurai. Being recognized as a consummate servant, you will be chosen by the chief retainers for special missions. They will even pardon your past blunders if someone more suitable is unavailable. What can be a greater example of loyalty than contributing ideas for supervising domain affairs? Your determination to be unequalled among peers will make you useful to your master even if you are not selected for a given task, and you may even be privately consulted on important matters. It is great loyalty to be able to placate such demands and offer guidance. An unfaltering retainer will not be discarded, even if only marginally superior to others. Keep this in mind and aim higher."

The recipient of this advice inquired, "Can I achieve this through my training?"

Master Jōchō replied, "It is easy. Stay alert every moment without ever letting your guard down. Seek higher reason with a pure and unadulterated mind. It is simple and totally attainable with effort.

"There is a way of gaining a reputation for excellence throughout the country within ten days. I once talked with a monk about this. Most people are afraid of the monk. He boasts fine standing for being able to discern the truth, and bludgeoning others into submission with his adroit quips of logic. Go and see him tomorrow. When he says something to you, rebut his reasoning square on, and unsettle him with your superior logic. People will be surprised, and rumors of your exploit will spread quickly. Nobody will take notice unless you take down a big dog."

He responded, "Yes, but that monk is clever indeed," to which Jōchō said, "You cannot accomplish anything of consequence because you say such feeble things. What is so special about the monk? Regardless of how formidable your foe may be, don't give him an inch. Otherwise you will never prevail.

"It is interesting that Yoshitsune[1] talked of 'valor,' 'wisdom,' and 'benevolence.' These three virtues are important for men under the age of 40, even in this day and age. Those over 40 who are not yet noticed by their lord should continue to attach value to these qualities, or they will remain unestablished to the end. This monk became famous simply because he was known for these three qualities.

"When it comes to your lord, chief retainers, or elders, avoid criticizing them publicly. Even if their remarks are unreasonable, do not pass judgment to others. The loyal course of action is to acquiesce, even if their logic is flawed, and sing their praises so that others feel a sense of attachment. It is disobliging to plant seeds of doubt in people's minds. People are fickle. If one person offers praise, others will quickly follow suit. The same can be said about criticism, and folk are hasty to lower their estimation when someone is brought into disrepute.

"I heard that somebody proposed that you transfer to another clan. You should feel repulsed, and rebuke your superior for ever suggesting it. Impress on him that in spite of the favor he has bestowed upon you in the past, you can never agree such a preposterous proposal. If you play along to maintain an affable relationship with him, you will be branded as being a dubious fellow lacking in sincerity. Friends will turn against you, and eventually your reputation will plummet beyond repair. Even if you are starving to death, remember that you are a retainer of the Saga clan. Decide in your heart to never renounce fidelity to your master, even though Buddha and the deities may instruct you otherwise, and just choose to perish in obscurity."

---

1 Minamoto-no-Yoshitsune (1159–1189), a principal figure in the Taira-Minamoto War. The younger brother of Yoritomo, founder of the Kamakura bakufu, Yoshitsune is exalted in legend as a great warrior and is still considered Japan's foremost tragic hero.

103. Never make flippant remarks that will cause offense. Take extreme care. When people are flummoxed by something that has happened in the world, not knowing what to do, they will reflexively talk about nothing else. Talking is pointless at such a time. A careless slip of the tongue may spark a quarrel. Or, you may make enemies who nurse feelings of indignation. At such times it is best not to venture out; stay at home instead and compose poetry.

104. It is inordinately amiss to gossip about the affairs of other men. It is not always appropriate to speak well of them either. It is best just to be cognizant of one's own capabilities, apply yourself in training, and be circumspect in speech.

105. A man of noble character has a calm mind and does not rush things. A lesser man is not peaceable, and incessantly clashes and quarrels with everybody.

106. It is discerning to behold the world as if it were a dream. You want to quickly wake up if you have a nightmare, and are relieved that it was only a dream. This world in which we exist now is no different.

107. A clever man will manipulate the truth combining elements of genuine and insincere 'wisdom,' and attaches reason to assert his point. This amounts to 'poisonous wisdom.' Nothing lacking sincerity has worth.

❀ ❀ ❀

108. There is such a thing as an honorable defeat, by losing quickly in litigation or an argument. This is like sumo wrestling. If one is preoccupied with gaining victory at all costs, winning by deceit is worse than losing [with dignity]. On the whole, it will amount to a deceitful defeat. (Changing residence. Conveyed verbally.)[1]

❀ ❀ ❀

109. Discrimination, harboring animosity, and causing others to feel estranged is born of a lack of compassion. Conflict won't rear its ugly head if everything is enveloped in compassion.

❀ ❀ ❀

110. A man with shallow knowledge will act as if he knows it all. This is puerile. A learned man is modest, and would never boast in this way.

❀ ❀ ❀

111. I told my adopted son, Gon'nojō, "Young men today are inclined to be effeminate. It is an age in which warriors who are approachable, sociable, non-confrontational, and gentle are glorified as being virtuous men. This proclivity means samurai are limited in their potential, and are unassertive. Above all, as men are absorbed with protecting their station and stipend, I think they are just wasting away.

"As an adopted son, you may think it inexcusable to squander the estate as it was attained not through your own labors, but through the hard work of your adopted father. Such is the standard way of thinking these days. Still, I offer a completely different view. I never thought about my own position or property throughout my years of service. As vassals we belong to the lord, so loitering in a mode

---

1 This is related to the episode mentioned in Book 1-26.

of self-preservation is unpardonable. While I am still alive, I would be more than content to see you expelled or commit *seppuku* in the name of service. Either of these two honorable fates represents the definitive end for a retainer.

"On the other hand, I would be mortified if you ruined our house through delinquent deeds such as falling behind [in the Way of the warrior], conduct unbefitting of a retainer, indulging in selfish desires, or being a nuisance to others. If our assets crumble for some other reason, then so be it. Acceptance of such a fate means your 'weapon hand' will move unimpeded and keenly as your heart brims with vim and vigor to serve."

❀ ❀ ❀

112. The reason why a man is devoid of the will to serve is because of pride. He is convinced that he is right, and reasons everything in his own favor, becoming set in immoral ways, and thinking himself as outstanding. It is worthy of severe condemnation. Powers of judgment, artistry, status, riches, aptitude, and inventiveness are all attributes in which pride is justified. Thinking these are enough, however, he will become narrow-minded, never ask others for their opinion, and squander his life on piddling trivialities. Indeed, conceitedness seems to be an unavoidable conclusion, and the most foolishly proud of our clansmen even bragged about his inanity: "Since I am stupidest of all, I have been able to live a rather peaceful life."

The will to serve your lord requires only that you attend in accordance with your status, expunge yourself of deluded pride, know your faults, find ways to better yourself, and keep seeking improvement throughout your life, without ever being satisfied until your last breath. Being aware of your imperfections and trying to remedy them is precisely the Way [of the warrior].

❀ ❀ ❀

113. It is advisable to contact a person in advance before calling on him. Without forewarning you may find the host somewhat predisposed, which would be impolite on your part. Generally speaking, it is not prudent to visit somebody unless invited to do so. Truly intimate friends are few. Be well-mannered if invited to their homes. The enjoyment may be paltry if your visits are too frequent. A get-together just for fun will often result in many a *faux pas*. Also, even if you are busy when somebody calls, do not neglect your responsibility as a host by treating the guest aloofly.

❀ ❀ ❀

114. Lord Ikoma Iki-no-Kami's[1] chief retainer, Maeno Sukezaemon, was guilty of perpetrating a crime. Ikoma Shōgen reported it to the shogunate, and after the court-martial, Sukezaemon was sentenced to death by decapitation. Lord Ikoma's domain was confiscated, and his stipend was downgraded to 10,000 *koku*.

I thought Shōgen's intentions were loyal when I read the report, but his actions resulted in his lord's ruin. If he hadn't notified the shogunate of the incident, his lord would have held out with two or three loyal vassals.[2] Together they could have continued to take steps to protect the clan come what may. If he felt compelled to take action, he could have slain Sukezaemon after revealing all to the other retainers. That way, his lord's name would not be dragged through the mud. There is a saying, "Killing the ox by trying to fix the angle of its horns." This applies to Shōgen's actions.

The monk Kaion[3] said: "When I asked Fushū[4] why he was the only retainer who didn't wish to take part in the gathering to remonstrate with the lord, he replied: 'There is a proper way to advise one's lord. If all the retainers congregate for this purpose, it is the same as announcing to the whole world that your master committed wrongs. In all probability, people of the highest status (lords) will mature into selfish men with many foibles because they have always got their

---

1 Lord of the Takamatsu domain of 70,000 *koku*.
2 Some versions of *Hagakure* say "two or three years" here, rather than indicating two or three vassals.
3 See Book 2-89.
4 See Book 1-7.

own way.[1] Still, most of them aren't venal enough to bring about the demise of their fief. In many cases, if the attendants fuss over trying to mend the lord's ways, the rest of the world will become aware of the problems, and the domain will be lost. The aforementioned deliberation was canceled in the end, but did anything bad happen as a result?'"

By and large, an ambitious vassal seeks to admonish his lord because it will be thought of as an act of merit, or because he has been coerced by others. A loyal remonstration should be courteous and discrete so that it is received with good grace. If your lord refuses to listen, then do your best to obscure his failings. Take his side as his advocate, and ensure that no rumors arise to defile his name. Often it is the case that retainers become belligerent, and they turn their backs when their lord doesn't heed their counsel. Making a commotion is the most perfidious kind of behavior for a retainer. Perhaps due to our curiously providential origins, even when something deleterious occurs, it somehow always ends well for the Nabeshima clan.

❈ ❈ ❈

115. Nothing excessive is good. Even Buddhist sermons, lectures, and lessons in moral behavior can be harmful if expounded on too much.

❈ ❈ ❈

116. A grovelling flatterer forcefully applies his knowledge for nefarious purposes, and misleads his lord to climb the ladder of success. At first glance, it is hard to determine the evildoing of a panderer who seeks only the favor of his lord. Because it is difficult to identify manipulative intentions, even the notorious Ōga Yashirō[2] was able

---

1 In this case, he is referring to Lord Mitsushige.
2 Ōga Yashirō (?–1574) is known as a traitor who plotted to allow the enemy, Takeda Katsuyori, into Tokugawa Ieyasu's castle in Okazaki.

to dupe Lord Gongen.[1] Sly men of this stripe are often found among newly employed retainers or upstarts, but are rare among hereditary vassals or those of high station.

❀ ❀ ❀

117. Jin'uemon used to say "One should not bother bringing up daughters. They may stain the family name, and disgrace the parents [after they are married off]. The oldest daughter is special, but any others should be discarded."

❀ ❀ ❀

118. According to the priest Keihō,[2] Lord Aki[3] once said that "Valorous exploits can only be achieved by becoming a 'madman.'" I was astonished to hear how close his belief was to my own, and it made me even more determined to become a "madman" (*kichigai*) in service.

❀ ❀ ❀

119. The former Nakano Kazuma[4] said: "The original purpose of the tea ceremony is to purify the six senses. The eyes are cleansed by looking at the scroll and flower arrangement in the tearoom, the nose by smelling the incense, the ears by listening to the sound of the hot water being poured, the mouth by the taste of the tea, and the arms and legs by correctness in etiquette and form. As the five senses have thus been cleansed, next, the mind's sensibilities will also be purified as a matter of course. The tea ceremony will sanitize the mind when it is choked with superfluity. I never deviate from the 'heart of tea' at any hour of the day, but not because it is simply a pastime. Also, the utensils used in the ceremony should conform to one's social standing.

---

1 Tokugawa Ieyasu.
2 A priest at the Kōdenji Temple.
3 Nabeshima Aki-no-Kami Shigemasa (1571–1645).
4 See Book 2-93.

There is a poem about plum blossoms: 'Beneath the deep snows in the village that lies before, many branches of the plum tree flowered last night.' The lavish phrase 'many branches' was changed to 'a single branch.' This conveys equanimity and refinement."[1]

❀ ❀ ❀

120. If a man to whom you are obliged to—a friend or an ally—has transgressed in some way, you should secretly admonish him, but cover for him by publicly praising him as a one-in-a-thousand ally with no peer. By reproaching a man privately, his faults can be remedied and he will eventually be rehabilitated into a worthy fellow. Offering praise will encourage him to redeem his ways, and he will cease any further wrongdoing. In this way, it is important to sit within the precincts of compassion and help him rectify his conduct.

❀ ❀ ❀

121. A certain man said, "There are two kinds of willpower: internal and external. A man who is deficient in either will be ineffectual. It is like a sword blade that's sharpened and then stored in its scabbard. Every so often it is unsheathed to test its cutting power on an eyebrow, wiped clean, and then put away again. If a man is constantly swinging his sword about, others will keep their distance, and he will make no friends. A sword always inside its scabbard, however, will rust and become dull. Analogous to this, people will belittle a man who never reveals his power of will."

❀ ❀ ❀

122. Undertakings cannot be accomplished solely through cleverness. You must be able to see things keenly from a wide perspective.

---

1 During the Period of Five Dynasties (AD 907–960) a period of upheaval in China, between the fall of the Tang Dynasty and the founding of the Song Dynasty, the famous poet Zheng Gu (?–896?) read the poem, and thought it would be aesthetically more pleasing if "many branches" was rephrased to "one branch."

It is ill-considered to make impetuous conclusions regarding matters of good and evil, although one should not be tardy either. A man is not a true warrior if he can't settle a matter promptly, without vacillating in his determination.

❀ ❀ ❀

123. When I was young, Ittei said to me: "I have great expectations for you. I just hope that you tend the clan satisfactorily after I die. It will be difficult, but please embrace the burden of caring for the domain." Weeping as he said this, his words pierced my heart, as he made me aware of my immense responsibilities. It is something I have never forgotten, as it was the first time I had been coached so articulately. Such advice is rare in this day and age. When moral precepts are imparted to young men by elders now, they are centered on matters of "deportment," "attitude," and "good service." Mentoring focuses on self-improvement, but the meaning of Ittei's lesson was completely different. Alas, there are no people left who can express things in words the way Ittei did.

❀ ❀ ❀

124. When a man harbors ill feeling or takes to litigation, there are ways for a peaceful resolution to be reached depending on how the situation is mediated. Two warriors met on a one-lane bridge but refused to give way, threatening to cut each other down if the other did not move. A radish seller came between the two men, and catching each one on either end of his shoulder-carrying pole, picked them up and spun them around to the opposite ends of the bridge. There are many ways of solving problems, and this counts as constructive service to one's lord. It is most unfortunate to see precious retainers die needlessly, or create needless discord.

One time in Kyoto, Genzō[1] forced his views on Ezoe Shōbei when

---

1 Ushijima Genzō Naotaka was an official for books of poetry (*kasho-yaku*) and was a custodian in Kyoto. When Mitsushige died, he also took the tonsure with Jōchō,

they were getting drunk. Genzō had a habit of becoming impertinent when indulging in alcohol. The next morning, Shōbei took his short sword and tried to force his way into Genzō's house to kill him. Motomura Buemon heard about this, and escorted Shōbei back to his quarters after calming him down.

Buemon then came to see me and asked, "What in heaven's name should I do?" Then Genzō also showed up and inquired, "Is Shōbei here. Apparently he came to my house before and made quite a hullabaloo, but my stupid servants didn't inform me. I decided to come here having only just heard about the commotion." He wanted to visit Shōbei's residence but I stopped him. "You should go back. Leave it up to me. First, I will ask Shōbei what is irking him, and then tell you what he said." He did as he was instructed.

When Shōbei was summoned, he relayed his side of the story. "Telling people of their errors in front of others does not equate to 'offering an opinion.' I'm convinced he's is trying to humiliate me because he holds a grudge. I wanted to ask him directly why he resents me."

I replied, "I see. A fair explanation. Nonetheless, Genzō does not bear a grudge against you. He has an annoying tendency to give 'opinions' when he is drunk. Nagayama Rokurō has a bad habit of drawing his sword after drinking too much. Habits come in various forms. Where is the loyalty in wreaking revenge over something as trivial as a drunken outburst resulting in the loss of two of the lord's precious retainers?[1] You are a man who has received His Lordship's largesse. Are you not duty-bound to repay this favor? There is no need to lose face. I will ask what was in Genzō's heart, and inform you of what he said." He then returned to his home to wait.

Telling Genzō what Shōbei said, he replied: "I have no recollection of what came to pass last night. I hold no antipathy towards him whatsoever." To which I replied, "I will pass this on to Shōbei. As he was so contemptuous to you, his captain, I ask that you take a lenient

---

assuming the name Itchū.

1 If Shōbei had killed Genzō because of the incident, custom dictated that he also commit *seppuku* to atone for his transgression.

stance on account of his young age. I will warn him to show more prudence from now on." I informed Shōbei of what transpired, and the matter ended there.

After this flare-up, Shōbei decided not to continue with his appointment to the accounting division. We tried to discourage him from taking this course of action, but he requested Kitajima Jinzaemon to organize his transfer to another post in the domain. Buemon got wind of the request, and once again came to me for counsel. I directed him to tell Jinzaemon to stop him for the moment, and called for Shōbei. In explaining his decision he said, "In any case, I will not be able to get along with Genzō, and would prefer to be transferred." I reassured him by saying, "I am sure you can get on well with each other again. Please consider what I say. If you change your post half-way through, rumors will abound that you became resentful of Genzō after a drunken rampage, and were transferred because of that. You will also be labeled a drunkard, and you may not find another post. It will also be detrimental to Genzō's reputation. Please hold your horses a little longer."

I implored him to make up: "You should swallow your pride and become best friends with Genzō." Shōbei replied: "Even if I wanted to, he will not open up to me." I responded, "Let me teach you how to open his heart. Don't concern yourself with his shortcomings, but look into your own heart and think, 'I acted badly. Reflecting on my actions, I find that I was mistaken. The way I reacted against my superior was unpardonable. While Genzō remains in this position, I must work my fingers to the bone.' If you can think like this, then he will recognize your sentiments, and you will be able to continue on friendly terms. Besides, you are a problem drinker. You too should refrain from booze for a while." He abstained from drinking after being repeatedly advised to do so.

After Shōbei talked with Genzō he said, "I am very grateful for your heartfelt apology, and embarrassed with my own behavior. I will not send you away for as long as I am your superior." Indeed, the two became inseparable, and when Genzō was assigned to another post, he recommended that Shōbei be promoted. This is what can happen depending on how situations are managed.

When somebody is intoxicated or talking nonsense, or says something rude which cannot be ignored, the best way to respond is with a witticism that suits the circumstances. How foolish is an incensed man who is too irascible to counter with a fitting comment there and then, and proceeds to unsheathe his sword feeling as though his honor has been challenged.

If you are called a "fool," merely counter by calling the other a "knucklehead," and be done with it. Shōbei could have alleviated the tension by saying, "Although I am grateful for your critique, I would prefer it be out of earshot of other men. With so many people present, I fear that your words may besmirch my honor. What's more, if I must be subjected to your censure, may I submit that you are also not bereft of blame? We all stray from the path of reason when intoxicated, but I would be happy to receive your admonishments when sober. Now, let's have another drink." There would be no shame, and no need to become irate had he responded in this way. If Genzō persisted with his abuse, the situation could have been be dealt with by suitable comebacks.

Let it also be said that a drunkard will find it difficult indeed to pick a fight with a deadly serious man.

A few years ago when two men were on guard duty at the castle, one teasingly called the other a "cross," an object upon which common criminals are executed, making his blood boil. Infuriated, the slighted man decided to kill him. Gorōzaemon[1] and Naridomi Kurando were on night duty and learning of the incident, they intervened and made the troublemaker apologize forthwith.

If the insulted man had retorted something like, "And you sir, are but a 'stake' for burning sinners," then nothing more would have happened. Remaining tongue-tied is a sign of weakness. Take care of how you say things, and what is articulated in the moment.

❋ ❋ ❋

125. When I heard that Genzō was to be investigated for transgres-

---

1 Yamamoto Tsuneharu, Jōchō's nephew.

sions, I went to a certain man and asked to speak in private. "What is it that you intend to interrogate him about? Luckily I am back in Saga, but I cannot possibly return to Kyoto without knowing the reason now. I apologize for my brashness, but I must be told. Please tell me why." Left with little choice the man said: "It's alleged that he's been using the lord's utensils for personal affairs. It has been reported to His Lordship that he sometimes took these items outside the residence gates on excursions with the maids, where he drank copious amounts of rice wine with them."

I replied, "Oh, thank goodness. I am very relieved. There is no need for concern. As the caretaker of the Kyoto residence for several years, he has no shortage of necessary utensils. You must have noticed that when you paid a visit. He may have borrowed some in order to perform his duties for public gatherings of 30 or 40 guests. It's busy work dealing with government officials and court nobles, or meeting caretakers of other domain residences, or negotiating with moneylenders. This posting also entails frequenting tea houses and theaters.

Regarding the maidservants, as you know, those stationed at the Kyoto residence for several years employ them in addition to *ashi-garu* (common foot soldiers) and menservants. It is no revelation that he drinks a lot of *saké*, but he has never become belligerent as a result of his imbibing. None of these acts are serious enough to warrant punishment. It is understandable that an inexperienced sub-inspector (*kachi-metsuke*) followed the letter of the law and reported what he assumed to be offenses, but a residence caretaker cannot fulfill his duties unless he is afforded some leeway. I am actually comforted to hear it." I then departed.

It came to pass that Genzō was pardoned of any wrongdoing, and continued in his role as the residence custodian in Kyoto. A matter can be delineated as being reasonable depending on how it is phrased. The tone in which you are heard is contingent on how you start the conversation.

❀ ❀ ❀

126. I whispered in the ear of a certain monk. "As I advised when you were banished from the temple, hole up for a while so that nobody knows of your whereabouts. When you are pardoned and come back to Saga, your influence will be greater than when you were the chief priest. People will not approve if you are spotted around Saga at the present time; and it will all amount to nothing if you are investigated by His Lordship's decree. When His Lordship heard of a 'certain monk' taking cover in the Kōdenji Temple after being banished, I was told to inform him never to show his face in Saga again. Reflect on this very carefully." I then took my leave. He seems to not know at all about his predicament.

❀ ❀ ❀

127. Once, five or six of the lord's pages[1] were traveling by boat. They collided with another transport vessel in the night. Five or six of the vessel's deck hands boarded the boat and insisted that they "relinquish their anchor in accordance with protocol." The pages replied angrily, "That 'protocol' is for seadogs like you. How can you dare to think to take equipment from a samurai ship? We will cut you all to pieces and throw you in the sea." Following this threatening outburst, the deckhands scurried back to their own boat.

There are ways in which a warrior should act at times. In trivial matters, it is best to resolve the problem by bellowing with a loud, forceful voice. If you overreact and take too long to clear up a petty problem, you will 'miss the boat' thereby slowing you down in your mission, and you will be worse off for it.

❀ ❀ ❀

128. A man came for help upon noticing a discrepancy when balancing the books. I sent a letter to his unit captain saying, "It would be unfortunate for a man to commit *seppuku* over money. As you are his superior, may I suggest that you send funds to cover the

---

1 *Kogoshō* (pages) were young pre-*genpuku* boys who served as attendants to the lord.

deficit." My request was deemed tenable, money was sent to balance the accounting, and the problem was solved. Transgressions can be dealt with without being brought into the open.[1]

129. Shōgen[2] always said: "Rooted in the word '*kan*' (remonstrance) are self-seeking desires. There can be no altruistic remonstration." Nobody knows if Shōgen remonstrated with his lord. He did not once attempt to influence him by forcing reason. He always conferred in private to elicit his understanding.

Also, Nakano Kazuma Masatoshi[3] never sought to take his lord to task with brash admonishments under the guise of "service." Instead, he would covertly offer advice at a well-timed moment, away from the ears of others. His guidance was always received graciously. The lord's iniquities were thus never exposed because nobody knew what went on.

To try and forcibly convince your lord through personal interpretations of reason is "great disloyalty." This is because the underlying motivation is to make a show of allegiance at the expense of the lord's reputation. As the details become known, the lord's honor will be sullied if he does not heed the petition; whereas the name of the 'loyal' retainer will be well-known. The outcome is worse than if no remonstrance is given in the first place.

If advice offered in private is not readily accepted by the lord, the retainer should realize that the task is beyond him, look to control any damage, and surreptitiously devise other ways for his supplication to be heard. After repeated appeals, the lord is sure to listen in the end. If he pays no attention to the advice and continues in his waywardness, the retainer should stay by his side with even more resolve ensuring that his lord's failings are not exposed to public scrutiny.

---

1 See Book 1-110, Book 2-16, and Book 2-114.
2 Nakano Shōgen Masakane was an elder councilor under Nabeshima Mitsushige.
3 A minister who served under Nabeshima Katsushige.

130. A retainer must pledge to "Amend the minds of all the people in the domain so that no one is disloyal or immoral, and serve his master well so that all can live peacefully." This was the aspiration of Yi Yin.[1] He was a paragon of "great loyalty" and "great compassion." To correct the ways of other people is harder than rectifying your own. First, you must be amiable with everyone. The key is to be "secretly loved" by being on good terms with those you are close to, as well as those you are not so well acquainted with. I can say from experience that it is easier to accept opinions from those whom you can empathize with.

When making a suggestion, it should be in accordance with his circumstances and character. Keep his temperament in mind, and start with something that he might like to hear. There are many ways to make your point. If you speak of a man's foibles in an accusatory manner, he most likely won't pay attention to you. Why would he feel gratified if you are condescending, and treat him as if he is flawed?

First, confess your own imperfections and make a statement along the lines of: "I have a long-standing desire to purge myself of my failings, but I am unable to do so on my own. I would like your opinion in confidence, as I consider you to be an intimate friend." The other person will likely respond, "I feel the same way." In that case, you could suggest that you both "exchange opinions," and with each other's feelings understood, bad habits can be mended.

If one has wholehearted intentions of repenting sins, traces of all transgressions committed eons ago will vanish. No matter how wicked the man, attempts for redemption must never be abandoned. There is nothing more wretched than an imprudent fellow. There is nobody beyond redemption if various tactics are tried. Failure is a consequence of the wrong approach, or your own apathy.

Because I was asked by the grandfather, I have been watching over the son of a man solitary and despised by others for his obnoxious personality. I keep a constant eye on the child, and pray to Buddha and the gods every morning in the hope that his situation

---

1 Yi Yin was a minister of the early Shang Dynasty (1600?–1046 BC), and was one of the most revered officials of the time. He helped Tang, first king of the Shang dynasty, defeat King Jie of Xia.

improves, instead of abandoning him as a lost cause. It is said that acts of sincerity are honored by the gods in heaven and earth, so good omens will come, I'm sure. This is my lifelong wish. I have become intimate with scoundrels in the clan who most people hold in contempt. Although most would never trust such blighters, I alone choose to serve as their advocate and sing their praises to others: "He is unquestionably a 'nonconformist,' but has as his most admirable trait an unyielding attachment to His Lordship." Such words can change people's minds. Everybody has redeeming qualities. Even if he is flawed in many ways, he should be encouraged to reform and augment his positive attributes to be precious to the clan.

I made the following a gentleman's agreement with my colleagues: "His Lordship will pass away before long. When that day comes, I will shave my head with the same resolve as following him in death (*oibara*), and hopefully rouse my 50 or 60 senior attendants. It may seem arbitrary to have been scolded by them so often, only to discard one's life when the time comes; but is this not incumbent of a truly devoted retainer? Without question, this is how a lowly servant who soldiers on unnoticed behind the scenes can surpass men of higher station, and bring honor to his lord. Let us take this to heart, and martyr ourselves in service."

Someone said to me "If a certain newcomer in the lord's employ swaggers and blows his own horn any more, we will put him out of his misery." I said: "You are completely wrong. Newcomers are just here to 'clean the lord's backside,' doing menial tasks. They will get their comeuppance in the end. Can you not see that? Do you really think it prudent for men of your stature, men who are destined to bring great honor to His Lordship in four or five years, to be at loggerheads with such depraved fellows?" With that, I was able to prevent any rash action, and encouraged them to remain on gracious terms for the sake of the lord. Thankfully, everybody amiably heeded what I said, and I allied myself with dozens of excellent men, from high-ranked vassals (*chakuza*) down to common foot soldiers (*ashigaru*). They were all primed to forfeit their lives gladly for the lord should the need arise.

If you see a man who has amended his comportment even a

little, nurture this further by lavishing praise. He will try even harder to improve himself.

❋ ❋ ❋

131. All men are predisposed to fail in important tasks through impulsiveness. Have a mind to persevere for as long as it takes, and your work will get done in due course, often sooner than you think. Your time will come. Think ahead about 15 years. The state of the world will be much different. It might not change as much as it is forecasted in books such as the *Miraiki*.[1] Still, the expedient men of today will no longer be around in 15 years, and only half of the young samurai with us now will still be alive then.

As the world deteriorates, men's capabilities are also waning. Just as silver replaces gold when the latter is depleted, copper will also eventually replace silver. The worth of men is fading with the times. Perseverance and grit shown now will help a young samurai surpass his peers. This means he will be a capable retainer in a mere 15 years. Fifteen years is in the middle of a dream. As long as one is able to remain in good health, an enduring wish to serve as a valuable retainer will come true. It's challenging to outshine so many exceptional colleagues now. But, it will be relatively straightforward to stand out in 15 years with so few rivals left.

❋ ❋ ❋

132. If you apply yourself in fixing somebody's bad habits, his behavior will change for the better. Like a digger wasp, it is said that even an adopted child's resemblance to you will eventuate through tenacious proselytizing to follow your example.[2]

❋ ❋ ❋

---

1 A book that prophesied about the future.
2 *Jigabachi*, or digger wasp, which is known for its ability to paralyze insects and implant their eggs.

133. When crafty retainers become powerful, or when some evil act committed by a superior, acrimony will often infiltrate the lower ranks of vassals who had nothing to do with it. They will become languid in their duties, and spend their time engaging in idle tittle-tattle. It is crucial to be particular with one's words at times such as this.

The retainer's attention should be fixed on one point. Namely, when the clan succumbs to the rot, what will the lord do? It is precisely in times of turmoil that you should spare no effort in aiding the lord.

No matter how many sycophants appear, or how much wrongdoing is committed by those in positions of authority, no illustrious clans with long traditions will see their demise within a ten year span. If the unruliness persists for 20 years, then there will be a huge degree of vulnerability. Understand this, and devise contingency plans to eradicate any malign conduct, and rebuild the organ of clan governance within a decade to sustain it. If left to degenerate further, even those not involved will lose motivation to be of assistance as whisperings of various scandals trickle down like water from a draining basket, exposing evildoing for the world to see. Most offenses are leaked from the inner circle, and the clan will surely collapse inside the next ten years.

It is best not to mock the transgressions of others. Needlessly making enemies will give rise to further damage. Invite even an evil man to trust you, and venture to put right his character.

❀ ❀ ❀

134. Strength of will aligns your words and deportment with the Way. You will be commended by others as being a true adherent. When inquiring into your own heart there is the last phrase of a poem that goes, "How will you reply when your own heart asks questions?"[1] This is the ultimate teaching for all arts, and it is a fine regulator of one's behavior.

❀ ❀ ❀

---

1 See Book 1-40.

135. Pin your ears back and respectfully pay attention when listening to stories of old men, even if you have heard them before. Certain things will strike at your heart after listening 10, 20, or 30 times. It is a special moment when the epiphany comes. They might be the ramblings of old men, but they contain the wisdom of samurai who achieved epic feats in their day.

❀ ❀ ❀

136. Depending on the situation, one may have to trample on one's lord's commands, or waive charity from other people to carry out your duty. Ultimately, you will never deviate from the right course so long as your sole desire is to serve your lord.

There was a man who attended his lord's wife. When Her Ladyship died, he did not shave his head, justifying his stance by proclaiming, "My Lord said I should not."[1] Nevertheless, other servants dispatched by her father, a lord in another clan, whose relationship was more distant than his, did shave their heads. It was not good form that only they take holy orders, so the attendant was forced to follow suit.

In this case, even though the lord declared that he need not relinquish his post and shave his head, he should have disobeyed him. It was immaterial what the lord and senior advisors thought. When Her Ladyship Denkōin[2] died, six of her male and female servants followed her in death, and long before this Yatsunami Musashi[3] also resolved to commit *oibara*.[4] Resolutely proclaim: "It affects His Lordship's honor, so I will disregard such a directive."

---

1 That is, to retire from service and leave the mundane world by taking the tonsure, and spend one's days praying for the repose of the deceased's soul.

2 Katsushige's daughter, who married Uesugi Sadakatsu (1604–1645). She died in 1635.

3 Formerly a retainer of Hata Nobutoki, he later entered the service of the Nabeshima clan.

4 This incident is related to when Yatsunami Musashi was tasked with escorting Oyasu, the adopted daughter of Ryūzōji Takanobu (1529–1584), to her arranged wedding with Hata Mikawa-no-Kami of Karatsu to form a familial alliance. She became very ill on route, and Musashi avowed to follow her in death to save the reputation of the province should she die on his watch. See Book 8-47.

❋ ❋ ❋

137. When visitors call upon me in the quiet depths of the mountain, I inquire of the affairs of the world. They tell me that relations between the Nabeshima domain and the shogunate are harmonious, and of the compassionate governance of the fiefdom. It is fortuitous indeed, and I think there is no other clan as magnificent as the Nabeshima anywhere else in Japan. It is an august house that will correct itself instinctively should calamity befall it. It is a portent of protection by the spirits of our ancestors for the fief to be administered so splendidly.

❋ ❋ ❋

138. A certain *rōnin* came to me and complained after being deposed from service. He said, "It is unfair that I should be forbidden from leaving this domain when I have no means to eat. I could at least find a way to eke out a living if permitted to seek employment in another fief. With no stipend to subsist on, I may soon be pushed into committing felonies."

I reasoned with him by saying: "Be pleased that you are forbidden from going elsewhere. The *rōnin* lifestyle that you are being forced to endure is a valuable lesson from your lord. That you are allowed to reside here instead of being exiled is proof that he still holds you dear. No other domain has such strong bonds of fealty. Your lord is certainly thinking of reinstating you after a period of chastisement. If your situation has not improved after several years, then you can start thinking of committing 'felonies.' It seems to me that you are just saying such things through privation, and the boorish resentment you have for your lord. You are in danger of being punished even more with such a repugnant attitude."

He retorted, "Retainers in the Saga domain these days sleep until late morning, and feign maladies to avoid their duties. They are exceedingly self-indulgent." I rejoined: "That is precisely the strength of this domain. A retainer from other clans who tries to influence matters with his guile and cleverness will become disgruntled if he does not receive due recognition. The loyalty of such a man tends to vacillate because he believes there are no rewards for him here, and he would be given a higher position elsewhere. On the other hand, hereditary vassals do not waver. Without ever having to be taught, we awaken when we please in the knowledge that we are kindred members of our domain, a big family, from the day we are born, to the day we die. Can such indomitable trust be found elsewhere?"

He then argued, "Even though we warriors of the Saga domain boast of our unmatched valor, is this not our own prejudiced view unknown to others? Is it written about anywhere other than here?" I answered, "The intrepid martial spirit of Nabeshima warriors has indeed been chronicled for posterity. Recall the battle at Shimabara saw 400 of our men slain.[1] This exceeds the number of men killed in action at the fall of Kamakura (Genkō Incident), which saw the demise of the Hōjō family.[2] Surely, this is testament to the Nabeshima fighting spirit. In addition, Lords Taikō[3] and Gongen[4] rewarded us for our valor on a number of occasions. Evidence of Nabeshima heroism is incontravertible."

A samurai who spends an extended period of time away from service, so it seems, will become jaded and harbor hatred against he who caused his suffering. He will talk disparagingly of his lord, which

---

1 Not to be confused with the Shimabara Uprising of 1637–1638 in which Nabeshima warriors were mobilized by the bakufu to quell the Christian-inspired peasant uprising. This "Battle of Shimabara" took place in 1584 and pitted the Saga forces against Shimazu Iehisa of the Satsuma province. The Saga warriors were defeated, and Ryūzōji Takanobu (1529–1584), daimyo of the Hizen province, was killed.

2 The Genkō Incident (1331–1333) led to the fall of the Kamakura shogunate. After returning from exile, Emperor Go-Daigo was determined to restore imperial rule and successfully enlisted the help of Ashikaga Takauji, the Kamakura general sent to suppress his rebellion. Nitta Yoshisada, who was in turn directed to punish them both, instead marched on Kamakura and destroyed the Hōjō regency and the Kamakura shogunate. Go-Daigo then instigated the Kemmu Restoration (1333–1336), which marked the formation of the Muromachi shogunate.

3 Literally meaning "retired regent," this was a commonly used name for Toyotomi Hideyoshi (1536–1598). Hideyoshi employed the services of Nabeshima Naoshige and his son Katsushige in his Korean campaigns.

4 Another name for Tokugawa Ieyasu (1542–1616) after his enshrinement in the Tōshōgū Shrine in Nikkō. At the Battle of Sekigahara in 1600, Nabeshima Katsushige changed allegiance to support Ieyasu, thereby contributing to this crucial victory, and paving the way for the establishment of the Tokugawa shogunate.

is why his luck expires rendering him unlikely to be reinstated.

❀ ❀ ❀

139. Revel in being discarded, or having exhausted all your energies in vain; only those who have endured hardship will be of use. Samurai who have never erred before will never have what it takes.

❀ ❀ ❀

140. As I mentioned in *Gukenshū*,[1] the highest level of service is to be able to advise the lord through the position of *karō* (chief retainer). Engaging in trivialities can be forgiven as long as one understands this. Still, nobody seems to grasp what this means. There are flatterers who curry favor with the lord and senior retainers through mercenary desires for advancement, but their aspirations are limited, and they do not seek the lofty heights of becoming a chief retainer. Some with more gumption disavow ambitions for success and become reserved in their service, preferring instead to read books such as *Tsurezuregusa*[2] and *Senshūshō*.[3] Kenkō and Saigyō were no more than lily-livered cowards. They masqueraded as writers because they were

---

1 See Book 1-19.

2 Translated into English as "Essays in Idleness," this book was written possibly between 1330 and 1332 by a famous monk named Yoshida (Urabe) Kenkō (ca 1283–ca 1352). It is a philosophical mishmash that remains one of the most admired examples of Japanese prose. In his youth, Kenkō served as a steward to Horikawa Tomomori, maternal grandfather of Emperor Go-Nijō (r. 1301–1308). For reasons unknown, he became a Buddhist monk in 1313. Retaining his connection with the imperial court, he was also a renowned adherent of the Nijō school of poetry in which he became one of the so-called "four deva kings." *Tsurezuregusa*, however, is prose rather than poetry, and consists of 243 brief passages of varying lengths. Characteristic of his writings is the theme of *mujō*, or the transience of worldly things.

3 *Senshūshō* ("Condensed Selection of Stories") was authored by Saigyō (1118–1190), a celebrated *waka* poet and Buddhist priest. It consists of 109 anecdotes contained in nine volumes, and was probably written in 1187. He was originally born into a samurai family in Kyoto. He served as a guard for Emperor Toba (r. 1107–1123), and later became a friend of the former Emperor Sutoku (r. 1123–1142). He took the tonsure at the age of 22, and became famous for his travels throughout the provinces, during which he wrote many poems about nature. He mainly resided in a temple on Mt. Kōya and in his later years, his prestige as a monk and a poet was such that many men, including

afraid to serve as samurai. A man who has renounced the world to become a monk, or old men retired from duty, may become absorbed in such books. But to be a useful vassal to his lord, a warrior must be completely devoted to him amidst his pursuit of glory, or even after falling into the chasms of hell.

❀ ❀ ❀

141. As my father was already 70 when I was born, he remarked: "I might just bequeath the lad to someone like a salt merchant." When Taku Zusho[1] overheard this, he chided him by saying, "Lord Katsushige often says that you, Jin'uemon, are a dedicated but unassuming retainer, serving from the shadows. Such dependable service will ensure that your offspring are looked after, and remain helpful to the lord." Following this, he bestowed upon me the name "Matsukame," and Edayoshi Rizaemon performed the *hakama-tsuke* ceremony on my behalf.[2]

From the age of nine, I was summoned as a page for Lord Mitsushige, whereby I was called "Fukei." When I attended Master Tsunashige I would jump onto the *kotatsu*,[3] creating mischief, and we would carry each other on our backs. Everybody viewed me as an out-and-out ragamuffin.

When I became 13, I was ordered by Lord Mitsushige to raise my forelocks.[4] I confined myself to my quarters for one year, after which I reported back for duty as a page on the first day of the fifth month with my new name of "Ichijū." After that, Kuranaga Rihei assisted me as my *eboshi-oya*[5] in the *genpuku* ceremony, and then

---

nobles, priests, and military leaders sought his tutelage. One of the main themes in his poems was the concept of *sabi*, or the lonely, austere beauty in things.

1 Jōchō's godfather.

2 The *hakama* is a traditional formal attire for men that resembles a divided skirt. The ceremony for fitting a *hakama* was conducted at the age of five.

3 A charcoal brazier in a floor well.

4 Hairstyles were changed as a symbol of coming-of-age. Growing forelocks enabled the fashioning of a topknot.

5 A person who puts an *eboshi* (black lacquered headgear) on a young man's head during his ceremony of attaining manhood (*genpuku*).

facilitated my appointment as his assistant scribe. Thanks to his gracious intercession, Rihei announced: "As you can also compose poetry Gon'nojō,[1] the young Prince Tsunashige has asked that you serve him." This meant a temporary cessation of my duties. I learned later that his intention was to have me replace him in this post.

In any case, being dismissed I was not invited to accompany Lord Mitsushige to Edo, so was left dangling in the wind and very disheartened about my prospects. At that time, the priest Tannen[2] was residing in Matsuse. As he was on friendly terms with my late father, he was asked to look out for me, and I often paid him a visit. I even contemplated becoming a monk myself.

Seeing my predicament, I heard that Yamamoto Gorōzaemon[3] had a private conversation with Nakano Kazuma about sharing some of the land left by my father. Just as I had sworn upon Hachiman, the god of war, that I would never accept such a handout, I was suddenly called to the domain administration office and informed that I would be receiving an extra rice stipend. (Two others received the same as me.)

As a samurai, it would not do to be looked down upon as lowly, so day and night I thought of ways to excel in service. I visited Gorōzaemon every evening to chat. Gorōzaemon said one night, "I heard from an old-timer that 'A man who seeks only fame and power (*myōri*) is not a true retainer. Then again, he who doesn't is not a true retainer either.' This contradiction warrants serious contemplation." After thinking about his counsel carefully, the answer suddenly dawned on me.

I realized the ultimate responsibility of a vassal is to petition his lord when necessary for the upkeep of the domain. One cannot do this while floundering at the bottom of the retainer ladder. Thus, working one's way to the top as chief retainer (*karō*) was the supreme paradigm of service. It became clear that a retainer should pursue fame and authority, not for personal gratification, but for the purpose

---

1 Gon'nojō was the name given to Jōchō after his *genpuku* ceremony. Not to be confused with Jōchō's adopted son, who was also given the same name.

2 See Book 1-39.

3 Jōchō's nephew, who was actually much senior in age and mentored him.

of singular service. I resolved to reach the exalted position of chief retainer. It has always been remarked that a young man promoted to a high position of responsibility too quickly generally betrays the expectations placed on him. So, I worked hard day in, day out, shedding not quite crimson tears, but yellow ones of grief, so that I might be recognized in my fifties. My training and procedures were consistent with the principles of the Kakuzō style[1] of *jūjutsu*.[2]

As I noted in *Gukenshū*, those retainers who were punished after His Lordship's death brought this divine retribution upon themselves through their narcissism. Although it may appear that this rendition of my life is immodest, providence has driven me to where I am, and I relate it to you unreservedly as a monk in idle conversation.

❀ ❀ ❀

The next morning:[3]

> *Partake of this simmering rice gruel, savoring the warm sentiment of this winter sanctuary* (Kisui)[4]

> *Wilted stalks of morning glory smoldering in the hearth, our hearts alight* (Komaru).[5]

---

1 In other words, simplistic but highly practical. See Book 2-2.
2 In the Yamamoto version of *Hagakure*, the following material is also included after this. "In spite of my undying efforts, my lord breathed his last before I could be promoted to this position. With his death, men who already occupied the highest posts were acting in a sordid manner, bringing nothing but disgrace to the lord, and so I became a monk in lieu of death to uphold his honor. When I think about it, although I was unable to meet my objective of serving as chief retainer, in a sense, the years of perpetual effort to reach this goal are equivalent to fulfillment. It is true that once a man establishes his purpose, he will eventually be able to realize his aspirations."
3 If one compares this with the two poems which appear at the beginning of the first book, it would seem that the next morning is referring to the sixth day of the third month, 1710. Although the dictation took place over many years, the intention of Jōchō and Tsuramoto is to give the reader the impression that all of the discussions were conducted overnight in one continuous sitting.
4 Tashiro Tsuramoto's pseudonym.
5 Yamamoto Jōchō's pseudonym.

Books 3~11
Selected Vignettes

闇書三~十一

PERTAINING TO FEALTY

3-1. Lord Naoshige once remarked: "Nothing is felt so profoundly as *giri*.[1] There are tragic occurrences, such as when my cousin died, that do not even elicit my tears. Then, for some reason I listen to tales of men who lived 50 years or even 100 years ago, with whom I have no affinity or relation to, and I cry from a sense of *giri*."

❊ ❊ ❊

3-9. A newcomer among Lord Naoshige's attendants was shown preferential treatment by His Lordship. One day, some of the older retainers decided to express their objections to Lord Naoshige. "Sire, we see that you are showing favoritism to a certain attendant who has not fought with us in battle, and we cannot see how he can be of use in a critical time of need. Pray tell, why do you treat him so kindly?"

After listening to them Lord Naoshige replied, "What you say is true. Although he may not be of use in battle, for some reason he caught my eye, and I feel comfortable apportioning him tasks of a menial nature. How can I ask men with proven service, such as your good selves, to toil away in tedious tasks? I need you most when danger threatens."

❊ ❊ ❊

3-16. Suffering in the throes of destitution, one day Saitō Yōnosuke's[2]

---

1 *Giri* is an important concept that refers to the "obligation" to act in accordance with established social protocols. In the context of samurai, the concept referred mainly to their obligation of service to their liege lord, even if it meant sacrificing their lives in their enduring quest to repay the favor (*on*) bestowed upon them. In this example, Naoshige is referring to the sense of obligation to unrelated ancestors allied to the clan who helped forge the culture and ways of his beloved domain.

2 Saitō Yōnosuke was a celebrated retainer of Nabeshima Naoshige who proved his martial prowess during the expeditions in Korea. Nevertheless, he appears to have been quite a problematic fellow in the ensuing peace of the Tokugawa period. Because of his brusque personality, he did not endear himself to many of his superiors, resulting in

wife bemoaned that had they run out of rice for the evening meal. Yōnosuke picked up his swords and left the house saying, "As the wife of a samurai it peeves me that you fret about such a trifle. There is rice everywhere. Wait here."

He came across horses laden with bags of rice. Yōnosuke asked the farmers, "Where are you headed with that cargo?" They replied, "To the servant's galley in the castle." "If that is so, bring your horses this way, to my house. I am Saitō Yōnosuke, and I am due to collect rice from the officials. It must be quite a burden for you to lug such heavy consignments hither and thither. Leave it in my care and present my receipt of delivery to your village headman."

His request did not win the peasants over, and they tried to continue on their way. Yōnosuke flew into a rage and unsheathed his sword. "I will not allow even one of you to pass!" The peasants were left with no choice but to haul the bales of rice into Yōnosuke's home in exchange for his receipt. Yōnosuke crowed to his wife, "Behold this mountain of rice! Use it as you please."

When news of the incident surfaced, Yōnosuke was interrogated and readily admitted his guilty conduct. After the trial he was sentenced to death. As was customary, Lord Katsushige told his aide: "Report the episode of Yōnosuke's wrongdoing to my father, Lord Kashū (Naoshige)."[1] The news was delivered to Lord Naoshige in the third citadel (san-no-maru) by the official.[2]

The retired lord listened to the account, and addressed his wife without responding to the messenger. "My dear, Yōnosuke is to be executed. This is terrible news. Putting his life on the line for me many times in a manner worth more than all the warriors of Japan and China put together, he fought tooth and nail in bloody defense of Hizen.[3] It's thanks to the service of valiant men like him that we

---

demotion and cuts to his stipend. A demonstration of his impetuousness can be seen in the following vignette, Book 3-17.

1 The first daimyo of the Nabeshima domain and Katsushige's father.

2 The Saga Castle consisted of four citadels referred to as *ichi-no-maru*, *ni-no-maru*, *san-no-maru*, and *nishi-no-maru*.

3 Hizen was the region that included the fiefs of Saga, Karatsu, Hirado, Ōmura, and Shimabara. In this context, Noashige is referring only to the Saga domain.

can now live in peace as lord and lady of the fief. He is a man with no peer who lays claim to countless feats of valor in battle. If anyone is guilty of a terrible wrongdoing, it is I. My neglect led such a dedicated vassal to be plagued by misery without even food in his bowl. How could I bear to see such a hapless vassal put to death?"

With tears in their eyes, both lord and lady grieved over Yōnosuke's fate. The official was shocked to see such an outpouring of heartache, and hurried back to Lord Katsushige to inform him of their distress. Lord Katsushige was moved. "How compassionate my parents are. I have been searching for ways to live up to my filial obligations, and it now seems unthinkable to execute Yōnosuke given their respect for him. Return to the third citadel and inform my parents that I have rescinded my decision."

When the retired Lord Naoshige heard of his son's intention to exonerate Yōnosuke, he put his hands together and prostrated himself in the direction of the inner citadel. "Though he is my son, I am deeply indebted to him for his show of clemency. This is a wonderful gift indeed."

❀ ❀ ❀

3-17. Lord Katsushige was observing a shooting practice for his vassals. When Saitō Yōnosuke stepped up to the mark, he aimed his arquebus high, and fired. Lord Katsushige was informed by the target attendant, "No musket ball, Sire." Yōnosuke stood tall and exclaimed for all to hear: "Of course there isn't! Until now, I have never shot musket balls into mounds of dirt; but, I have a curious habit of never missing the torso of a live enemy. This can be corroborated by the fact that Lord Hida[1] is still alive!"

Lord Katsushige was incensed by this outburst, and was inclined to cut Yōnosuke down in his tracks. He returned to the castle fuming instead, putting a damper on what had otherwise been a good day. Upon returning to the castle, Lord Katsushige visited his father in the third citadel, the retired Lord Naoshige, and angrily relayed the

---

1 Nabeshima Naoshige.

incident. "This is what happened… Yōnosuke didn't treat me as his lord and went out of his way to embarrass me. Although tempted to kill him there and then, your long and treasured relationship with him stayed my hand. I ask you now, how is he to be castigated for his insolence?"

When Katsushige had at last calmed down, Lord Naoshige responded, "Indeed, your anger is understandable. Thus, I advise you to have his unit captain commit *seppuku* immediately." Lord Katsushige was flabbergasted by this response. "It was not the unit captain at fault. It was Yōnosuke. I am inquiring how I should punish Yōnosuke." Lord Naoshige was insistent. "I recently instructed the unit captains that 'Young warriors tend to let their guard down, and forget how to wield their weapons in this extended period of peace and tranquillity in the realm. They will not be able to perform in battle should the need arise without regular training to augment military preparedness. Let's avert this problem by first having the men practice on the firing range in front of Shinano-no-Kami.'[1] My intention was to make this exercise for young untrained warriors; but to insist that an old warhorse like Yōnosuke shoot together with inexperienced men is offensive, and so the unit captain should be held culpable. What Yōnosuke said was on the mark! I bear witness to his past exploits. The unit captain is to be sentenced to death immediately." Lord Katsushige apologized for his thoughtlessness, and the problem faded away.

❀ ❀ ❀

3-52. Since his youth, Saitō Sado was an outstanding martial artist who performed countless meritorious feats of courage. He was noticed by Lord Naoshige, and brought into his service. Nevertheless, although a fearless warrior in war, he lacked the skills to serve expediently during times of peace. Unable to make ends meet, he and his family were on the verge of starvation. As it was doubtful

---

1 "Shinano-no-Kami" was an honorable name for Nabeshima Katsushige, literally meaning "Lord of Shinano."

whether Sado could survive until the eve of the New Year, he announced: "The only thing left for me to do is cut my gut." His son Yōnosuke tried to stay his hand by saying, "Let's try and find an alternative first." Sado said, "There's really no point in going on, constantly worrying about little things. Let's do something shockingly evil, and then go meet our deaths." His son assented, "All right then, let's do it."

They went to the Takao Bridge. As they waited for an opportunity to stage their sinful swan song, they saw horses lugging sacks of rice pass by. Disregarding convoys of only one or two packhorses, when a column of ten traversed the bridge they unsheathed their swords, chased the drivers away, and stole the cargo of rice.

News of the wicked incident spread far. A report was made by Inuzuka Sōbei, the inspector in charge of transporting rice. The magistrates deliberated on the matter and recommended to Lord Katsushige that Sado and his son be sentenced to death forthwith.

The magistrates went to the third citadel, and Fujishima Shōeki reported the verdict to Lord Naoshige. He and his wife were both distraught to hear the news, and were rendered speechless. Shōeki withdrew, and reported their reaction to Lord Katsushige. He was taken aback and decided to annul the death sentence. Instead, he released Sado and Yōnosuke from his service. He sent the magistrates to the third citadel again to convey his decision.

Lord Naoshige called the magistrates before him and declared: "It's as if I forced Sado to commit daylight robbery. Sado accomplished many praiseworthy exploits in battle and made quite a name for himself. Alas, as he was not as adept in service in normal times, I didn't afford him an adequate stipend. I must confess, I had forgotten about him in this era of peace. I can only assume that he committed the unlawful act out of exasperation. I am ashamed, but also thankful and overjoyed that Shinano-no-Kami (Katsushige) took face-saving measures out of filial duty by dismissing them instead of condemning them to die. I was dumbstruck when I heard of their malefaction, thinking it out of place for me to request leniency."

The magistrates took their leave. Shōeki was subsequently ordered to present Sado with 10 *koku* of rice. Later, when Lord Naoshige passed away, Sado and his son submitted to martyr themselves in his wake, to which Lord Katsushige said, "If you feel so inclined, continue serving me." Still, Sado persisted in seeking permission to die, and both committed *seppuku*. Yōnosuke's second son, Gon'uemon, martyred himself when Lord Katsushige passed. Three generations died with their lords.

❀ ❀ ❀

4-2. When Lord Katsushige was about to retire, he recommended that Hyakutake Iori, Ikuno Oribe, and Iwamura Shin'uemon should continue to serve at his grandson Lord Mitsushige's side. Apparently he said: "Iori is a logician. Oribe is compassionate and works diligently without making a fuss. Shin'uemon is conscientious, and exerts himself without erring. Each has a necessary attribute to closely attend a daimyo."[1]

❀ ❀ ❀

4-49. Lord Katsushige was known to say, "There are four different types of retainers: swift-sluggish, sluggish-swift, swift-swift, and sluggish-sluggish." According to Lord Katsushige: "The swift-swift retainers can understand instructions quickly, and carry them out in an expedient manner. These are the best vassals, but are few and far between. Men like Fukuchi Kichizaemon are of this caliber.[2] The sluggish-swift retainers are slow in understanding, but are able to execute their orders quickly. Nakano Kazuma is a good example. Swift-sluggish retainers are diligent in obeying instructions, but are often slow at completing their duties. These are many. The rest all fall into the category of sluggish-sluggish."

❀ ❀ ❀

---

1 All of these men were elders.
2 See Book 7-43 below.

4-60. During Lord Katsushige's reign, each boy would start attending at the age of 11 or 12, regardless of his father's high or low station. They received instruction in all manner of assignments, enabling many of them to be employed as attendants. Over 70 attendants are said to have been in his service. Soejima Hachi'uemon retained his forelock and continued serving as a page until he turned 42, and Nabeshima Kanbei until the age of 40.[1] As long-standing servants, they knew Lord Katsushige intimately, were very familiar with the positions and duties both in Edo and the domain, and were accustomed to entertaining feudal lords, and knew them all. Following Lord Katsushige's example they were highly disciplined samurai. As soon as they underwent the *genpuku* ritual and they removed their forelocks [to officially mark their coming of age], and made excellent samurai. Back in those days, young lads were not permitted to inherit their family headship and its assets when their fathers died, so they worked conscientiously to make their own way in the world.

One day, on the way to Edo to fulfill *sankin-kōtai* obligations,[2] a message needed to be sent from Odawara to the shogunate. The senior attendants intended to appoint a messenger from their coterie, but no one was deemed capable of articulating the information properly. Saitō Sakutayū was selected from among the pages, and a *genpuku* ceremony was conducted to remove his forelock; then he was set off with a rank suitable for the task.

❀ ❀ ❀

5-66. One year, while traveling to Edo for the first time after retirement, the lord [and his entourage] stayed overnight in Osaka. Mawatari Kakubei and Yajima Hikobei were designated as nightwatchmen. Kakubei fell asleep when Hikobei went to the privy. His Lordship woke up and beckoned to the guards, but there was no response. He tried to get up but was unable to on account of his sore back, so he crawled to the next room. It was at this moment when Hikobei

1 See Book 1-112.
2 See footnote for Book 1-194.

returned. His Lordship asked: "Who is the other guard?" But sensing his wrath, Hikobei refrained from saying anything. Kakubei could be seen asleep in a seated position, with his face and chest pressed against the floor. His Lordship relieved Kakubei and Hikobei of their guard duties, and summoned the elders. When they came, His Lordship said: "Those two are incapable of carrying out their duties. I will not tolerate such insubordination. Are not the night watchmen the only ones we can rely on during the hours of darkness? They do not have the right mental attitude for this life-or-death task. Interrogate them thoroughly and report back to me."

After grilling the men, the elders reported, "We express regret for their misconduct, and ask that they be sent back to Saga to be judged by Lord Tsunashige." Then His Lordship said, "It was not Hikobei's fault. As for Kakubei, find out whether or not he was sleeping with his head on a pillow." Another investigation was conducted, but it was obvious that Kakubei did not use a pillow, and His Lordship was informed that he inadvertently fell asleep in spite of his best efforts, and sank to the floor. His Lordship replied, "If that is the case, then he wasn't as slipshod as I thought. He must have been exhausted, so it can't be helped if he slept while on duty, dropping to the floor as he did. We should send him back to Saga to rest; but then Kakubei will be ordered to commit *seppuku* if Lord Tsunashige finds out the reason for his early return. Send them both to Edo first as punishment."

Whenever His Lordship thought offenders had reasonable pretexts for their actions, he would first interrogate them, hear what they had to say, and then forgive them. If he thought the accusation had no justification, he would look for extenuating factors and formulate an explanation on the perpetrator's behalf to exonerate him. Everybody was thankful for his merciful disposition.

❀ ❀ ❀

5-98. A few years ago, the status of the Ogi, Hasuike, and Kashima lords became high enough to be awarded prestigious duties by the shogunate.[1] They were also expected to present the government with gifts, as was the custom for lords, of the same level as the main family.[2] At that time Prince Tsunashige had still not succeeded the clan headship and was living in Edo. He complained to his father, Lord Mitsushige, upon hearing of the situation, saying that the hierarchical relationship between the main family and branch families would be jeopardized. Lord Mitsushige warned the three branch lords, but they refused to comply. The problem worsened, creating discord between the main family and the three branches. The chief retainers discussed the issue day and night, but were unable to find a solution.

Nakano Shōgen[3] appeared before Lord Mitsushige, saying: "In spite of our deliberations we cannot agree on an adequate settlement. I have given it considerable thought, as antagonism between the main family and branch families constitutes a clan emergency. I have formed some opinions and would like to offer them to you.

"You show me great munificence by taking me into your service and even allotting stipends for each of my children, which is much more than I could ever ask for. This bespeaks your paternal affection for us. When considered in this light, I have come to realize the state of affairs surrounding our three branch families is different from the three [Tokugawa] families of Owari, Kii, and Mito, or the allotment of fiefs in other domains. As it is Lord Katsushige's offspring who serve the government, you should always regard them as your children, and cherish them as your treasures, as you do Lord Shinshū (Tsunashige). The better they conduct their duties for the government, the more it should gratify His Lordship. The fact that the three lords are fulfilling their obligations well does not harm the clan in any way. On the contrary, it brings us prestige.

"People have misunderstood this, and have become incensed at

---

1 Records indicate that the third lord of the Ogi sub-domain, Nabeshima Mototake, was appointed as *gochisō-yaku*, or the official tasked with entertaining important visitors to Edo Castle, in 1692. This date is at odds with what is recorded in this section of *Hagakure*.

2 See Book 1-101.

3 See Book 2-129.

the branch families for doing a fine job. The three lords are angry at this pitiful treatment, and criticized you for allowing it. Nobody knows how this situation will end for our clan if such discord continues. Until the age of Taiseiin (Lord Katsushige), all retainers designated to serve the lords of the three branch families would come before His Lordship without hesitation. There was never any distinction made between samurai of the main family and branch families on festive days and the like, and they were afforded the same esteem.

"Recently, however, retainers of the branch families have been treated disparagingly as 'servants of the three lords,' and being offended, many have left Saga. Consequently, their masters are also becoming indignant despite our previous good relationship. I'm sure it must be perplexing for the three lords that people should be maddened simply because they are serving the shogunate commendably.

"Thus, I think the weight of blame lies with us. You need to invite Lord Kashū[1] [of Ogi] and say: 'We express regret for our misconduct. Some young men made senseless remarks, and their elders agreed. The bitter recrimination is unbearable. This preposterous situation is largely due to my oversight. I am to blame, and I take full responsibility. From now on, it behoves me to make amends, and unite the families. Hereafter, you will treated the same as Shinano-no-Kami (Tsunashige) so that we can foster everlasting peace in the fiefdom. As you are a senior counselor with considerable experience, I call upon you to help convince the other lords to join me in setting right this most disagreeable predicament. I will talk sense into Shinano-no-Kami in person.' If you frame it like this, Lord Kashū will be vindicated, and the problem can be resolved."

Lord Mitsushige agreed. "This is very true. I was wrong. Please go and meet Kashū and relay this sentiment."

As the quarrel was still in full swing, Shōgen wasn't sure if Lord Kashū would be prepared to grant an audience to him, even if he went to Ogi. He thought it prudent to send Fukae Tōemon in his place, as he was related to the lord through marriage. Tōemon was

---

1   Nabeshima Kaga-no-Kami Naoyoshi (1623–1689). Motoshige's son, and second lord of the Ogi sub-domain.

asked to explain: "Shōgen would like to come to Ogi for counsel, and what he has to say will be in your best interest, so please lend him your ear." Shōgen then departed for Ogi and Kashū agreed to meet him straight away. Shōgen said to him: "Tanshū (Lord Mitsushige) would like you to come to Saga within one or two days. I know not what this is regarding, but I feel it would be good for all families." Shōgen returned after confirming which day Kashū would visit.

On the day of the appointment, Lord Kashū came to Saga with his son, Kishū.[1] He told him, "Wait in the west citadel as I am sure you will also be summoned later." He then proceeded to the castle for an audience with Lord Mitsushige.

Lord Mitsushige started with the following speech: "A trouble-some quarrel has erupted with the three lords, and regrettably the problem is yet to be resolved. After careful rumination, it is clear that we are at fault…" He offered a comprehensive explanation of his thoughts, prompting Kashū to shed many tears. He interrupted, "Please say no more. I understand what you are saying, and am humbled. Given my position, I must also take responsibility for allowing the young men to say the things they did. I will take care of the problem from here, so please worry no more. I have brought my son, Kii-no-Kami, with me. Please let him hear your views directly." He brought his son without delay to Lord Mitsushige. Kashū swore an oath on a *Kumano goō* talisman,[2] and father and son sub-mitted a blood pledge (*keppan*) of reconciliation.

Shōgen never sought credit for this successful resolution.[3] He kept it secret forever, and simply reported that His Lordship had devised the whole plan himself. Showing himself to be a truly con-siderate, loyal servant, it was only to me that he divulged the real course of events in strict confidence.

As it was a secret, Yamamoto Jōchō only confessed it to me on

---

1   Nabeshima Kii-no-Kami Mototake (1662–1713).

2   Distributed by Kumano Sanzan, the three major shrines (Kumano Hongū Taisha Shrine, Kumano Hayatama Taisha Shrine, and Kumano Nachi Taisha Shrine), these talismans were used for *kishōmon* (sworn oath) from the Heian period through to early modern times.

3   See Book 2-129.

the seventh day of the twelfth month, Shōtoku 3 (1713) in his peaceful abode.

He said: "Many times over the years have I observed talented servants expounding clever ideas who take the credit and bring their lords into disrepute. Your recommendations should be communicated quietly, and make it seem to others as if it was his idea when the result is favorable. A loyal retainer whose family has served for generations should be prepared to take the fall for all the wrongful deeds committed by his master. It is understandable, then, why Nakano Takumi never revealed that he was the first to reach the Arima Castle at the time of the Shimabara Rebellion, or why a servant would secretly offer advice to his lord as I mentioned. According to some senior retainers, if the Nabeshima clan is to fall, it will be through discord with the three families."

An old samurai once recalled: "The three families in Lord Katsushige's era were his offspring, and they were treated equally. It was like having four young lords, and so it added to the prestige of the clan. The three lived in their residences inside the castle precincts, and the men appointed to serve in Ogi were trusted retainers of Lord Naoshige, and several trustworthy men were attached to the Hasuike and Kashima lords. These excellent samurai lived around the castle, and whenever they needed to speak with Lord Katsushige, they would simply proceed to the antechamber, announce 'There is business to discuss,' and appear before the lord. When men were needed for various duties or tasks, they were summoned regardless of whom they served under, and on festive days and the like, all retainers participated and were treated on equal terms.

"After Lord Katsushige passed away, Lord Mitsushige took over headship of the domain. As he had been raised in Edo, he had little knowledge of the old customs and lore of the clan. Even the elder Okabe Kunai was dismissed as a bannerman (*hatamoto*) of the Tokugawa shogunate, and Sagara Kyūma was appointed from outside the clan, so they had no veritable knowledge of the Nabeshima family traditions. This is why they transferred Lord Getsudō's[1] mausoleum

---

1 Nabeshima Motoshige, founder of the Ogi sub-domain.

in the Kōdenji Temple and partitioned the grounds with a hedge wall. They copied the 'Three Family' system of the Tokugawa family, and dealt with their retainers as if they were servants of servants, and not of the main family. When they visited the Saga Castle they were forced to wait by the entrance. Kunai and Kyūma made it increasingly difficult for them to be granted an audience with the lord, excluding them in all matters. Those who served the three lords became outraged saying, 'It was us who brought serenity to the clan through our generations of service. There is nothing we can do if these newcomers insist on being so contemptuous, so we shan't visit Saga again.' With this, they all departed Saga. Their lords also confined themselves to their own castles. With the mausoleum for Lord Getsudō being moved again to Sōchiji Temple, the sense of alienation became even greater.

"The Nabeshima clan is distinct from other daimyo houses regarding sub or branch families; but the fractious events that transpired were regrettable, and it was not what Lord Katsushige would have desired. Recently, it seems as though the families have come closer together, which is a great relief.

"The attendants of the branch families started referring to Lord Mitsushige as the 'head family' and their own masters as their true 'lords.' When Lord Katsushige was leading the clan, the branch system was comparatively good. The new lord's retainers put an end to this, but I am happy to see that the situation has improved of late.

According to Yamamoto Jin'uemon (Jōchō's father), 'All of the men in Ogi were deeply trusted by Lord Naoshige. Half of them followed him in death at the time of his passing. The remainder were trustworthy fellows who served in outstanding fashion. Despite being halved in number, they were still unable to be outdone.'"

※ ※ ※

7-6. With the passing of Lord Kōkokuin,[1] his aide Ezoe Kinbei took his ashes to Mount Kōya to be consecrated. Kinbei then shut himself

---

1 Nabeshima Hizen-no-Kami Tadanao. Nabeshima Katsushige's heir.

away in a hermitage and carved a figurine of his master from wood, and another of him prostrating before him. Kinbei returned home, probably on the first anniversary of his death, and committed *oibara*.[1] The statue he carved was brought from Mount Kōya and enshrined at the Kōdenji Temple in Saga.

❀ ❀ ❀

7-43. A story about Fukuchi Kichizaemon and the meal of crane. Crane meat was served when Lord Katsushige entertained guests. A guest remarked, "Sire, I hear that you can tell whether the meat is from a white or black crane just by tasting it. Is this true?" Lord Katsushige replied, "It is indeed the case." The guest then inquired, "Which variety is on today's *carte du jour*?" "It is *manazuru*, white crane." The guest was still doubtful. "Can it really be true? I would like to verify this claim with somebody in the galley." Lord Katsushige summoned Fukuchi Kichizaemon from the kitchen. It just happened that Kichizaemon was secretly listening to their exchange. He rushed back to the kitchen and swigged several large bowls of *saké*, before finally making an appearance after repeated requests. By this time, Kichizaemon was heavily intoxicated and his slurred words were barely legible. "It's errr, umm, black, white… no, it's a blackish…" Lord Katsushige reprimanded him for being drunk and sent him back to the kitchen…[2]

❀ ❀ ❀

8-22. Yamamoto Gorōzaemon[3] protested to the priest Chōon when he was serving in Edo. Before Lord Tsunashige succeeded his father in becoming head of the clan, he received instruction in the teachings of Buddha from the priest Chōon.[4] He was to be awarded an

---

1 In 1626.
2 This section continues with exactly the same content as 4-49 regarding the four types of retainers.
3 Tsunetomo's nephew.
4 Also referred to as Kaion.

inka by the priest, confirming his awakening in Buddhism. It was an event that stirred much rumor among the senior retainers in the mansion. Hearing the tittle-tattle surrounding the affair, Yamamoto Gorōzaemon, who was serving as one of Tsunashige's attendants and was an inspector (*o-metsuke*), was displeased by the timing of events and decided to pay the priest a visit at his temple in Edo. His intention was to convince the priest to cancel the bestowal, or cut him down with his sword if he refused.

The priest greeted him in a dignified manner as a worshipper to the temple. Gorōzaemon said, "There is something that I must talk with you about in private, so please send your acolytes away." Moving closer he whispered sternly, "It is rumored that you intend to present Shinano-no-Kami[1] with an *inka*. Having been born in the province of Hizen, I am sure that you are aware of the history and customs of the Ryūzōji-Nabeshima clan. Compared to other domains, ours has a long history of successive generations, and must continue with the lord and his men working together harmoniously. Until now, no leader of the Nabeshima clan has been endowed with an award of advanced knowledge in Buddhist teachings. If His Lordship was to be presented with an *inka*, he would become fixated on his 'enlightenment,' and the lord-follower relationship will unravel through his condescension of his retainers' opinions as if they were insects. This would cause a rift between the lord and his men and, it must be said, would be terribly harmful to the wellbeing of the clan. Men in high positions are predisposed to arrogance, so I implore you by all means to desist from awarding him the *inka*. If you refuse my request, I will be forced to take action."

A little flustered at first, the priest recovered his equanimity. "I admire your intentions, and I fully understand the condition of the domain. You sir, are a retainer of commendable loyalty." Gorōzaemon interjected saying, "Stop with your ruses. I did not come to receive acclaim from you. I only want to hear that you will abandon your plans to present His Lordship with a Dharma transmission." The priest responded by saying, "What you ask is reasonable. I will not

---

1 Nabeshima Tsunashige.

present him with the transmission, ever." After confirming the priest's promise one more time, Gorōzaemon left the temple. Master Jōchō was told of this episode by Gorōzaemon.

❀　❀　❀

8-24. Lord Katsushige went falcon hunting at night. Walking here and there, he encountered someone fishing with a net in the river. Lord Katsushige asked, "Have you had any luck tonight?" Not recognizing that it was Lord Katsushige he replied holding up his net: "Indeed, I have a fine catch this evening." There was a big carp in the net. Lord Katsushige said, "Behold, what a magnificent carp." The fisherman said, "I caught two as big as this in the past." Katsushige said, "You'll get to eat this one tomorrow. I'm envious." The man retorted, "That is not so, old man. I have a master. He likes carp. I always offer the first big carp to him, and we eat the small ones. It would be unforgivable if I ate the first big carp of the season." Lord Katsushige replied as he left, "I respect your attitude."

The following morning, when the cook in the kitchen asked Lord Katsushige about his meal, he said, "Wait for a while. I suspect a carp will arrive before long." Then, news came that Ishii Hachirōzaemon had come bearing a carp. "This was caught last night. It is hereby presented to you, Sire." In Lord Katsushige's era, even if people were too low to be granted an audience, they would always bring their first catch or harvest to the castle as an offering. Villagers would bring nuts saying they were from the grafted trees.

❀　❀　❀

8-70. As Nakano Takumi teetered on the cusp of death, he gathered everybody in the family and said: "In preparing for service, a retainer must consider three factors: obedience, dedication to duty, and the way he dies."

❀　❀　❀

10-67. The family history of Lord Sōma[1] is recorded in a scroll called the *Chiken Marokashi*. It was an unequaled family genealogy in Japan. The lord's mansion suddenly caught fire one year. Lord Sōma lamented, "I do not bemoan the loss of the manor and its fittings. They can all be replaced if they are destroyed in the fire. Regrettably, though, I couldn't retrieve our treasured heirloom, the family tree."

One of his attendants declared, "I shall enter the flames and save this treasure." Lord Sōma and the other retainers chortled incredulously, "How can you salvage it now when the building is engulfed by this fire?" This retainer was never effusive in service, nor had he ever been exceptionally useful, but for some reason his lord was fond of him as he was diligent. "By no means have I been an effective servant to His Lordship because of my clumsiness. Nevertheless, I have always been ready to sacrifice my life for something useful should the opportunity arise. I believe that time is now." With that, he stormed into the blazing inferno.

As soon as the fire had been put out, Lord Sōma instructed his men, "Find his body. It is such a shame!" They searched through the burnt ruins and finally located his charred remains in the garden area next to the residence. Blood gushed from his stomach as they turned his prostrated body over. Evidently, he had slit open his belly and inserted the document inside, protecting it from the flames. Henceforth, it became known as the *Chi-keizu,* or "Blood Genealogy."

❧ ❧ ❧

10-157. When a retainer of Takeda Shingen named Amari Bizen-no-Kami was killed in battle, his 18-year-old son, Tōzō, replaced his father as *yoriki.*[2] When a warrior in his unit was wounded in battle and the stream of blood would not clot, Tōzō ordered him to drink watered-down dung of a gray-haired horse. The injured warrior

---

1 Iwaki Nakamura domain.
2 In Japan's medieval period, the position of *yoriki* was to serve as an assistant to the lord or unit commanders during military campaigns. During the later Tokugawa period, however, *yoriki* were administrative assistants in governmental offices. This passage is referring to the former.

protested, "Although life is precious, how can I drink horse dung?!" Tōzō overheard his aside and responded, "You are a truly brave warrior, and what you say makes sense. The real meaning of loyalty, however, means we are duty-bound to try and stay alive to contribute to our lord's victory. Now, I will drink some also." After gulping down a mouthful of the concoction, he gave the cup to the wounded warrior, who consumed the remedy gleefully. It is said he quickly recovered from his injuries.

❦ ❦ ❦

11-28. On loyalty. Rather than exploits in battle, a retainer can exhibit magnificent loyalty by correcting his master's mind-set, and thereby contribute to the stability of the domain. It is not difficult to be the first warrior to attack the enemy line or achieve a meritorious feat, as all one needs to do is risk life and limb by charging forth. This is a solitary action, and is over when you die. On the other hand, correcting the lord's faults requires many years of devoted toil—not brief, sacrificial missions. It is only after one has been promoted to the position of elder councilor or chief retainer following years of dedicated service, earning the trust of one's colleagues and lord and receiving his favor, that a man earns the right to offer counsel. This demands inestimable hard work until promotion is granted.

Even elevation through the ranks fueled by self-aggrandizement involves considerable effort; but promotion based solely on a motivation to assist the lord requires more determination to keep calm and carry on. One who is oblivious to this selfless mission will never be accepted as a genuinely faithful servant.

PERTAINING TO DEATH AND WAR

4-46. When Lord Katsushige was a young man, his father Lord Naoshige told him: "Executing criminals who have been condemned to die is good cutting practice for you." Following this ultimatum, ten convicts were aligned inside the western gate, and Katsushige proceeded to cut their heads off one by one, until he reached the tenth. When he saw he was a young man of robust health, he said, "I am weary of cutting for the moment. I will let this wretch live." His life was spared.

❋ ❋ ❋

6-5. When Takagi Akifusa[1] turned his back on his lord, Ryūzōji Takanobu, he requested to take refuge with Maeda Iyo-no-Kami Iesada. Akifusa was a peerless and valiant warrior, and a master of the sword. He was accompanied by his loyal retainers Ingazaemon and Fudōzaemon, also daring warriors (*kusemono*) who never left their master's side.

Lord Takanobu sent a message to Iyo-no-Kami instructing him to slay his guest through concern of the damage his former retainer could inflict. When Akifusa was sitting on the porch with Ingazaemon washing his feet, Iyo-no-Kami crept up from behind and chopped off Akifusa's head. Before his head fell to the ground, Akifusa was able to unsheathe his *wakizashi* and spun around to counterattack, but mistakenly took off Ingazaemon's head instead. Both of their heads tumbled into the washbowl, but Akifusa's head then hovered into the middle of the room. It seems that he had acquired magical abilities.

❋ ❋ ❋

6-58. When the castle at Arima[2] was captured, Mitsuse Genbei[3] sat on a wall near the inner citadel on the twenty-eighth day.[4] Nakano Takumi Shigetoshi happened by, and asked what he was doing sitting there. Mitsuse said, "I was suddenly overcome by stomach pains and cannot go any further than this. The other members of my unit have gone ahead, so I must call on you to lead them."

When this act was conveyed to the inspector, it was declared to

---

1 Noto-no-Kami. A son of Ryūzōji Moriie.
2 During the Shimabara Uprising (1637–1638).
3 An inspector (*o-metsuke*).
4 Twenty-eighth day of the second month, 1637.

be an instance of cowardice. Mitsuse was consequently ordered to commit *seppuku*. In the old days, the debilitating malady of stomach cramps was referred to as "cursive cowardice" because it suddenly rendered the victim unable to stand [like a brush that doesn't leave the paper when writing in cursive script].

❀ ❀ ❀

6-201. In Meireki 3 (1657), our clan was to accept custody of some Ōmura Christians. Ōki Hyōbu and Nagayama Jūbei were sent to escort them. On the first day of the twelfth month, they picked up 80 Christians in Isahaya. A new prison was erected in Imaizumi-mura and the 80 Christians were incarcerated there. Hyōbu, Nakano Kazuma, Nakano Matabei, and Jūbei were ordered to oversee the prisoners. On the twenty-seventh day of the seventh month the following year, the prisoners were put to death. Their heads were displayed on the prison gates in Takao.

An examiner arrived from Nagasaki. He was looked after by Nakano Ka'uemon (later known as Nakano Matabei), Nagayama Jūbei, inspector Ōki Hyōbu, and Nakano Kazuma. The executioners were foot soldiers (*okachi*) selected for their sword skills, and each of them cut off three heads. When it came to the last three, Mitani Senzaemon completed his assignment with much flair… The bodies were transported to the sea off Higo by boat and dumped in the ocean.

❀ ❀ ❀

7-14. At the age of five, Yamamoto Kichizaemon[1] was told by his father, Jin'uemon, to kill a dog with his sword. He was then ordered to execute a convict when he turned 15. Without fail, all young warriors were expected to behead a human when they reached the age of 14 or 15. Lord Naoshige also ordered his son Katsushige to hone his cutting skills. He is said to have decapitated ten convicts in a row.[2]

---

1 Tsunetomo's half-brother.
2 See Book 4-46.

This practice was commonplace long ago, even among sons of lords; but nowadays even the children of the lower samurai do not refine their skills through performing executions. This is a sign of willful neglect. It is simply an excuse to claim that 'this kind of practice is not needed,' or that 'killing a tied-up felon is not meritorious,' or 'the act itself is a crime,' or it is 'sinful.' In the final analysis, as the way of martial valor is disagreeable to them, all they are concerned with is polishing their nails, and having nice things.

Scrutiny of a man who considers such practices as 'disgusting' reveals that he cleverly composes justifications simply because he is frightened. Lord Naoshige ordered his son to do it because he deemed it necessary training. The previous year, I went to the execution ground in Kase for a beheading, and experienced a frisson of excitement. To be unnerved by executions is confirmation of cowardice."

❀ ❀ ❀

7-15. Tomoda Shōzaemon's *seppuku*. Shōzaemon was Lord Mitsushige's page, and he was always in attendance. He was an unfaithful fellow, however, and became so infatuated with the leading actor in a theater troupe, Tamon Shōzaemon, that he substituted not only his name, but also his family crest for Tamon's. He was so besotted that he sold his clothes and belongings to be his patron, but as he used all of his money, he stole Mawatari Rokubei's sword and had a servant spear-carrier (*yarimochi*) pawn it. The spear-carrier reported this to the authorities. Shōzaemon was investigated, and both he and his attendant were sentenced to death.

Yamamoto Gorōzaemon[1] conducted the interrogation. When reporting his findings to Lord Mitsushige, he proclaimed, "It was the spear-carrier who snitched on his master. His name is so-and-so." Lord Mitsushige said without hesitation, "Have them both killed."

When sentencing Shōzaemon to commit *seppuku*, Gorōzaemon told him: "There is no way for you to save face other than through death. Die honorably as a samurai." Shōzaemon replied, "Thank you

---

1 Jōchō's nephew.

for your kind words. Indeed, I will do as I am told with equanimity."

Nobody knows who came up with the wicked plot, but Shōzaemon was lied to regarding who was to be his *kaishaku,* or second, to finish him off. Naozuka Roku'emon, a lowly foot soldier (*okachi*), was ordered to administer the *coup de grâce.*

Shōzaemon sat upright in position, and very calmly acknowledged the man he thought was his second sitting across from him. However, at the sight of another man at his side drawing his sword, he stood up and said, "Who are you? I'm not going to let you cut off my head!" He completely lost his composure and behaved in a regretful manner. He was eventually held down and beheaded with his hands and feet held by others. Gorōzaemon mentioned in confidence that "Shōzaemon would have met his quietus admirably had he not been tricked in such a way…"

❀ ❀ ❀

7-16. Noda Kizaemon's opinions on *kaishaku.* "If a [condemned] samurai starts writhing through losing his nerve at the place where he is to commit *seppuku,* it is likely that the *kaishaku* role will not be performed well. When this happens, wait for a while and encourage the man to compose himself. The deathblow will be clean if you can deliver it quickly during a moment of calm."

❀ ❀ ❀

7-18. A story about Ushijima Kyūjibei. At a performance by a troupe of actors in Shōzu village, Kyūjibei was walking among the audience wearing his braded straw hat. He tripped and lurched forward, and his sandal flew off, ricocheted off a hedge and hit a man on the head. Kyūjibei picked himself up, and reaching for his sandal he said: "I'm terribly sorry about that. I didn't do it on purpose. Dear me, I have even dirtied my clothes. So sorry." The spectator and a gang of two or three men who seemed to be his companions barked back: "Oi! Just because you carry a sword don't think you can throw a sandal at someone's head and get away with a 'so sorry." Turning around,

Kyūjibei discarded his hat and retorted, "What unreasonable fellows you are. Although I didn't do it on purpose, I expressed regret as a courtesy, as it was my sandal after all. Not to accept my apology and accuse me in public in such a way is unforgivable. There are too many people in here. Step outside. I will cut you all down to size!" The men were overwhelmed by his spirit and hesitated. Kyūjibei continued in a gentler tone, "Just accept my apology. If you don't, you will lose your head, and so will I. Hush and enjoy the *kyōgen*."[1] Then he put his hat back on and departed. There was nothing faint-hearted about his conduct. He must have been a very brave man.

❈ ❈ ❈

7-24. On day eleven of the eleventh month, in the second year of Tenwa (1682), Sawabe Heizaemon[2] was ordered to slit his belly.[3] Hearing of this decree on the evening of the tenth, he dispatched a request to Yamamoto Gon'nojō (Tsunetomo) to be his *kaishaku,* to which he wrote the following reply. Gon'nojō was 24 years of age. "I empathise with your resolution, and agree to perform this honorable task out of my respect for you. It was my first instinct to decline your request out of courtesy, but there is no time to excuse myself for any reason as the ceremony is to take place tomorrow, and so I humbly accept. I am greatly honored that you should choose me from among so many. Rest peacefully tonight in preparation for tomorrow. It is late now, but I will visit you in person soon to make arrangements. Tenth day, eleventh month."

Heizaemon commented that it was an outstanding letter. Since olden times, it was inauspicious to be asked to perform *kaishaku*. It is a difficult task not readily acknowledged, even if it is performed in an excellent fashion; but if the second slips up, it will generate a lifetime of embarrassment. Master Jōchō keeps a copy of the letter.

---

1 A form of traditional Japanese comic theater usually performed as an intermission between acts in Noh performances.

2 Son of Nakano Masayoshi, and Jōchō's cousin.

3 Also see Book 1-16.

❀ ❀ ❀

7-25. Ōno Senbei's *oibara*. Senbei's older brother and some black-smith from Hasuike were engaged in a pledge of male love relation-ship.[1] One day they started to argue and their relationship deteriorated. Family and friends attempted to intercede but to no avail, so they appealed to the lord. Lord Katsushige was on duty in Edo, so Lord Kōshū[2] presided over the case.

After hearing both arguments he declared, "You shall fight it out with no assistance. Anybody who tries to help you will be punished by death." Fences were erected in Takao Nawate and the two were to fight within. The venue became packed with spectators, dotted around like nails on the back of a shoe. The blacksmith arrived first, and then Ōno, who said: "I apologize for keeping you so long. It took me forever to take my leave. Now let's begin." They drew their swords and sparks flew from the tips as they clashed. The spectators watched with bated breath. Just then, Ōno's upper thigh was cut through and he fell to the ground with a thud. With this, somebody burst through the fence screaming, "You will not get away!" The blacksmith was cut down with a single blow of a sword. The assailant was Ōno's younger brother, Senbei. But the older Ōno had been killed outright.

When the incident was reported to Lord Kōshū, he disapproved: "The insolence, after I strictly forbade any outside interference. Execute him." As an investigation was being made, Lord Katsushige returned to Saga. When he heard what had transpired, he said: "Senbei is a cut above other men. He did well. If your own brother is killed before your eyes, could you stand there and not do anything because you value your own life?" With this, Senbei was pardoned. Lord Kōshū was admonished sternly. "The incident was managed with little consideration, and setting up a site for the fight by the road for all and sundry to see was an appalling decision."

Senbei later rose through the ranks, becoming a favored servant in charge of falconry and raising the birds. To repay his lord's largesse,

---

1 *Shudō*. See Book 1-180 and 181.
2 Nabeshima Naozumi. Katsushige's son, and a later lord of the Hasuike sub-domain.

he martyred himself by following Lord Katsushige in death…

❀ ❀ ❀

7-36. Matsuura Dōun's comment on the Arima offensive.[1] Dōun said, "When I was a young man, I participated in the Arima offensive, but in retrospect, whether one is able to achieve a meritorious feat in combat depends on the course of events. Your preparedness in battle is what matters. By preparedness, I mean the closer you sit to the enemy's camp, the more brave people will think you are. Stories told at night during campaigns emphasize how those who go to the encampments near the front seem fearless, but those who remain in the rear appear to be all the more cowardly. It would be wise to remember this when you are young." (This was relayed by Baba Gontarō.)

❀ ❀ ❀

7-40. Whenever the members of Ōki Hyōbu's unit gathered, he would always say after business had been completed: "Young warriors should aim to be courageous. You can be brave if you devote every thought to building your nerve. If your sword breaks in the thick of battle, fight with your bare hands. If your arms are cut from your body, wrestle your adversary to the ground with your shoulders. If your shoulders are also sliced off, you still have the ability to bite the heads off 10 or 15 enemy warriors." He often said this.

❀ ❀ ❀

8-48. The making into a samurai of Hirohashi Ichiyūken. Ichiyūken worked as a manservant in Lord Ryūzōji Takanobu's kitchen. Due to rancor incurred in a sumo bout, he drew his sword and killed seven or eight men, and was subsequently condemned to commit *seppuku*. When Lord Takanobu heard news of the fracas, he exonerated his

---

1 The Shimabara Uprising of 1637–1638.

servant. "Men of valor are important in these troublesome times we live. He seems to be one with a gallant heart." Lord Takanobu took Ichiyūken to the battle at Anegawa, where he was unmatched in courage and demonstrated many commendable exploits.[1] At the Battle of Takagi, Ichiyūken penetrated so far into enemy territory that his lord became concerned and detained him by his horse's side. Still, wanting to be the first into the fray he broke off into a run when they had come to a standstill, and the lord was barely able to catch hold of the sleeve of Ichiyūken's armor. Ichiyūken sported many wounds on his head, which he staunched with leaves and bound with a cloth.

As there were no physicians present, a potion called Ichiyūken's "black medicine" was mixed with ointment and applied to swellings. This concoction was made from grinding navel lint with grains of boiled rice and salt. When somebody developed a lesion, it was cut open at the top and the ointment was rubbed into the wound. The patient often fainted during this treatment.

When a swelling appeared on Lord Naoshige's arm, Ichiyūken requested: "Do show it to me, my Lord." When His Lordship showed him, Ichiyūken pulled out a hidden needle and suddenly proceeded to pierce the lump. "What are you doing?!" cried Lord Naoshige. He replied, "Does a minor prick like this cause you pain?" Lord Naoshige snatched the needle and slashed Ichiyūken's cheek with it. They did not get along with each other afterwards. Ichiyūken was slain in battle under Naoshige's command during the Hirai offensive at the Suko Castle in the second year of Tenshō (1574).

❀ ❀ ❀

8-56. Horie San'uemon was warden of the Edo mansion warehouse. San'uemon committed the crime of raiding the Nabeshima domain's warehouse, and fled to another province with stolen money. He was eventually caught and acknowledged his knavery. It was declared,

---

1 A major battle fought on July 30, 1570 near the Anegawa River in northern Ōmi Province (now Shiga Prefecture) between the allied armies of Oda Nobunaga and Tokugawa Ieyasu, who defeated the combined forces of Asai Nagamasa and Asakura Kagetake.

"Given the serious nature of the offence, he must be tortured until death." Nakano Daigaku[1] was appointed as the official to confirm his execution. First of all, the hairs on his body were burnt off, all of his fingernails were pulled, his tendons were severed, he was punctured with holes, and subjected to all manner of torture. Still, he whimpered not once throughout the ordeal, and his complexion remained unchanged. In the end, his back was slashed, and he died with his torso folded back as boiling soy sauce was poured over him.

❋ ❋ ❋

8-82. Leaving some skin when performing *kaishaku*. When a certain man committed *seppuku*, the second cut through his neck, but there was a strand of skin left so the head was not completely severed. The *o-metsuke* (observer) exclaimed, "There is a bit left!" This angered the man who dealt the mercy blow. He took the head in his hand and cut it completely from the neck. Holding it above eye-level, he bellowed: "Behold!" It was quite a disturbing scene.

There are stories in the past of heads flying through the air when the *kaishaku* performed his task. For this reason, it was regarded better practice to leave a tag of skin on the throat to connect the head to the body, preventing it from rolling towards the officials. Now, it is considered better to make a clean swipe through.

A man who experienced cutting off 50 heads said: "Depending on the neck, it may offer as much resistance as if one were cutting through the breast (*ichi no dō*). You will not detect any resistance for the first three heads you sever, and the neck is easy to slice through. After cutting four or five necks, however, the resistance becomes quite pronounced. In any case, as it is a matter of immense importance, you will not mess it up if you cleave through the neck aiming to hit through to the ground each time."

❋ ❋ ❋

---

1 Tsunetomo's uncle.

8-86. When his lord returned to Saga, Ishii Jinzaemon remained as caretaker in the Edo mansion and took to gambling with Ishii Mokunosuke, winning a pair of swords in a bet. The two men were ordered to commit *seppuku* when details of the incident surfaced. The living quarters guard, Matsuo Kihei, was also executed in Edo. His father, Jūrōdayū, was handed a dishonorable discharge. It was Jūrōdayū who brought his son to Edo. Jinzaemon was called back to Saga and was incarcerated after being cross-examined. At the inquiry, he gave a detailed explanation to the chief retainers about his gambling: "The transgression I committed has led to my internment, and now I wait for the verdict of my impending death. Thus, I sit with no regrets of the past. There is, however, one thing that I find to be unacceptable. There is a hollow under the guttering of my room that has been blocked by chains. I am dumbfounded that some people think a samurai in my position might try to escape through a hole in the drain!"

Fujii Kaheiji visited him at the temple where the *seppuku* was to take place. They exchanged cups of *saké* together, and then Jinzaemon bit into a slice of taro. Chewing through half of the morsel he whispered, "Will this emerge when I am decapitated?" Kaheiji asked, "Why on earth would it?" Jinzaemon put it down and said, "I have a lump in my throat, and cannot swallow anything. It would be most unbecoming should it come out when I am cut."

He confided to Kaheiji: "Although I am renowned for my courage, I must actually be a coward given the ignominious state I am in now. If I squirm shamefully from the pain of the incision, I wish for the *kaishaku* to deliver the mortal blow quickly so that my weakness does not betray my brave reputation. It is said that the face of a genuinely gallant warrior (*kusemono*) does not change when confronted by his mortality. I was composed as always until the final evening, when I was brought to this place. I am sorry to say this is not the case now." Ōtsuka Sadasuke acted as his second. Jinzaemon was praiseworthy to the very end. (From Kaheiji's account.)

❀ ❀ ❀

9-12. Ōkubo Kannosuke's retribution. Ōkubo Tōemon from Shiota was a *saké* dealer for Lord Nabeshima Kenmotsu. Lord Kashū's[1] son, Lord Ōkura,[2] was physically disabled and shut himself away in a place called Minō. He entertained sumo wrestlers, and was fond of cavorting with ruffians. The wrestlers were often disorderly, causing disruption in neighboring hamlets. Two of them visited Tōemon's establishment, and chatted away raucously in crude banter as they indulged in rice wine. Tōemon was drawn into an altercation, but they cut him down as he defended himself with a *naginata*.

Tōemon's 15-year-old son, Kannosuke, was studying at the Jōzaiji Temple at the time. When he heard about his father's murder, he jumped on his horse and galloped to the scene with a *wakizashi* that was 1-*shaku* 3-*sun* in length.[3] He challenged the two large wrestlers and vanquished them quickly, but suffered 13 wounds in the process, from which he eventually recovered. He was later known as Dōko, and became skilled in the art of massage.

❀ ❀ ❀

9-15. They say that the late Tokunaga Kokichizaemon[4] often grumbled, "I am so old that I wouldn't be able to do anything, even if there was a battle I was mobilized for. Even so, I yearn to die by charging headlong into the enemy ranks and being struck down in a blaze of glory. What a pity it would be to simply perish in bed!"

❀ ❀ ❀

9-26. Yamamoto Jin'uemon's last days.[5] Yamamoto Jin'uemon became ill when he was 80 years old. Looking as if he was about to groan, I said, "Go ahead and cry out. You will feel so much better." Jin'uemon

---

1 Nabeshima Naozumi (1616–69), the first daimyo of the Hizen Hasuike domain, and the fifth son of Nabeshima Katsushige.
2 Nabeshima Ukon Naomori.
3 Approximately 15 inches (39cm).
4 A retainer of the Taku clan in Saga.
5 Jōchō's father.

snapped, "I will do no such thing! Everyone knows the name of Jin'uemon, so how would it look if a man considered more outstanding than the rest was to let out an audible groan in his final moments?" He never cried out to the very end.

🌸 🌸 🌸

9-30. The son of Mori Monbei[1] got into a fight and came home with wounds on his body. Monbei asked, "What happened to your foe?" "I cut him down." "Did you finish him off?" "Of course I did." Then Monbei declared, "Well done. You should have no regrets. Although not right away, you will have to commit *seppuku*, so prepare to cut your belly when you are settled. Allow me to be your second rather than die by the hand of somebody else." Not long after, Monbei performed *kaishaku* for his son.

🌸 🌸 🌸

10-63. A vassal of Lord Matsudaira Sagami-no-Kami of Tottori,[2] was dispatched to Kyoto to procure money for his domain. He rented a townhouse to live in. One day when he went out to explore the surrounds, he happened to overhear a passerby say, "The samurai in that brawl is a retainer of Matsudaira Sagami-no-Kami." He was alarmed as he knew that some of his fellow clansmen were in town on their way up to Edo. He asked the man where the brawl was, and made haste to the scene only to find his associate bleeding and about to be finished off. He immediately confronted the two antagonists, killed them outright, and then returned to his townhouse.

The magistrate's office got wind of the incident and summoned the Tottori samurai to a hearing. "You are charged with illegally joining your comrade in a fight. How do you plead?" He replied, "As I am but a bumpkin from the provinces, I am afraid I do not understand what you mean. Please repeat the charge."

The irate official barked back at him, "Are you deaf? The fact that

---

1 A warrior with the rank of *teakiyari*.
2 Ikeda Mitsunaka (1630–1694), the first daimyo of the Inaba-no-Kuni Tottori domain.

you participated in a fight and killed some men is a flagrant contra-vention of the law (*hatto*) and rules (*okite*)!" The accused countered, "I am starting to understand what you are saying. Although you accuse me of flouting the law and values, I contend that I did no such thing. There are no living creatures, most of all men, who don't want to be alive. I also cherish my existence very much. I was told 'your colleague is in a fight,' and thought it would dishonor the military way if I ignored the situation. That is why I dashed to the scene. What's more, it would have been unforgivable had I done nothing after witnessing the murder of a fellow clansman. I would extend the duration of my own life, but the spirit of bushido would perish in me. Thus, I dispensed with my cherished life to preserve the Way of the samurai. By forfeiting my life, I have observed the law of the samurai and upheld the warrior spirit. I have already laid down my life, and therefore humbly request that my punishment be meted out swiftly." The magistrate officials were stirred by his demeanor. The incident was brought to a close without further ado, and the officials notified Sagami-no-Kami that "Your retainer is a praiseworthy fellow and should be treasured."

❀ ❀ ❀

10-90. An old retainer stated that killing an enemy in battle is akin to a hawk catching a small bird as its prey. Even though it charges into a flock of a thousand birds, the only one in its sight is the one it targeted from the outset. Incidentally, the head of an enemy taken after declaring, "That armored warrior with the such-and-such bind-ing is mine!" is called a *kezuke-no-kubi*—a "head with hair."

❀ ❀ ❀

10-91. In the *Kōyō-gunkan*[1] a certain warrior said, "When I face my enemy, it feels as if I have entered the shadows, and so I inevitably get

---

1 The term *bushidō* first appeared in the *Kōyō-gunkan*. This treatise, concerning the life and times of Takeda Shingen, is a treasure-trove of information for understanding the

stricken with wounds. Even though you have achieved many exploits in battle, you have never been injured. How can this be so?" The other warrior[1] answered, "Of course, it is like being in darkness when I face the enemy; but if I can calm my mind, it becomes like night-time illuminated dimly by moonlight. If I attack then, I know I will not be wounded." This is the defining moment of a warrior's true strength.

❀ ❀ ❀

10-111. A retainer from Satsuma was walking as if in a sleepy daze when he passed by the guard house. A constable saw him, and saying "You can't be asleep," he poked him in the face with a staff, making him bleed. The Satsuma warrior wiped the blood off and left. He returned on horseback around evening accompanied by several others, and waited for the constable to appear. When he found the guard with his attendants, he jumped off his horse. He then addressed him before clefting him in twain. The other guards took off in terror. The incident was reported immediately, but the Satsuma side denied any association, and the episode ended there.

❀ ❀ ❀

10-134. When serving as a second during *seppuku*, if you are using a *katana* (sword), place your right foot about 1-*shaku* 4 or 5-*sun* away from his knee. If you are using your *wakizashi* (short-sword) your right foot should be 1-*shaku* away.[2] Step forward on the same angle as your knee is pointing, and keep your hands low as you cut keeping the blade edge perpendicular to the neck.

Sengoku warrior ethos. Due to many historical inaccuracies, however, scholars tend to view the text as untrustworthy. There is even controversy over who wrote the book. Most of the chapters are signed by Kōsaka Danjō Masanobu (1527–1578), a Takeda house elder. However, some scholars have contested that the author was the military scholar Obata Kagenori (1572–1663). Research by Sakai Kenji into the language used shows that it is reminiscent of the Muromachi period, and was therefore probably written by Kōsaka Danjō, and compiled by Obata Kagenori.

1 Baba Minō-no-Kami.

2 Approximately 17–18 inches (43–46cm) and 12 inches (30cm) respectively.

❀ ❀ ❀

11-1. Written in the *Gunpō-kikisho*, "Win first, then attack" is the essence of certain victory. Resourcefulness in peacetime means preparing for war. You must be able to defeat an enemy of 100,000 men with a force of 500.

Be sure to withdraw via the byroads rather than the highway when assailing an enemy castle. Lay the wounded and dead bodies of your allies face down in the direction of the enemy.

When attacking the enemy encampment, keep in mind the shadows of trees to quantify the distance from an embankment or bridge as you go by. When your allies are in retreat, you can wait under the landmark trees to check the number of men as they pass by and guard the rear. Face the retreating forces and cry out, "I have the rear guard. Assemble here if you wish to join me!"

Naturally, the warrior's focus should be in the front of the attack, and at the back of the retreat. Don't forget to wait for the best time to attack; and don't forget to attack while you wait.

❀ ❀ ❀

11-5. A *kabuto* (helmet) is typically thought to be heavy. Nonetheless, when one is rushing a castle and attacking with bows, guns, rocks, big pieces of wood and so on, the *kabuto* does not seem so heavy at all.[1]

❀ ❀ ❀

11-6. Lord Getsudō[2] bequeathed a document explaining how to win a sword fight. When shogun Iemitsu thought of practicing *kenjutsu*,[3] he asked Kimura Sukekurō,[4] a retainer of the Kii house, and Getsudō

---

1 A possible alternative in interpretation is to translate "attacking with" as "is being attacked with."
2 Nabeshima Kii-no-Kami Motoshige of the Ogi sub-domain.
3 Traditional Japanese swordsmanship.
4 1581–1650. A celebrated master of swordsmanship in the early Edo period. A student of Yagyū Munenori.

to write down their formulas for how to prevail in the military ways (*hyōdō*), with the intention of appointing one of them as his *kenjutsu* teacher. Sukekurō prepared a three-page document and offered it to Iemitsu. Getsudō simply wrote: "It is wrong to think it's right, and it is wrong to think it's wrong. They are both wrong. It is right to not think of anything." Lord Iemitsu was impressed by this, and chose Getsudō as his sword master. Their practice together, however, never eventuated as Lord Getsudō died soon after.

❀ ❀ ❀

11-8. When the sword master Yagyū Tajima-no-Kami[1] met with the shogun, several *shinai* (bamboo swords) suddenly dropped from the ceiling. Master Yagyū clasped his hands overhead to avoid being struck. Another time when he was called for, the shogun concealed himself in the shadows with a *shinai* in hand, ready to take him by surprise. Master Yagyū shouted: "The shogun is practicing *kenjutsu*. Don't spy!" Just as the bewildered shogun turned to see who was there, Master Yagyū moved forward and appropriated his *shinai*.[2]

❀ ❀ ❀

11-18. When appointed to seek and kill. Wherever you are, accomplish your mission forthwith, without going back to your house or somewhere else first. The same applies to when you are summoned for duty on regular days. For this reason, a samurai must always be prepared, ready to respond at a moment's notice.

❀ ❀ ❀

11-46. Nagahama Inosuke offered the following advice: In sword combat, the warrior should simply surrender concerns for his life

---

1 Yagyū Tajima-no-Kami Munenori.
2 This is referring to the famous teaching in the Yagyū Shinkage-ryū school of swordsmanship, called *mutō-dori*. That is, to take the sword away from the opponent without cutting him down.

and strike at the enemy. The contest will be neck-and-neck as the opposition will do the same. Victory is decided by faith and fate. Never show one's sleeping quarters to others. The moment you start nodding off to sleep, or when you leave your room, are both critical times when you are at your most vulnerable. Be heedful of this.

❁ ❁ ❁

11-55. A general once declared: "Apart from unit captains, all warriors should take care of the front of their armor and their helmets." Also: "The armor itself does not need to be ornately decorated, but the *kabuto* (helmet) should be of excellent quality, as it will be claimed by the enemy along with your head."

❁ ❁ ❁

11-56. When you take your enemy's head, slice a cross in the neck below the knot in his hair using a knife. In the past, when a certain samurai claimed his opponent's head, he removed three molars as proof. Another samurai stuffed paper in the gap between the teeth [to arrogate the trophy]. A fight erupted, and the samurai who inserted the paper won bragging rights.

❁ ❁ ❁

11-67. About execution sites. Setting up an execution site near where travelers pass by is not wise. Capital punishment conducted in Edo and the Kamigata region is intended to set an example for the whole of Japan; but executions carried out in the respective provinces are local matters. It's a poor reflection on the domain if too many criminals are put on display. How would this look to other clans? Also, even a felon will forget the nature of his offence with the passing of time. A crime should be punished where it is committed.

❁ ❁ ❁

11-133. Begin each day pondering death as its climax. Each morning, with a calm mind, conjure images in your head of your last moments. See yourself being pierced by bow and arrow, gun, sword, or spear, or being swept away by a giant wave, vaulting into a fiery inferno, taking a lightning strike, being shaken to death in a great earthquake, falling hundreds of feet from a high cliff top, succumbing to a terminal illness, or just dropping dead unexpectedly. Every morning, be sure to meditate yourself into a trance of death.

An elder decreed: "If one steps out of his house, he will be in the midst of corpses; if he steps out of his gate, he will meet the enemy." The point here is not vigilance; but rather to kill one's self from the very outset.

❁ ❁ ❁

11-149. The story of an old warhorse. Warriors in olden times used to grow mustaches because their ears and noses would be removed and taken by the enemy as proof of their triumph in battle. The mustache was cut off together with the nose to confirm that the trophy head was that of a man and not a woman. If the head was found to be clean-shaven, it was just left to rot in the mud. A samurai cultivated his drooping mustache to ensure that his head, once removed, was not unceremoniously discarded. Master Jōchō said, "A man's complexion will not change after being killed in battle, so long as he washes his face every morning."

PERTAINING TO WOMEN

3-29. After breaking up, Lord Naoshige's former wife[1] visited often with her attendants for the purpose of *uwanari-uchi*[2] or playing pranks on his new wife. Lady Yōdaiin[3] handled her with such courtesy, His Lordship's former wife always went away reluctantly mollified.

---

1 Keien Myōyo.
2 *Uwanari-uchi* was the practice in which a divorced woman assembled her female relatives or attendants to play pranks on her husband's new spouse to "get even."
3 Nabeshima Naoshige's new wife.

3-42. Following the death of her previous husband, Nōdomi Jibedayū, in battle, Lady Yōdaiin withdrew to her father Ishii Hyōbudayū's home in Isakari.

One day, Ryūzōji Takanobu's men called upon the Ishida house on their way to battle and requested they prepare lunch. Hyōbudayū told his servants, "Grill some sardines." They set about the task, but it was taking too much time as there were so many to prepare.

Lady Yōdaiin was observing them from behind the curtain. She stepped out and scraped the burning embers from the bottom of the oven and emptied the basket of sardines over them. Heating the fish with a large fan, she then gathered the entire pile into a winnowing basket, shook the ash away, and distributed the fish to the men. Lord Naoshige watched her work and thought to himself, "I want a quick-thinking wife like her." He soon started to court her.

One evening when Lord Naoshige was visiting Lady Yōdaiin, someone chased him away shouting, "Thief!" He jumped over a ditch to get away, but got nicked by a sword. He suffered a minor cut on the sole of his foot. He was also slightly wounded during a night raid in Taku.[1] There is also speculation that he was injured in the second month of the fourth year of Tenshō (1576) while attacking Yokozawa Castle.[2]

3-43. When Toyotomi Hideyoshi stayed in Nagoya[3] while on campaign, he threw a party and invited the wives of the Kyushu lords. Lady Yōdaiin's presence at the festivity was also requested, but she asked Hideyoshi's maid, Kōzōsu, to get her pardoned from the gathering. Kōzōsu managed the situation so that Lady Yōdaiin was exempted. However, Kōzōsu requested "Please make an appearance

1 1570.
2 It should read "Yokozō" Castle.
3 In Kyushu, not to be confused with the city in modern-day Aichi Prefecture.

once, lest your actions be seen as setting an example." Shaving her forehead and doing her hair in a way that looked as if she had horns, she appeared looking particularly ugly. She never had to join them again. (Relayed by Kanemaru.)[1]

❀ ❀ ❀

5-91. When the big fire broke out in the year of the monkey (1668), Lord Mitsushige went to the house of Doi Toshikatsu, the husband of his daughter O-sen, in Yanagihara. Lord Mitsushige inquired, "The fire has spread to the tenement houses. Where is the lady of the house?" He was told, "She is still inside the residence." He went inside and asked her what she was doing. "I have already been telling my servants to leave, but my husband is away, and it would not be appropriate for his wife to abandon the house in his absence. I am prepared to burn to death." Mitsushige left the building without her. (Relayed by Kanemaru.)

❀ ❀ ❀

6-70. Daizen's[2] wife was Nabeshima Ichisuke's daughter. She was bequeathed to Daizen after her adoption by Lord Katsushige. During the Arima offensive in the Shimabara Uprising, Daizen's actions spawned his lord's rancor, and he and his wife were forcibly divorced.[3] She sent letters via a messenger, but he left them unread saying, "As much as my heart pines, even away from the prying eyes of others I can't bring myself to read the letters of one ripped from me by my lord." He told others, "I no longer have anything to live for." He stopped eating and started to drink heavily. He died after he started to vomit blood. Following his death, the lord contributed 150 *koku* of rice to his former wife to compensate her living expenses…

---

1 Kanemaru Gun'uemon was a scribe.
2 Nabeshima Masayuki.
3 Daizen was ordered to guard the Edo residence at the time of the Shimabara Uprising, but disobeyed and went to the front.

❀ ❀ ❀

6-127. The shogunal red seal (*shuin*) for pottery in Takagijuku. When Lord Toyotomi Hideyoshi was encamped in Nagoya (Hizen), he had to return to Osaka because his mother had taken ill. On his way back, he took the upper road in Saga. The reason why the place where the ferryboat departs to traverse the Kawakami River is called "Nagoya ford" is because this is where Lord Hideyoshi crossed. According to the people who witnessed the event, Lord Hideyoshi was a small man with big oily eyes, and his face and limbs were red, as if they had been painted in vermillion. He was clothed in magnificent garments and straw footgear, and was carrying long and short swords in red-lacquered sheaths with gold threads, with an extra pair of half-sandals slung from them. He was traveling on horseback, as were all members of his entourage, with no palanquins to be seen.

At that time, Lady Keigin[1] told people: "Collect all of the doors from the houses and create tables out of them by attaching four bamboo sticks as legs. Then make firm rice balls and place them on plates in the street. Hideyoshi saw them as he passed and said, "This must be the work of Lady Keigin, as she's an astute woman. Normally there is no food available around these thoroughfares, and the people in my procession are getting hungry. That she should care for us like this is wonderful." He then reached out and picked up a rice ball saying, "Behold. This rice ball is dense. In a samurai family, the women are considerate." He also noticed the earthenware that the rice balls were placed on exclaiming, "Behold again, these plates are outstanding." He summoned the potter to Nagoya and issued him with a shogunal red seal [indicating official patronage of his craftsmanship]. This shogunal seal is still treasured. The imprint reads: "The pottery made by this man is incomparable. He is worthy of designation as the eminent potter in Kyushu Nagoya. Issued to Pottery Master Ienaga Hikosaburō, Twenty-sixth day, seventh month, Tenshō 20 (1592)…"

---

1 Nabeshima Naoshige's mother-in-law. She was Ryūzōji Takanobu's mother and remarried Naoshige's father.

❀ ❀ ❀

7-38. About the wife of Ushijima Shingorō.[1] Ushijima Shingorō was a favored vassal of Lord Tsunashige, and was treated cordially by him. In spite of this, it became known in the community that the brother of Shingorō's wife, Gondō Shichibei, was frequenting establishments of ill repute. He was sentenced to death in Edo to atone for his transgression. Wanting to set an example, Lord Tsunashige had all of Shichibei's extended family placed under house arrest. As Shingorō was Shichibei's brother-in-law, he too was subjected to punishment, and was sent back from his post in the Edo estate to Saga, and confined to his house for a period of three years.

During this time, Shingorō's relatives and others in his unit implored him: "Good man, sever ties with your wife so that you can resume your duties. How is it possible to survive on a mere 4 *koku* of rice?" Unfazed, Shingorō avowed, "I will never divorce my wife. I am not weakened by affection, but as a samurai I am loathe to detach myself from her when she has done no wrong, as it is a contravention of *giri*.[2] Leave me be to die of starvation." This episode was relayed and verified during Shingorō's confinement.

❀ ❀ ❀

8-47. Hashino Shōgen's agreement to *seppuku*. When an [adopted] daughter of Lord Ryūzōji Takanobu was betrothed to Lord Hata Mikawa-no-Kami of Karatsu for marriage, Yatsunami Musashi-no-Kami[3] came to fetch her.[4] However, she had become gravely ill, with only a one-in-ten chance of survival. "As I have been requisitioned to escort Her Ladyship to Karatsu, I resolve to commit *seppuku* should she die before my mission is complete." Others tried to persuade him otherwise, but to no effect.

---

1 This episode happened in 1697.
2 See footnote for 3-1.
3 Lord Hata's vassal.
4 See Book 2-136.

Lord Takanobu's chief retainers deliberated on the predicament. "It would be culpable if no one from our clan also follows Her Ladyship in death. Alas, there doesn't seem to be anybody prepared to embrace this fate other than, perhaps, Hashino Shōgen."

Shōgen was immediately called before the chief retainers. "As you can see, although this is an imposition, we must ask you to sacrifice your life by cutting your belly in the event of her death." Shōgen responded: "This is indeed a surprise. I wonder if the *seppuku* of a man with such low status as mine can serve to assuage such a serious situation in which the very reputation of the domain is at stake. Surely it would be more appropriate for high-ranking officials to kill themselves." But he consented: "I will happily do as I am commanded." He then went to Musashi-no-Kami's lodgings and informed him of the directive. "Being greatly obliged to Her Ladyship, I will follow her to the netherworld." As luck would have it, she made a full recovery and Shōgen did not have to die.

❀ ❀ ❀

9-19. Slaying an adulterer. Once, a certain man returned home late at night to discover that a stranger in his house in an illicit tryst with his wife. He killed the lover. Then, he smashed the wall of his house and knocked over a bale of rice, and informed the authorities that he had "despatched a burglar." The matter went no further after their investigation. In time he divorced his wife, resolving the affair magnificently.

❀ ❀ ❀

9-20. About a man who killed his wife. When a certain man returned home one day, he discovered his wife engaged in an act of infidelity in the bedroom with an attendant. He made for the inner room as his attendant took flight to the kitchen. He then stormed into the bedroom and smote her with his blade. Calling for the maid, he impressed upon her: "In order to prevent shame befalling my children, I ask you to make it seem as though my wife's death is a result of illness. Should you disagree, I will kill you too, as an accessory." She replied, "Please do not kill me, sire. I will do what I can to ensure that the secret is not divulged." She then tidied up and dressed the body in nightclothes.

A physician was sent for two or three times, but then a message was dispatched saying that the woman had already died, and there was no need for him to come anymore.

The wife's uncle was summoned and briefed of the incident. He agreed with the measures taken to disguise the facts. Thus, the wife's passing was put down to a sudden affliction, and the truth behind the actual cause of death was not disclosed. The attendant was expelled from the house. This affair happened in Edo.

❧ ❧ ❧

9-27. The clever handling by Tashiro Riuemon's wife of a servant's advances. One day when Tashiro Riuemon was away from home, one of his servants declared his love to his wife. "I have tried many times to stifle my feelings, knowing full well that I am guilty of apostasy to my master. But I see it as karma, and can no longer contain myself." Riuemon's wife was angered by his declaration, and rebuked him harshly, but to no effect. In the end she said to him, "If you feel so strongly, then I submit to you. Go to the storage room in the back and wait for me there. I will fulfill your desires."

Delighted by her response, he did as she requested. When they had gone inside, she said, "I will join you after tidying up," and then locked him in the storeroom to await her husband's arrival home. Before long he returned, and she told him what had happened. The forlorn fellow was hauled from the outbuilding and executed by Riuemon after hearing what he had to say.

❧ ❧ ❧

9-39. Once, a man called Takagi became embroiled in a quarrel with three local farmers. He was beaten into submission and chucked into a paddy field. When he returned home in his miserable state, his wife asked accusingly, "Have you forgotten how to die [like a samurai]?" "Absolutely not!" he retorted. Leaving the house she remarked, "All men are destined to die at some stage. There are a number of ways one can die, such as from illness, in battle, *seppuku*, or by being beheaded with one's hands tied behind one's back; but to die dishonorably would be most regrettable."

Before long she came back and put both the children to bed, made a torch, and equipped for the coming fight when it had become dark. "I found the three men talking together when I went out before. Now is our chance to attack. Let's go." Walking a few steps in front of her husband with the torch in one hand and a short sword in her sash, she forced her way into the cabin. They attacked the farmers, feverishly slashing with their swords. Two farmers were killed outright, and one was wounded and chased away. The husband was later ordered to commit *seppuku*.

❀ ❀ ❀

10-5. Once, a certain man said, "I know the shape of 'reason' (*ri*) and 'women.' "[1] When somebody asked what shape these things were, he replied: "Reason is a square, and will not budge at all. Women are round. Women do not discriminate between good or evil, wrong or right, and will roll into any position."

❀ ❀ ❀

10-17. The Ii family did not have a designated lawful wife. Naomasa's last words were: "Our clan always takes the vanguard in battle. By virtue of his birth mother, even an incompetent son stands to inherit the clan headship. We can't hope to serve any purpose following a lord incapable of leading valiantly from the front. There's

---

1 In some versions of *Hagakure*, the character for "fault" or "wrong" (非 = *hi*) is used instead of "woman" (婦 =*fu*). This actually makes more sense as it contrasts with "reason" (理 = *ri*), but I have chosen to remain faithful to the text I am basing this translation on. It may have been done purposefully in jest, or as a cynical comparison between "women" and "reason."

little that can be done to prevent a weakling son conceived to a lawful wife from becoming the clan's 'rightful heir.' Instead, it is best to single out a worthy contender sired to a concubine."

❀ ❀ ❀

10-101. On the qualities of a dog for hunting wild boar. Does it have glaring eyes, a tail that stands up like a pole, fur like needles, and a backside big enough to rest Japan on it? Also, there is a teaching that if a dog has only one whisker by its mouth, then it is jumpy; two whiskers is good; and three whiskers means it is timid. If you feed it boar meat as a puppy and its appetite is voracious, then it is destined to become a great dog. Be sure to weigh a litter of pups after birth. The heavy ones will grow into good dogs. Furthermore, don't beat them, scold them, or pat them. Feed them often, but only a little at a time.

❀ ❀ ❀

11-36. The story about the time when Hyakutake Shima-no-Kami[1] did not show when Shigenami was killed.[2] As Shima-no-Kami remained at home, despite the insurrection that broke out near Tsujinodō[3] following Shigenami's slaying, his wife threw his armor at him and screeched: "Are you so afraid that you can't join the rumpus and fight with your allies?" Staying where he was, Shima-no-Kami replied: "I shed tears of sorrow for Shigenami's downfall, and am unable to rouse myself to enter the fray."

Another time, because of a disagreement with her husband, Shima-no-Kami's wife neglected to feed the men one morning. Her husband and his troops were suddenly mobilized for battle, and departed quickly. The repentant wife prepared some food, and dress-

---

1 Hyakutake Shima-no-Kami was respected as one of Ryūzōji Takanobu's four greatest warriors.
2 This is referring to the incident in which Ryūzōji Takanobu assassinated Kamochi Shigenami, lord of the Yanagawa castle, in 1581.
3 Saga City.

ing as a man, she hurried to the meeting point with her servant girls, carrying caskets of water and morsels.

Also, after the battle at Shimabara, the Satsuma forces were approaching Chikugo when Shima-no-Kami's wife was inside the Kamochi castle.[1] To ensure that the castle did not look like it was only lightly guarded, she improvised by making many insignia flags, and lined them up on top of the walls. She protected the castle valiantly and saw the enemy off. It seems that the flags were used for all manner of purposes thereafter. Shima-no-Kami's earlier residence was behind the west citadel, but is now where the Denbei mansion is.[2] Shima-no-Kami's wife was undeniably a feisty woman.

❖ ❖ ❖

11-77. A samurai was traveling through the village of Yae in Saga when he was suddenly gripped by stomach pains, and hurried into a nearby house in search of a lavatory to relieve himself. A young woman alone in the house said the privy was in the back, so he hurriedly removed his *hakama* in the house while rushing out to the toilet. Just then, the woman's husband returned home. Seeing the *hakama* strewn on the floor, he accused the two of adultery, and the case was taken to trial. Lord Naoshige heard about it and commented, "Even if the two perpetrators are innocent of committing the act, the fact that the man removed his *hakama* without considering that the woman was alone, and the fact that she let him do so when her husband was away, makes it the same as adultery." They were both sentenced to death for their poor judgment.

❖ ❖ ❖

11-162. In raising a boy, the first priority is to encourage valor. From his youngest days, the child should be taught to respect his father as his lord, as well as matters of protocol and etiquette, service, proper

---

1 This was the battle in 1584 between Ryūzōji Takanobu and Shimazu Iehisa. The Ryūzōji forces were defeated, and Takanobu and Shima-no-Kami were killed in combat.
2 Nabeshima Denbei Zōfusa.

speech, self-control, and even how to walk down a road. Warriors of old did this. If he is lazy, he should be scolded and not fed for a day. This is all training to be a good retainer.

With a girl, it is critical to impart to her the importance of virtuousness from a young age. She should not get closer to a man than 6-*shaku*,[1] nor should she meet his eyes, or receive things from him by hand. She should not visit attractions nor go to temples on her own. A woman who has withstood a strict upbringing at home will not falter when she is married.

When managing servants, reward or punish them appropriately. If one is negligent in enforcing instructions, servants will become selfish and eventually make mistakes. Be on the watch for this.

MISCELLANY

3-22. Once, when Lord Naoshige went through a little hamlet called Chiriku, he was informed: "A man who is over 90 years old lives here. As he must be such a lucky chap to enjoy such longevity, can we not pay him a visit?" Lord Naoshige retorted, "No one can be more wretched. How many of his grandchildren do you suppose he has seen die? What could possibly be lucky about that?" He didn't pay him a visit.

❀ ❀ ❀

3-26. When Lord Naoshige developed an abscess on his ear, it was suggested by someone that "it will come off if bound with threads from a spider's web and pulled forcefully." Admitting that the protuberance was "extremely bothersome," Lord Naoshige reluctantly followed the advice. Yet the scab began to fester and rot. He convalesced for a period, but it would still not heal.

Naoshige lamented: "Everything I have done until now has been for the benefit of the people. Alas, I must have been mistaken in my reckoning of what others have told me, and have inadvertently erred

---

1 1-*shaku* = 12 inches (30cm).

many times as a result. The problem of my festering ear must be divine retribution. If I should putrefy and die, this would bring shame on my descendants, so I would sooner expire before my malady gets too serious and I rot to death." Simply claiming "I am ill," he hid himself away, refused to eat, and turned down any medicine.

Lord Katsushige implored him repeatedly: "People will judge me later as a dishonorable son if I don't give medication to my father as he teeters on the verge of death. Please take some medicine." Lord Naoshige agreed. "For you, Shinano-no-Kami (Katsushige), I will take a little medicine." He asked Hayashi Eikyū to concoct a potion. Eikyū obeyed, and when he presented it, His Lordship reproached him angrily saying, "I show you favor because you are an honest man. What you have done is quite outrageous. You mixed rice in the tonic, did you not? Answer me truthfully!" Eikyū conceded remorsefully. "You hadn't been eating for days, Sire. I assumed you lacked strength, and thought that if I put some rice in the mix it would give you strength to aid your recovery. So that's what I did." Lord Naoshige declared sternly, "Don't do such a devious thing again!"

Lord Naoshige called for Ishii Shōsatsu when he had taken ill. "I would like to have the study completely dismantled this evening. Do you think it is possible to keep the workers quiet?" Shōsatsu assured him, "That will be easy, My Lord." The study was disassembled and tidied without a sound. The next morning, Lord Naoshige asked him, "How were you able to prevent any noise being made?" Shōsatsu replied, "I had the workers bite down on brushwood leaves." Lord Naoshige commended him: "Jolly good show. That's why I asked you to manage the task. By the way, I would like to have a rock on the island in the lake to be placed where the study was so I can hold a Buddhist service for myself.[1] My mother and wife warn that 'If one uses an unmarked rock as a monument, one will not be able to produce offspring.' So, although it may be unnerving to people, I need an epitaph inscribed on the back…"

---

1 The practice called *gyakushu*, or "pre-emptive funeral," was a Buddhist service conducted during an individual's lifetime as a reminder of the transience of all things, and to pray for happiness after death.

He then started thinking what to engrave, and decided on NABESHIMA KAGA-NO-KAMI TOYOTOMI ASAOMI NAOSHIGE. The building is where the Sōchiji Temple was built [in 1618]. His grave is located there. It was constructed one year prior to his death.

❀ ❀ ❀

3-27. Lord Naoshige once imparted the following truism to his grandson, Lord Motoshige: "Regardless of the status of your house, be it high or low, the time will come when it will crumble. The downfall will be ignominious if you display exasperation, trying to avoid the inevitable. Accept your ruin with dauntless dignity when that time is upon you. With such mental preparation and acceptance of the inevitable, it may actually prove to be a remedial setback." Lord Getsudō[1] conveyed this story to Master Zenkai-in.[2]

❀ ❀ ❀

3-46. Lord Aki[3] went on official business to see Lord Naoshige in the third citadel. Lord Naoshige was away, and no one knew where he was. He visited again the next day, but still Lord Naoshige was nowhere to be found. After searching the castle, he was finally spotted in a corner turret. Lord Aki ascended the tower and inquired,"Pray tell, what are you doing up here?" "I have been observing the manners of the people in our domain for the last two or three days." Asked, "Why would you do such a thing?" Lord Naoshige replied, "I have been surveying peoples' attitudes as they pass by, and pondering. Alas, it appears that warriors of Hizen have already lost the 'sting' in their spears. You must listen to what I say. Most men who pass by have their eyes cast to the ground. It seems that they have become somewhat docile. The thrust of one's spear will be ineffective if lacking in fighting spirit. A benign man who is always polite but re-

---

1 Nabeshima Motoshige.

2 Motoshige's second son, Nabeshima Naoaki.

3 Nabeshima Shigemasa (1571–1645).

strained, cannot do manly tasks. A true samurai sometimes needs swagger in his step, and an aura of haughtiness." From this time on, it is said that Lord Aki was prone to speaking boastfully.

❀ ❀ ❀

3-49. Lord Nippō[1] said to his attendants, "A samurai should never let his guard down, even in ordinary times, as you may be confronted by a crisis when least expected. You will fall down if you are not alert. Also, don't pour scorn on someone just because others do. In the course of service you should be proactive in offering instruction, but step back and wait for invitations to participate in diversions and sightseeing outings [rather than organizing them yourself]. It's fatuous to feign knowledge of something you don't know when others talk of it. Also, it's inappropriate to abstain from telling others of things you do know when asked."

❀ ❀ ❀

3-53. The unrivaled spearman Yokoʻo Kuranojō received preferential treatment in the service of Lord Naoshige. Lord Naoshige would praise him unreservedly to his grandson, Lord Getsudō. "I only wish you could see for yourself how magnificently Kuranojō wielded his spear in battle when he was in his prime. It was a sight to behold." Kuranojō, acutely aware of the favor bestowed upon him, wrote an oath to his lord, pledging to follow him immediately in death by cutting his belly (*oibara*).

One day, Kuranojō became enmeshed in a lawsuit with a farmer, and the circumstances were deliberated on in his lord's presence. Kuranojō lost an impossible case. Outraged by the verdict, he beseeched, "I request that you annul my oath, as a samurai outdone by a lowly farmer couldn't possibly follow his lord in death." Lord Naoshige sighed, "One side wins, and one side will lose. Although a master of the martial arts, it's such a pity Kuranojō knows little

_____

1 Nabeshima Naoshige.

about the ways of the world." He released Kuranojō from the pledge.

※ ※ ※

4-18. Lord Naoshige enjoyed a nightcap every evening. Before retiring for bed, he was sure to spend time conversing until he sobered up. When he was ready to turn in, he would tighten his underwear; then, unsheathing his *wakizashi*,[1] he would hold it close to his face, trim his eyebrows as he inspected the blade, then put it back in its scabbard. He never neglected this ritual throughout his lifetime.

※ ※ ※

4-22. Lord Katsushige made his ten footguards (*go-kachi*) carry swords 3-*shaku* 3-*sun* in length.[2] He would catch them unawares by ordering them to draw their swords at any given moment. Eventually, all of his servants were so well trained, that they could draw the instant he opened his mouth. Then, they were made to carry swords approximately 1-*sun* longer. When they were proficient at drawing these, they reverted back to their old swords [which were much easier to use].

※ ※ ※

4-25. During Lord Katsushige's reign, on the first day of each year he wrote down his supplications and submitted them to the three shrines in Yoka, Honjō, and Hachiman. He would pay homage at the shrines to thank the deities for prayers answered. The content of his supplications were:

1. May distinguished attendants emerge.
2. May there be no attendants who need to be dismissed.
3. May there be no illness among attendants.

---

1 Short-sword.
2 Approximately 3 feet 3 inches (1 meter). 1-*shaku* = 12 inches (30cm); 1-*sun* = 1.2 inches (3.03cm).

This list of Lord Katsushige's supplications from the year he died remains at one of the shrines. (As told by Ittei.)

❋ ❋ ❋

4-40. Lord Katsushige felt cold when he was hunting in Shiroishi. He entered a farmer's house in search of a hearth to warm himself. The solitary inhabitant was an old lady who said, adding more straw to feed the flames, "This morning is particularly cold. Please do come and sit by the fire." After a while, he thanked her and left. As he stepped out of the house, he trod on rice in the yard. The old lady smacked his feet with a broom, saying angrily, "That is rice for the lord. What a terribly clumsy man you are." He replied "Please forgive me," and left. Being very impressed by the old lady, he decided to include her family in the "ten [leading] farm households" in Shiroishi who were permitted to have a surname and carry a sword.[1]

❋ ❋ ❋

4-41. When Lord Katsushige successfully landed a huge boar at the Shiroishi hunt, everybody raced forth saying, "My oh my, His Lordship has bagged such a rare and large specimen." Suddenly, the boar jumped to its feet and started to escape. The onlookers took flight in the commotion, but Nabeshima Matabei drew his sword and killed the beast. While this was happening, Lord Katsushige shielded his face with his sleeve saying, "Dust is getting in my eyes." He was considerately averting his gaze from the disgraceful sight of his bewildered men.

❋ ❋ ❋

---

1 The Tokugawa shogunate and domains restricted people from carrying swords and adopting surnames (*myōji taitō*). Although sword-carrying privileges and surnames were granted to select commoners by daimyo as a reward for praiseworthy service, their official status remained the same. Sometimes, samurai were forced to relinquish their status, and in such cases, the right of *myōji taitō* was renounced.

4-54. Before passing the reins of power to his son Mitsushige, Lord Katsushige presented him with a scroll consisting of 20 articles. These were Lord Katsushige's principles. Included is an account of a discussion held between father and son on day twenty-six of the fifth month [in Genwa 4 (1618)], when Lord Katsushige visited Lord Naoshige on his deathbed.[1] Lord Naoshige implored him: "The most important aspect in governing the domain is to retain good men." Lord Katsushige then asked: "Should I pray for capable vassals?" Lord Naoshige replied, "People offer prayers making pleas to the Buddha and gods for things they have no capacity to obtain. But recruiting fine attendants is something within your powers." "How can I do this?" Lord Katsushige asked again. "Things tend to be drawn to a man who is partial to them. For example, if a man who has never kept a plant before suddenly starts to love flowers, before long he will be surrounded by them, even the odd rare genus. In this way, if you are enamored of people, then good men are sure to appear. So, just be caring of others."

Apparently Lord Naoshige also said, "Being devoid of sincerity will render you incapable of success." A number of other topics were also covered.

❀ ❀ ❀

4-64. Lord Katsushige professed, "Men who have risen from humble beginnings should never forget their past." He also said: "Place the past in front of you, so that you do not put it behind you and forget from whence you came."

❀ ❀ ❀

4-65. Lord Katsushige apparently said to his chief retainers: "I remember well how Lord Naoshige would always say, 'Listen to the circumstances carefully in lawsuits and trials to try and circumvent a sentence of death.' I relay this to you all." Also, "Never drink during

---

1 He died on day three of the sixth month, 1618.

an emergency. Alcohol is usually not good in any case. This was also an admonition from Lord Naoshige."

❀ ❀ ❀

5-70. When Lord Mitsushige was a young man he was interested in all manner of amusements,[1] and would immerse himself in anything that took his fancy. Elders sought to discourage his obsessions with this and that, thinking it would serve no good purpose in the future.

He grew fond of books on poetry around the age of 19. The elders thought it was acceptable for him to enjoy something along these lines, so let him do as his heart desired. Because of his infatuation with poetry, however, he subsequently abandoned all else. Lord Katsushige was enraged when he heard about this. Scolding him severely, he gathered all of his poetry books, and burned them at the Uchikoshi mansion.[2] He dismissed the two elders[3] serving Lord Mitsushige, and made him write a divine oath promising that he would never again look at books of poetry. "Poetry is for court nobles in Kyoto, not for men of warrior houses. How can you become head of the clan when you have neglected your duties as a samurai? You only need to be knowledgeable in military affairs and politics."

Lord Mitsushige stopped reading poetry after this. He realized after several years had passed: "It is only natural that my grandfather, Lord Katsushige, prohibited me from reveling in poetry, lest it prove detrimental to my ability to govern. If he were alive today, I think he would permit a diversion in my free time so long as it didn't interfere with my duties. My ancestors were born in the age of the 'country at war,' and left honorable reputations as valiant warriors in the realm. Having been born a samurai, it would be sad if I was unable to leave my name for posterity. However, now is an age of peace—I have no recourse to seek glory in battle. If the country was at war, I would perform valiantly in a manner not inferior to my ancestors. To make

---

1 See Book 2-68.
2 One of the Nabeshima residences in Edo.
3 Mawatari Ichinosuke and Fukushima Gorōzaemon.

a name for myself now, I could become a master in 'the Way of poetry' to the extent that I am esteemed as the foremost expert in Japan. I want to become the only warrior, other than [Hosokawa] Yūsai,[1] to inherit the secrets of *Kokin-denju*[2] and make it my legacy. Providing it doesn't hinder governance of the domain, then surely it would be acceptable to my late grandfather, and would not be lambasted as undutiful."

Thus, he made great efforts studying the 'Way of poetry,' and was finally able to obtain the secrets of *Kokin-denju* on his deathbed, which was really quite miraculous. He said, "As I was prohibited by my grandfather, I must continue my studies behind closed doors." He was always concerned that his poetry fixation would be leaked to the world.

It is said that Yūsai did not obtain the secrets in their entirety, but Lord Mitsushige inherited Nishi-Sanjō's legitimate tradition, and received a perfect certificate of which there are but two others in the world. It is remarkable that these esoteric writings now rest in the possession of our clan. There are only three families who own the secrets of *Kokin-denju*—the imperial family, the Nishi-Sanjō family, and the Nabeshima family.

❀ ❀ ❀

---

1 Also known as Hosokawa Fujitaka (1534–1610), Yūsai was a well-known daimyo and poet who served as a crucial go-between for the shogun Ashikaga Yoshiaki and Oda Nobunaga. When Nobunaga was assassinated in the Honnōji Incident of 1582, Yūsai went into retirement and passed on his domain (Tango) to his son, Hosokawa Tadaoki. After this, he became known as an authority on *waka*, and even instructed Toyotomi Hideyoshi (1537–1598) in classical Japanese poetry. He is also known for teaching Prince Hachijō Toshihito (1579–1629) the secret traditions of the tenth-century *Kokin-shū* anthology (*Kokin-denju*).

2 *Kokin-denju* ("Transmission of the *Kokin-shū*") is a corpus of secret teachings concerning the poems of the imperially commissioned classic tenth century poetry anthology known as the *Kokin-shū*. These coveted teachings were usually passed on from the teacher to a chosen student. *Kokin-denju* began when the highly prominent Nijō and Kyōgoku-Reizei literary families of Kyoto disputed the bequeathal of Fujiwara no Sadaie's (Teika, 1162–1241) traditions of poetry. Both families were descendants of this legendary bard.

5-74. Some lords were discussing whether it was possible to shoot pigeons nesting in the watchtowers of Edo Castle. One daimyo asked Lord Mitsushige what he thought. "Do you think you could bag them?" Mitsushige replied. "I can shoot pigeons with no difficulty, but am loathe to say if I could do the same to the ones roosting in Edo Castle." His answer impressed the other lords.[1]

❀ ❀ ❀

5-81. When Lord Tsunashige was given a reprieve from duty in Edo for the first time, Lord Mitsushige traveled with him back to Saga. All of the villagers lined the roads, prostrating with their hands clasped in prayer to welcome the young lord whom they were seeing for the first time in the fief.[2] Lord Tsunashige later commented to his father, "They were kneeling in prayer to me as I passed by." Lord Naoshige told him off sternly. "Understand this, son. We are no more worthy of veneration than other people."

❀ ❀ ❀

5-143. On the twenty-fifth day of the fifth month, Empō 1 (1673), three vessels from England came to Nagasaki port with the intention of trading, but we turned them away.[3] Because of the kerfuffle , Kumashiro Sakyō (and many others) was dispatched to Nagasaki to guard Fukahori… Sakyō sent notification that it would be unwise for many people to descend at once as it might draw attention, so the new arrivals used plain-looking palanquins to reach their destination, one at a time. Thinking it critical to prepare for any situation, Sakyō mobilized the guards with a strategic plan.

---

1 The inference being that it was strictly prohibited for anybody to use arms in the shogun's Edo Castle.

2 Due to the *sankin-kōtai* system in which daimyo were obligated to leave their families in Edo as hostages, this was the first time that Tsunashige was able to visit the domain he was destined to lead. He was 21 years of age. See Book 1-194.

3 The ships belonged to the English East India Company.

Directives:

1. Covertly arrive in positions not far from the English vessels when mooring the boats the night before they set sail.

2. No. 1: Nabeshima Shima is to take up his position in Shirosaki. Deploy just before Nishihama-kita.

   No. 2: Nakano Kurōbei's crew shall take up their position in front of Kaminoshima Island. Crew in same position. Launch after Shima.

   No. 3: Nabeshima Aki's crew will take position offshore of Kaminoshima Island. Deploy after Nakano Kurōbei's crew.

   No. 4: Sakyō and his crew, Taku Hyōgo, Daiki Shōemon, and Nishi Gotaiyū, shall take up positions between Bakuchishima and Hitotsuya. They will deploy in front of Ōhato.

   No. 5: Kitashima Geki, Doi Kurando, Hara Jirōei and five gunboats should take up positions to the north of Takahoko fort. Deploy from under Makome.

3. Regarding meals for the soldiers and the crews, one day's worth of provisions should be prepared the night before. The men may be required to camp out depending on the situation, so a sufficient amount of provisions should be arranged and meals prepared each night for the following day.

4. For boat insignias, paper banners with clan markings alone will suffice. There is no need for individual boat insignia or flags.

5. No brushwood covers are to be used, even if it rains.

6. Each vessel should be equipped with boat hooks and iron rakes.

7. Do not carry any guns. Remain empty-handed.

8. Concerning signals. A large flag will be waved from Sakyō's boat and a conch shell will be blown. With this signal, all ropes should be cut and the boats deployed. No boats are to move before the signal is given.

   Additionally: Gunboats should not deploy with the other boats.

9. Cannons should only be fired after the bell on Sakyō's boat has been rung.

10. Do not shoot from the rear of the gunboat.

11. Vessels armed with arrows should proceed together with cannon boats. Arrows are to be fired using the same signal.

12. If an English ship is commandeered or sunk, surround it with other boats and secure it. Should something happen to Sakyō at this time, the remaining unit leaders are to report the situation to the Nagasaki magistrate's office as well as Saga. As long as Sakyō is unharmed, he (I) will continue to give orders. The English ships are to be handed over to the magistrate, and all crews will return to Fukahori in a systematic fashion.

13. If the English vessels leave port without any trouble, all boats are to remain stationary until Sakyō signals with his conch shell, even after the boats assigned by the shogunate envoys have left. With the first signal, weigh the anchors and lower the oars. With the second signal, Sakyō's vessel will lead and each unit will follow in the order of Nabeshima Aki's men, Nakano Kurōbei, Nabeshima Shima, Kitajima Geki, Doi Kurando, and then the cannon boats and bowmen.

14. Boats should be moored tidily in Fukahori.

15. Nishi Godaiyū will instruct the boatmen well in advance regarding when to deploy.

Written by Sakyō Kumashiro on the nineteenth day of the seventh month.

The English ships left port on the twenty-fifth day of the seventh month without incident. Sakyō and everybody else left Fukahori on the twenty-seventh day of the seventh month, and arrived back in Saga on the twenty-ninth day. There were 30 boats. Totoki Settsuno-Kami, an elder of the Yanagawa clan, visited Sakyō on his boat and complimented his procedures.

❈ ❈ ❈

6-21. Tannen used to say the following: "If a Buddhist monk is not compassionate on the outside and courageous inside his heart, he will never become enlightened in the Buddhist Way. In the case of a samurai, unless he is courageous on the outside and bursting his gut with great compassion on the inside, he will be unable to execute his duties. Through mingling with samurai, the Buddhist monk is able to understand courage, and conversely, the samurai learns compassion from the monk.

"Over years of traveling I have met with many sagacious priests throughout the country, but not one was useful in my study. If I got wind of some heroic samurai nearby, I would visit him without carping about the difficult road to find him. I remember how listening to warrior tales helped me greatly in my quest to study the Buddhist Way. First of all, with his weapons in hand the warrior has the strength to charge forth into the enemy lines. The monk has only his rosary beads, and can't storm into a wall of spears and long swords with only an attitude of gentleness and compassion.

"One cannot advance without great courage. As proof of this, priests are sometimes seen trembling nervously when offering incense at a large Buddhist gathering. It is because they lack courage. The priest needs to be incredibly brave to trample down the evil spirits trying to return, and to hoist the dead from the chasms of the netherworld.

"Nevertheless, monks in the present day concern themselves with trivialities, and are wrapped up in becoming 'docile' and 'gentle', making them unable to realize the Way. It is also regretful to see monks encouraging samurai to seek enlightenment through Buddhist teachings, transforming them into hopeless wimps. It is a mistake for a young warrior to obsess for Buddhist teachings as it makes him perceive the world in two [contradictory] perspectives. A warrior will never achieve anything unless he holds true to a single direction.

"A samurai who has retired from his duties to lead a life as a recluse may venture to attend sermons on the Way of Buddhism. A warrior in service must unremittingly bear the bone-breaking burden of loyalty [to his lord] and filial duty [to his parents] on one shoulder, squared with courage and compassion on the other, and fulfill his calling to stand as an honorable samurai.

"Chanting 'My Lord! My Lord!' during morning and evening

worship, day in and day out, is surely just as meritorious as a priest citing the sacred Buddha's name or mantras. Also, *ujigami*[1] should be worshiped as this will augur good fortune. Many examples are known from the old days, and now, of warriors brimming with valor but lacking in compassion, who spiral downward into their destruction."

❀ ❀ ❀

6-63. Ittei was dismissed from duty and lived in Umenoyama. He transferred his stipend to his son, Yasuzaemon. One day, when he had an errand to run in Kyoto, Shimomura Saburōbei, the residence caretaker said, "Being a *rōnin* means you can't have had any wine for a long while." Ittei said, "I haven't come across any in the mountains where I reside. More than that, though, there is no rice. I keep barley, buckwheat, barnyard millet and the like in a cooker and eat it when I want to. I haven't had any soup either, come to think of it." Saburōbei replied, "Well then, it must be difficult to fall asleep on cold nights without a drink. I warrant it is also hard to eat something so plain." Ittei responded, "I don't sleep if I can't fall asleep. I sleep when I can. I don't eat if I can't eat. I eat when I can. It's as simple as that." Ittei also mentioned, "Saburōbei has a tendency to be terse, if not a tad overbearing. He must be an aggravating influence to have around, and is not like an "*Azuma otoko*" as depicted in *Tsuzuregusa*."[2]

❀ ❀ ❀

6-81. Originally there were no *ashigaru*[3] in the Nabeshima clan. During the campaigns to invade Korea, various houses utilized *ashigaru* in their armies to great effect. The Nabeshima leaders decided to make second and third sons serve as *ashigaru*, and this

---

1 Clan or local deity. See Book 2-80.
2 *Essays in Idleness*, or *The Harvest of Leisure* is a well-known collection of Japanese essays or "random jottings" written by the monk Yoshida Kenkō between the years 1330 and 1332. *Azuma otoko* refers to men or warriors of the Eastern provinces who were known for being unpretentious and pragmatic.
3 Low-level foot soldiers.

was the beginning of the rank in the Saga domain. (It is also said that laborers for the construction of Edo Castle were temporarily appointed as *ashigaru* during the siege of Osaka Castle.[1] The two theories are at odds. Verification is needed.)

❀ ❀ ❀

6-109. Nakano Uemon'nosuke Tadaaki was slain on day twelve of the eighth month in Eiroku 6 (1563) when Gotō and Hirai from Suko clashed on Kabashima Island in Kishima. As Uemon'nosuke was departing for battle, he hugged his infant son Shikibu (later named Jin'uemon) in the yard and said, "When you reach adulthood, be sure to seek glory in the military way." Consequently, Yamamoto Jin'uemon would also bring the children close, even if they were but infants, and whisper in their ears: "You must grow into a brave warrior (*kusemono*) who is relied upon by his lord." He also advised: "It's constructive to say such things in a child's ear, even if they don't yet have the capacity to understand."

❀ ❀ ❀

7-1. Naridomi Hyōgo[2] said, "Attaining victory means to win over one's allies. Winning over one's allies requires defeating the self. To defeat the self necessitates triumphing over one's body with the mind. That is, you must forge your body and mind so that even with tens of thousands of allied warriors behind you, nobody can keep up as you charge forth on your own."

❀ ❀ ❀

7-5. On Tazaki Geki's armor. When the assault took place on the Hara Castle in Shimabara, the warrior Tazaki Geki was wearing a

---

1 Katsushige was appointed as a construction official for the building of Edo Castle. See Book 1-201 regarding the sieges at Osaka Castle.

2 Naridomi Hyōgonosuke Shigeyasu (1560–1634).

dazzling set of armor.[1] Lord Katsushige was displeased by his ostentatiousness, and whenever he saw something garish from then on, he would remark, "Ah, just like the armor of Geki." In light of this anecdote, pretentious military equipment or attire will be condemned as flimsy and lacking resilience. People will see through it.

❀ ❀ ❀

7-46. Ikuno Oribe's precepts. When Tsunetomo was young and having a drink one night in the castle, Ikuno Oribe came to talk with him. "Nakano Shōgen asked me of the basic attitude required for a man in service. As we are friends, I gave my honest opinion. I know not much, other than any man is capable of executing his duties expediently when things are going well. He will feel dejected when instructed to engage in tedious duties he perceives as being below his station. Such an attitude is lamentable. It is a waste. I believe that if a man in a high position is ordered to draw water from the well or cook rice, he should do it happily, without brooding. This especially applies to you Tsunetomo, as you are still young and so self-assured."

❀ ❀ ❀

7-48. On knowledge gleaned by Shida Kichinosuke through the course of his life.[2] Kichinosuke remarked: "It is exhausting to run until out of breath; but it feels particularly good when one is standing after finishing. It is even more pleasurable to sit. Furthermore, it is better still to lie down. And even more than that, how wonderful it is to take a pillow and doze off. This is the way a man's life should be. Ideally, you should apply yourself and work vigorously in your youth, and then sleep in your old age, or when on the verge of passing away. If you sleep first you will have to 'break your bones' working later. Even if you work your fingers to the bone later, it would be most unfortunate to die after spending [the latter part of]

---

1 During the Shimabara Uprising of 1637.
2 See Book 1-48.

your life bogged down in exhaustive toil." (This anecdote was relayed by Shimomura Rokuzaemon.) Kichinosuke also had a similar saying. "The more hardship, the better."

❖ ❖ ❖

7-52. When Harada Shirōzaemon slayed a giant snake. When Harada Esquire, a member of a Takeo [Nabeshima] family, was 15 years old, he was walking across a field with a falcon on his arm when a large serpent appeared. Perhaps with its eye on the bird, the snake lunged and wrapped its tail around Harada's chest three times. Harada drew his short sword as he held the falcon, and waited in the ready position for the serpent's head to approach. When it was in reach he sliced it off. The limp body of the serpent flopped to the ground. It was approximately 3-*ken* in length.[1] Harada's ribs were injured in the encounter and he took some time to recuperate. He says his ribs hurt to this day when it gets cold. (Told directly by Harada.)

Yet another man who went hunting in Takeo came across an unfamiliar creature with its mouth wide open. It was attempting to bite him, so he removed his hunting knife, approximately 1-*shaku* 2 or 3-*sun* long,[2] and plunged the blade deep inside its mouth up to his elbow. It was a snake measuring 1.5-*ken* or so.[3] Its face looked like that of a guardian lion-dog, and about 4-*shaku*[4] of its torso was like that of a cat. Its scales were like coins, and white hair extended from its jaw to its belly. It had eight feet that looked like those of a rat. Its body tapered towards its tail. He preserved the creature in salt and took it back to Saga. This happened about three or four years ago. For a while nobody could pass where the reptilian beast was discovered because the mountain trembled violently, and the paths were cut off.

If a snake assails you, quickly leap to the side so that it slithers straight by. It will come towards you with its head raised, so strike to break its back. If you cut it in two, it may still slither away. Cutting

---

1 Approximately 18 feet (5.5m).
2 Approximately 14–16 inches (36–40cm).
3 Approximately 8 feet 9 inches (2.7m).
4 Approximately 3 feet 11 inches (1.2m).

it below the head will snuff it out. If you cut low on its tail, it will progress another 2 or 3-*ken*[1] and stop. It is said that snakes will jab humans with their heads, and can penetrate through one side and out the other. Furthermore, a *mamushi*[2] will come back at you and take revenge if you fail to cut off its head.

❧ ❧ ❧

8-14. When the former Yamamoto Jin'uemon met with his men he would say, "Go ahead and gamble, and brag if you wish. If you can't unleash seven tall tales while walking 1-*chō*, then you are not a real man!" In the old days, achieving meritorious deeds in battle was all that was required of a warrior, and decent men would not be able to perform important manly tasks. He pretended not to see the way-ward antics of his men, saying instead they were "doing something of value." Sagara Kyūma also turned a blind eye to vassals who com-mitted acts of larceny or adultery, and cultivated them into good men by degrees insisting, "If they are not yobs to start with, they cannot be made into reliable samurai."

❧ ❧ ❧

8-20. Ikuno Oribe remarked, "If a retainer can think that his service will finish in a day, he will be able to soldier through anything. Anybody can endure backbreaking work for a day. Tomorrow is another day."

❧ ❧ ❧

8-77. Uchida Shōemon's riposte about performing *kaishaku*. Once, a group of warriors congregated in the greeting room of the main citadel. A man passed comment to Uchida Shōemon:[3] "I hear that

---

1 Approximately 12–18 feet (3.6–5.5m).

2 Japanese pit viper.

3 A master of the Tetsujin-ryū school of swordsmanship.

you are a skilled teacher in the art of swordsmanship. But I do declare that your teaching style must be rough, judging by the way you carry yourself. I'll wager that if you were to perform the *kaishaku*, you would probably lop the top of the poor fellow's head off [rather than slice through his neck]." Shōemon retorted, "Au contraire! Let me mark your neck with a spot of ink, and I'll show you just how precise my cutting is."

❈ ❈ ❈

8-79. What Nagayama Rokurōzaemon said to the *rōnin*. When Rokurōzaemon was on the Tokaidō road traveling through the township of Hamamatsu, a vagrant was begging outside an inn. He approached Rokurōzaemon's palanquin saying, "I am a *rōnin* from Echigo. I have no money and am destitute. As we are both samurai, I would be ever so grateful for assistance." Angry at the request, Rokurōzaemon refused him by saying, "How insolent of you to proclaim that we are both samurai! If I were you, I would slit my gut open. Instead of disgracing yourself with no money, cut open your stomach now!" With this, the vagrant meekly slunk away into the shadows.

❈ ❈ ❈

9-3. When Shimomura Shōun was attending at the castle, Lord Naoshige commented, "It is wonderful that Iheita[1] is so burly and strong beyond his years. He wrestled some of the attendants and defeated those older than he." Shōun replied: "Although I am an old man, let's have a seated wrestling bout with him." He pulled Iheita in close and threw him down with force. Taking his leave, Shōun said: "He will shame himself as his bones have not yet set, but he is immodest regarding his strength. He is weaker than he looks."

❈ ❈ ❈

---

1 Nabeshima Katsushige.

9-21. An opinion offered to a certain warrior intent on killing his superior. When the lord was residing in Edo, a certain retainer who had risen to a position of prominence harshly scolded another man to perform his duties properly. The insulted samurai withdrew from the scene without uttering so much as a word. It seemed as though he was preparing to kill his superior.

Another samurai invited him into a hut. "You cannot be blamed for harboring enmity and wanting to teach him a jolly good lesson. At the risk of sounding rude, I believe your rancor may be because you have a different view of service. His Lordship looks to depend on us should the need to deploy for battle arise. So, he shows restraint in how he uses us in service in peaceful times. His Lordship is cordial to minions like him to wipe his backside, or do menial tasks.[1] But he is a discourteous fool who is not aware of this, and misguidedly thinks he is a trusted retainer. Because he is a fool, he serves in a carefree manner, but is no more than a fly that has landed on His Lordship's head. To fight with an idiot such as him, when you are a warrior trusted by the lord to excel in times of crisis, is no better than beating a leper to death with a staff. Furthermore, it would be disloyal to inconvenience His Lordship by causing a fracas. An admirable samurai would not do anything drastic. You must act as your heart dictates, and as this is just my opinion, I have no intention of forcing you to stop." The samurai stopped thinking about killing the man.

❀ ❀ ❀

9-36. Ōkubo Dōko's observations about flowers. "People say that there are no real experts of anything left in this degenerate age, but I disagree. Over time, so many wonderful tree peonies, Chinese peonies, azaleas, and camellias have been produced. As time goes on, the more beautiful the flowers become. Just like these flowers, I am convinced that true masters of the artistic ways will also continue to appear as the world nears its end. It's a pity that people don't exert

---

1 See 3-9.

themselves, blaming instead the depraved epoch in which they live, with the world nearing its end. It has nothing to do with the world, as much as the people themselves."

❖ ❖ ❖

10-8. The essential point for correct etiquette is to perform it swiftly at the beginning and end, and serenely in the middle. Mitani Senzaemon [Masamichi] commented: "That's how I perform *kaishaku*."[1]

❖ ❖ ❖

10-26. The priest Ryōzan wrote a summary of Lord Ryūzōji Takanobu's military exploits. Another priest saw his record and censured him by saying: "It's ill-advised for a priest to write about a military general. Notwithstanding how eloquent his writing may be, he will most likely misunderstand a famous general's mind on account of his unfamiliarity with military affairs. Accordingly, it would be woeful to convey false impressions of a famous general to future generations [through an amateur's interpretation]."

❖ ❖ ❖

10-56. A certain man said, "There is a poem from the shrine [of Sugawara no Michizane][2] that goes: 'If one follows the path of sincerity in his heart, although he may not pray, will the deities not watch over him?' What can 'path of sincerity' possibly mean?" Another man answered. "As you appear to be partial to poetry, allow me to respond in verse. 'Inasmuch as all things in this world are

---

1 In 2-50, he is referred to as Yozaemon.

2 Sugawara-no-Michizane (845–903) was a prominent court scholar and famous poet during the Heian period (794–1185). After he contested the powerful Fujiwara hegemony in court, he died in exile for being accused of "plotting against the throne." A number of subsequent misfortunes at court were attributed to his angry spirit. He was posthumously pardoned and awarded the highest court rank to pacify his ghost. He is revered now as the patron saint of scholarship.

deceptive, sincerity is revealed only in death.' Living as if already dead is how to embody the path of sincerity."

❧ ❧ ❧

10-74. Priest Daiyū Oshō of Sanshū went to visit a sick man, but was informed that he had just passed away. The priest asked: "He was not the sort of man who would 'suddenly pass.' Did this happen from a lack of adequate medical attention? It is truly unlucky." The man's physician happened to be listening from the other side of the sliding door, and his wrath knew no bounds. "I heard your Holiness infer that his death was due to inadequate care. Your assertions may not be entirely groundless in the case of a quack. I understand that priests are supposed to have special powers drawn from Buddhist Law. If this is so, demonstrate this power by bringing him back to life. If you cannot, it is proof that Buddhist teachings have no value."

Although troubled by this outburst, the priest felt it indefensible for the reputation of Buddhist Law to be tarnished by his own folly. "I will revive this man through prayer. Wait, as I must get ready." He then returned to his temple to make preparations, and came back to sit in prayer next to the body. Before long, the sick man astonishingly started to breathe, and made a full recovery. They say that he lived for another half a year. Priest Tannen Oshō inquired if it was true, and how he prayed. Daiyū confessed: "There is no way for reviving the dead, and I am not acquainted with any particular method of prayer. I made up my mind for the sake of Buddhist Law, and when I returned to my temple, I sharpened a donated *wakizashi* and tucked it away in my robe. Facing the dead man, I beseeched: 'If the power of the Buddha exists, then wake now!' As I said this, I intended to cut my stomach open and die with my arms around the dead man's corpse..."

❧ ❧ ❧

10-123. When the priest Ungo Oshō from Matsushima was traversing through the mountains one evening, he was ambushed by a bandit. Ungo exclaimed: "I am from this region. I am no itinerant priest. I have no money. I will give you the clothes I wear, but entreat you not to take my life." The bandit reacted, "This is a wasted effort. I have no need for clothes," and moved on. After walking a distance of around 1-*chō*,[1] Ungo turned and hailed him back. "I have broken my vows by telling an untruth. As I was so flustered, I forgot about this piece of silver in my purse, even though I claimed to have no money. Do not be angry with me. Here it is, please accept it." The bandit was awestruck by his admission. He shaved off his hair on the spot, and became a disciple.

❀ ❀ ❀

10-125. Once, there was a group of ten blind monks walking through the mountains. As they passed around the top of a cliff, their legs began to tremble, and although they took extreme care, they were overcome by fear. The leader staggered and then fell off the edge. The rest all cried, "Oh what a terrible end!" They were unable to take a step further. The blind monk who had fallen off the cliff yelled up from below: "Do not be frightened. Falling was not so bad. I am now quite unperturbed. I worried about what would happen if I fell, and was somewhat apprehensive. But now I am very calm. If you want to put your minds at ease, quickly fall [and get it over with]."

❀ ❀ ❀

10-127. Hōjō Awa-no-Kami[2] gathered his students of military science and requested that a popular Edo physiognomist come and ascertain which of them were strong, and who were cowards. He made each one of his students sit before the man. "If you are 'strong,'

---

1 358 feet (110m).

2 Hōjō Awa-no-Kami Ujinaga (1609–1670) studied the Kōshū-ryū school of military studies (*gungaku*) under strategist Obata Kagenori (1572–1639). Ujinaga held a number of important posts in the bakufu, and taught a radically new interpretation of military strategy to powerful political figures, making him highly influential in the redefining of the samurai peacetime role.

strive to better yourself even more; if you are a 'coward,' be even more determined to sacrifice your very life into your training. As you were born with these traits, it is nothing to be ashamed of." Hirose Denzaemon was only 12 or 13 years old at the time, but sat in front of the physiognomist and raised his voice, saying: "If you declare that I have the countenance of a coward, I will smite you with a single blow of my sword!"

❀ ❀ ❀

10-137. It is best to say in a public discussion or tribunal: "Allow me to defer my reply until I have given it due consideration." Even if offering only a tentative response, it is prudent to retain some flexibility by declaring, "I would still like to ponder this matter a little more, if I may." With this margin of latitude, one should discuss the matter with others and solicit advice. An astute fellow may impart an unexpected tenet of wisdom that adds reason to your cause. Even if an ill-informed man learns the circumstances of the affair, the gist can then be spread throughout the community to your advantage.

Also, if you rehearse your argument with your servants or maids, "When they say such-and-such, I will say this," you will be able to speak articulately with an air of confidence, adding to the persuasiveness of your case. Your chances of failure are increased if you keep it to yourself and do not prepare. Whatever the case, one should seek the counsel of others. If there is nobody judicious to talk with, a solution will appear in one's mind through discussing it with one's wife or children. Such insight only comes with age and experience. (Relayed by Mura Josui.)

❀ ❀ ❀

11-26. Aki-no-Kami's[1] contention that his children need not study military tactics (*gunpō*). "Nothing can be achieved by analyzing too

---

1 Nabeshima Aki-no-Kami Shigetake was the lord of the Fukabori branch of the Nabeshima clan.

much on the field of battle. Discernment (*funbetsu*) prohibits a warrior from charging frenetically at the enemy. Indiscretion is what is needed in the thick of battle. To have a smattering of knowledge in military tactics will make a warrior indecisive as he ponders his options. Thus, my offspring should not study military tactics."

❀ ❀ ❀

11-40. Regarding regrets. There is nothing worse than having regrets. All samurai should take care not to do anything they will repent later. People become elated when their luck is up, and not seeing ahead, they drop their guard and come unstuck when things take a turn for the worse. This is a cause for regret. Always remain alert, and keep your feet firmly planted on the ground, especially when things are good.

❀ ❀ ❀

11-42. The following are teachings of Yamamoto Jin'uemon.[1]

1. Young men should not engage in poetry, reading graphic novels, *gō*, *shōgi*, or other such activities that will cause listlessness. Members of the Nakano clan should carry an oaken sword and hone their military preparedness for service.

2. Anything is achievable through single-minded endeavor (*bannō-isshin*).

3. Dog skin inside, tiger hide outside.

4. The end phrase of a letter will not wear your brush out. You won't break your back by bowing politely.[2]

5. Be sure to secure even a broiled chicken.[3]

6. Whip even a galloping horse.[4]

7. A man who asks questions candidly to your face holds no malice.

---

1 Jōchō's father. See 1-60. Although the gist is generally the same for some of these precepts, the wording is slightly different than those quoted in the first book.

2 You can never be too polite.

3 You should not let your guard down under any circumstance.

4 Don't take things for granted, especially if they seem to be going well.

8. A man lives for one generation, but a name forever.

9. Money is there for the asking, but [good] men are not.

10. A man who feigns laughter is a coward. A woman who does so is prurient.

11. A real man will be able to tell tall tales seven times in 1-*chō*.[1]

12. It is not rude to ask even when you know the answer, but an imperative if you don't.

13. If you can see one direction, you can see eight.[2]

14. If you know one truth, you will awaken to everything.

15. Wrap your will in pine needles.[3]

16. A trustworthy man is a *kusemono* (heroic warrior).

17. Don't insert your hands in the sides of your *hakama*. It is careless.

18. Don't open your mouth and yawn in front of others. Conceal it behind your sleeve or fan.

19. A straw hat or *kabuto* should be worn with the front part low.[4]

20. When he was dying he said: "Everyone knows the name of Jin'uemon. It would be regrettable to groan because of the pain." He never groaned until the very end.[5]

❀　❀　❀

11-48. On breaking free from life and death. A warrior who cannot detach himself from matters of life and death will be useless. The axiom, "Anything is achievable through single-minded endeavor" appears to be a form of attachment, but actually means to break free from concerns of life and death. With this mind-set, any meritorious feat is achievable. The [martial] arts are a vehicle into the Way [of detachment from life and death].

❀　❀　❀

---

1 1-*chō* = 358 feet (110m).

2 As long as you are careful in your observance, you will be able to perceive all things.

3 If you are sincere, the gifts you send as tribute are allowed to be small as it's the thought that counts.

4 To conceal where one is looking.

5 See Book 9-26.

11-74. Matsudaira Izu-no-Kami said to Mizuno Kenmotsu [Tada-yoshi]:[1] "You are an expedient man, but it is a pity you are so short." Kenmotsu retorted: "Indeed it is true. Some things turn out contrary to one's liking. I would be a little taller if I was to chop your head off and attach it to my feet, but I am unable to have it my way."

❀ ❀ ❀

11-124. The requisite for speaking is to not speak. If you wish to settle something without words, it can be accomplished without talk. If one is commanded to speak, do so with as few words as possible so that it sounds reasonable. It is opprobrious conduct to blurt impulsively and superfluously. You will likely be forsaken by others.

❀ ❀ ❀

11-167. It is said that, "Great enterprise does not dwell on trifles." As long as a retainer serves his lord with singular loyalty (which I have written about exhaustively in *Gukenshū*), he will be forgiven, even if he is careless in other matters, or makes a nuisance of himself in having his own way. By contrast, perfection in every respect makes a man somewhat disagreeable. He will be stretched to breaking point in important matters. One cannot achieve remarkable deeds without flexibility. It is said, "When a man achieves something great, minor blunders are not to be dwelt upon as 'undutiful.'"

---

1 Lord of the Okazaki domain.

MAIN EVENTS IN THE HISTORY OF THE SAGA DOMAIN AND YAMAMOTO JŌCHŌ'S LIFE

YEAR	EVENT
1530	Ryūzōji Iekane and Nabeshima Kiyohisa combine forces for the first time at the Battle of Tatenawate against the Ōuchi and Kanzaki armies.
1545	Ryūzōji Iekane is killed in Kawakami and Ryūzōji Chikaie is slain by Baba Yorichika.
1570	The Ōtomo army of Bungo province (modern day Oita Prefecture) attack the Ryūzōji stronghold of Saga Castle. Nabeshima Naomasa (later named Naoshige) makes a night raid on enemy forces in Imayama which serves to revitalise the Ryūzōji clan.
1584	Ryūzōji Takanobu is killed at Shimabara fighting against Shimazu and Arima forces.
LORD RYŪZŌJI MASAIE (1556–1607)	
1588	Toyotomi Hideyoshi endorses Ryūzōji Masaie's sovereignty over the Hizen province.
1590	Hideyoshi orders Masaie to relinquish control of the Saga fiefdom to his relative, Nabeshima Naoshige.

LORD NABESHIMA NAOSHIGE (1538–1618)	
1592	Naoshige leads his troops into battle in Hideyoshi's campaign in the Korean peninsula. His exploits of valor are lauded.
1597	Naoshige returns to Korea in the second expedition with his son Katsushige.
1598	Hideyoshi dies. Naoshige returns to Saga from Korea.
1600	Naoshige initially sides with the Toyotomi forces, but switches to become a Tokugawa ally. After defeating Tachibana Muneshige and contributing to the Tokugawa victory at the Battle of Sekigahara, Tokugawa Ieyasu officially sanctions his control over the Saga domain.
LORD NABESHIMA KATSUSHIGE (1580–1657)	
1607	The Ryūzōji line ceases after Takafusa's death, and Nabeshima Katsushige is permitted by the bakufu to appropriate all of their former lands.
1610	The Kashima sub-branch of the Nabeshima domain is created for Katsushige's younger brother, Tadashige.
1611	The Nabeshima domain is ordered to provide manpower for the construction of the shogun's castle in Edo.
1614	Katsushige and his troops are mobilized to take part in the Winter Siege of Osaka castle to quell any last resistance from Toyotomi supporters.
1615	The Nabeshima domain is directed to provide manpower for the rebuilding of Osaka castle.
1617	The Ogi sub-branch of the Nabeshima domain is created for Katsushige's oldest son, Motoshige.

1618	Nabeshima Naoshige dies at 81. Thirteen of his retainers follow him in death (*oibara*). Katsushige's eldest son, Motoshige, becomes a licensed instructor of the prestigious Yagyū Shinkage-ryū school of swordsmanship.
1619	Resources from the Nabeshima domain are mobilized in the construction of Edo Castle which was to be the seat of government and residence of the shogun.
1620	Nakano Kiyoaki (Jōchō's grandfather) is killed at Imari Momonokawa.
1628	Men from the Nabeshima domain are mobilized in the restoration of Osaka castle.
1629	Nabeshima Naoshige's wife, Yōdaiin, dies. Eight of her retainers follow her in death. Nabeshima Katsushige's second son, Tadanao, also dies. Five of his retainers follow him in death. The Hasuike sub-domain is established for Katsushige's fifth son, Naosumi.
1637	Katsushige's army participates in the Shimabara Uprising to subdue the Christians.
1642	The shogunate assigns Katsushige as supervisor of Nagasaki.
1647	Yamamoto Shigezumi (Jōchō's father) becomes the first governor of Arita.
1648	Katsushige's grandson undergoes the coming of age ceremony.
1652	The book of Saga domain laws known as "Torinoko-chō" is written.
1657	Mitsushige takes over the headship of the Nabeshima domain following the retirement of Katsushige.

LORD NABESHIMA MITSUSHIGE (1632–1700)	
1659	Yamamoto Jōchō (Tsunetomo) is born on the eleventh day of the sixth month. Birth name is Matsukame.
1661	Mitsushige bans *junshi*, or the self-immolation of retainers to follow their lord in death. This was to prevent retainers of Shiraishi Yūshu Nabeshima Naohiro committing suicide after his death.
1667	Mitsushige employs Tsunetomo into his entourage of apprentice pages. Name is changed to Fukei.
1669	Tsunetomo's father dies.
1672	Promoted to personal pageboy of Mitsushige. Name is changed to Ichijūrō.
1673	Saga warriors are summoned to Nagasaki to bolster defences after the unwelcome arrival of English trading ships.
1678	Undergoes the coming of age ceremony (*genpuku*) and becomes a scribe for Mitsushige. Takes the name Gon'nojō. Tashiro Tsuramoto is born.
1679	The Monk Tannen Oshō confers Tsunetomo with a *kechi-myaku* (certificate of "blood-lineage" in the school of Zen) for his understanding of Buddhist law. Is bestowed the Buddhist name Kyokuzan Jōchō. Antagonism between the main Nabeshima domain and the three sub-domains intensifies.
1680	Tannen Oshō dies.
1682	Tsunetomo becomes a page and then an officer of document writing. Marries the daughter of Yamamura Sukedayū Naritsugu.
1686	Appointed as a clerk in the Nabeshima Edo residence and then in the Kyoto mansion.

1687	Tsunetomo is temporarily suspended from duty because of Yamamoto Tsuneharu's (his nephew) suicide to atone for a fire that broke out in Saga in 1686.
1691	Assumes his late father's name, Jin'uemon.
1693	Ittei dies.
1695	Nabeshima Tsunashige becomes the third head of the domain after his father Mitsushige retires.
LORD NABESHIMA TSUNASHIGE (1652–1707)	
1696	Tsunetomo is dispatched to Kyoto to acquire the *Kokin-denju* teachings on poetry teachings for Mitsushige. Tashiro Tsuramoto becomes a scribe for Tsunashige.
1700	Nabeshima Mitsushige dies in the Kōyōken at 69 years of age. Jōchō (Tsunetomo) takes the Holy Orders and becomes a reclusive monk in a hermitage in Kurotsuchibaru.
1702	Jōchō takes Tominaga Tsunetoshi as his adopted son. Tsunetoshi is later named Gon'nojō.
1706	Nabeshima Tsunashige dies.
LORD NABESHIMA YOSHISHIGE (1664–1730)	
1707	Nabeshima Yoshishige becomes the fourth lord of the domain.
1708	Jōchō writes the *Gukenshū* and presents it to his adopted son.
1709	Tsuramoto is removed from his post as his lord's attendant. Jōchō's mother dies.
1710	Tsuramoto makes his first visit to Jōchō's hermitage, and dictations for *Hagakure* commence. Jōchō is 52 years of age and Tsuramoto is 33.

1713	Following the death of Mitsushige's concubine, Ryōju-in, Jōchō moves from Kurotsuchibaru to another hermitage in Daishōkuma.
1714	Jōchō writes a treatise called "Osorenagara Kakioki no Oboe" regarding the correct attitude for a daimyo for the fifth Nabeshima ruler, Muneshige. He presents it to him in 1715.
1716	Eleven books of *Hagakure* are completed.
1719	Jōchō dies at age 61.
NABESHIMA MUNESHIGE (1687–1754)	
1730	Nabeshima Yoshishige dies. Muneshige becomes the fifth lord.
1731	Tsuramoto becomes Lord Muneshige's secretary.
1748	Tsuramoto dies at 71 years of age.

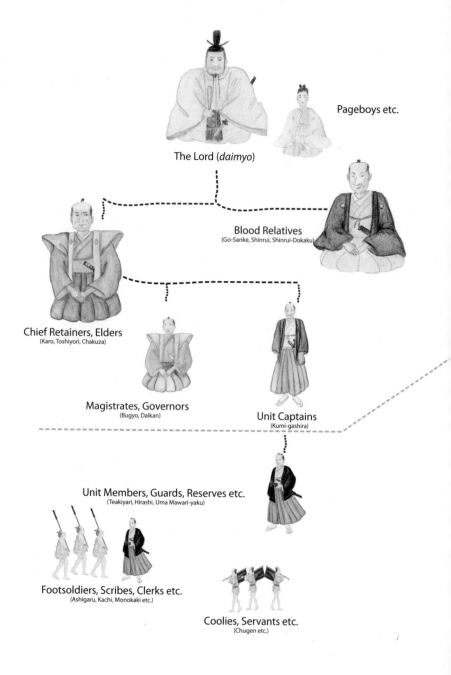

The Lord (*daimyo*)

Pageboys etc.

Blood Relatives
(Go-Sanke, Shinrui, Shinrui-Dokaku)

Chief Retainers, Elders
(Karo, Toshiyori, Chakuza)

Magistrates, Governors
(Bugyo, Daikan)

Unit Captains
(Kumi-gashira)

Unit Members, Guards, Reserves etc.
(Teakiyari, Hirashi, Uma Mawari-yaku)

Footsoldiers, Scribes, Clerks etc.
(Ashigaru, Kachi, Monokaki etc.)

Coolies, Servants etc.
(Chugen etc.)

Loyalty of Counsel

Great loyalty

Upper level samurai

> Honor found in good counsel and remonstrance through selfless advice for the good of the lord and domain, wisdom and discretion, preparedness to protect or die to take responsibility even if the lord is a fool.

Pure Will (Ichinen)

"The Way of the warrior (bushido) is found in dying"

Pure Will (Ichinen)

Mid to low level samurai

"Death Frenzy" (Shini-gurui)

> Honor found in courage, secret love (shinobu-koi), selfless dedication to duty, preparedness to die for the lord, martial spirit, reliability...
> **– KUSEMONO**

When faced with the choice of life and death....

High chance of death   Low chance of death

> Higher chance of living and fixing the problem.
>
> Even if you die, your honor and reputation will live on.

> May live for longer but will be thought of as a coward.
>
> Will have to commit seppuku anyway because of the shame.

Based on Oliver Ansart, "Embracing Death. Pure will in Hagakure" and Yamamoto Hirofumi, Zukai Bushido.

Symbolic Loyalty

REFERENCES

ENGLISH

Ansart, O. "Embracing Death: Pure will in *Hagakure.*" *Early Modern Japan: An Interdisciplinary Journal,* Vol. 18 (2010): pp. 57–75.

Befu, H. *Japan: An Anthropological Introduction.* HarperCollins College Division, 1972.

Bito Masahide. "Introduction of Studies on Bushi." *Acta Asiatica,* 1985.

Conlan, Thomas. "Largesse and the Limits of Loyalty in the Fourteenth Century." *The Origins of Japan's Medieval World* (ed. Jeffrey P. Mass), pp. 39–64. Stanford University Press, 1997.

Dale, Peter N. *The Myth of Japanese Uniqueness.* Croom Helm, 1986.

Davis, Winston. "The Civil Theology of Inoue Tetsujirō." *Japanese Journal of Religious Studies* 3, No. 1 (March 1976): pp. 5–40.

Day, Stacey B. *The Wisdom of the Hagakure.* Kyushu University Press, 1994.

Doak, K. *A History of Nationalism in Modern Japan: Placing the People.* Brill Academic Publishers, 2006.

Friday, K. "Valorous butchers: The art of war during the golden age of the samurai." *Japan Forum* 5 (1), 1993: pp. 1–19.

_____ "Bushidō or Bull? A Medieval Historian's Perspective on the Imperial Army and the Japanese Warrior Tradition." *The History Teacher* 27, no. 3 (May 1994): pp. 339–349.

_____ *Legacies of the Sword*. University of Hawai'i Press, 1997.

_____ *Samurai, Warfare and the State in Early Medieval Japan*. Routledge, 2003.

Furukawa Tetsushi. "The Individual in Japanese Ethics." *The Japanese Mind: Essentials of Japanese Philosophy and Culture* (ed. Craig Moore), pp. 228–244. University of Hawai'i Press, 1967.

Garon, S. *Molding Japanese Minds: The State in Everyday Life*. Princeton University Press, 1997.

Gluck, Carol. *Japan's Modern Myths*. Princeton University Press, 1985.

Hobsbawm, Eric J. and Terence Ranger. *The Invention of Tradition*. Cambridge University Press, 1983.

Howes, John F. *Japan's Modern Prophet: Uchimura Kanzo, 1861–1930*. UBC Press, 2005.

Hurst, C. G. III. "Death, honor, and loyalty: The bushido ideal," *Philosophy East and West* 40, 1990: pp. 511–527.

Ikegami, E. *The Taming of the Samurai: Honorific Individualism and the Making of Modern Japan*. Harvard University Press, 1995.

Koga Hideo and Stacey B. Day (eds.). *Hagakure: Spirit of Bushido* (Proceedings of the International Symposium on *Hagakure*, November 1992, Saga, Japan). Kyushu University Press, 1993.

Lafleur, William R. *Awesome Nightfall: The Life, Times and Poetry of Saigyō*. Wisdom Publications, 2003.

Mukoh Takai (trans.). *The Hagakure: A Code to the Ways of the Samurai*. Hokuseido Press, 1980.

Nitobe Inazo. *Bushido, the Soul of Japan: An Exposition of Japanese Thought*. Leeds & Biddle, 1900.

Ohnuki-Tierney, Emiko. *Kamikaze, Cherry Blossoms, and Nationalisms: The Militarization of Aesthetics in Japanese History*. University of Chicago Press, 2002.

Sadler, A. L. *The Code of the Samurai*. Charles E. Tuttle Company, 1988.

Varley, Paul. *Imperial Restoration in Medieval Japan*. Columbia University Press, 1971.

_____ *Warriors of Japan: As Portrayed in the War Tales*. University of Hawai'i Press, 1994.

Wilson, W. S. (trans.). *The Book of the Samurai—Hagakure*. Kodansha International, 1979.

JAPANESE

Bennett, Alexander. *Bushi no Etosu to sono Ayumi: Bushidō no Shakai Shisōshi-teki Kōsatsu*. Shibunkaku Shuppan, 2009.

Furukawa Tetsushi. *Nihon Rinri Shisō Shi Kenkyū. Volume 2: Bushidō no Shisō to sono Shūhen*. Fukumura Shoten, 1957.

_____ *Hagakure no Sekai*. Shibunkaku Shuppan, 1993.

Hiraizumi Kiyoshi. *Bushidō no Fukkatsu*. Shibundō, 1933.

Inoue Tetsujirō. *Bushidō*. Heiji Zasshisha, 1901.

_____ *Bushidō Sōsho*. Hakubunkan, 1906.

Kamura Takashi. *Hagakure Ronkō*. Sōeisha-Sanseidō Shoten, 2001.

Kanno Kakumyō. *Bushidō no Gyakushū*. Kōdansha Gendai Shinsho, 2004.

Kasaya Kazuhiko. "*Bushidō Gainen no Shiteki Tenkai.*" *Nihon Kenkyū* 35 (May 2007): pp. 231–274.

Koga Takeshi. *Bushidō Ronkō*. Shimazu Shobō, 1974.

Koike Yoshiaki. *Hagakure: Bushi to Hōkō*. Kōdansha Gakujutsu Bunko, 1999.

Kurihara Arano. *Hagakure no Shinzui*. Hagakure Seishin Fukyūkai, 1935.

_____ *Hagakure Kōchū*. Naigai Shobō, 1940.

Mishima Yukio. *Hagakure Nyūmon*. Shinchōsha, 1983.

Morikawa Tetsurō. *Hagakure Nyūmon*. Nihon Bungeisha, 1973.

Motoki Yasuo. *Bushi no Seiritsu*. Yoshikawa Kōbunkan, 1994.

_____ *Bushi no Rinri: Kinsei kara Kindai e.* Perikansha, 1993.

Nakamura Ikuichi (ed.). *Hagakure.* Teiyūsha, 1906.

Naramoto Tatsuya. *Bushidō no Keifu.* Chūōkōronsha, 1975.

Sagara Tōru. "*Kōyōgunkan, Gorinsho, Hagakure-shū.*" *Nihon no Shisō* (Vol. 9), Chikuma Shobō, 1969.

Saiki Kazuma, Okayama Taiji, Sagara Tōru (eds.). "*Mikawa Mono-gatari, Hagakure.*" *Nihon Shisō Taikei* 26, Iwanami Shoten, 1974.

Sakurai Shōtarō. *Meiyo to Chijoku.* Hosei University Press, 1971.

Ujie Mikito. *Bushidō to Erosu.* Kōdansha Gendai Shinsho, 1995.

Watsuji Tetsurō and Furukawa Tetsushi (eds.). *Hagakure.* Iwanami Bunko, 1940.

Yamamoto Hirofumi. *Hagakure no Bushidō: Gokai Sareta "Shini-gurui" no Shisō.* PHP, 2001.

_____ *Zukai Bushidō no koto ga Omoshiroi hodo Wakaru Hon.* Chūkei Shuppan, 2003.

Yoshida Yutaka. *Hagakure Nyūmon.* Tokuma Shoten, 1975.